After suffering childhood sexual abuse for many years, it's fair to say it's been a dark cloud in my life. Like the weather, it can be better some days than others, but I and many like me are survivors. You can recognize survivors of abuse by their courage. When silence is so very inviting, they step forward and share their truth so others know they aren't alone.

I'd like to dedicate this book to my brother and to all the other survivors out there.

Chris Hawkins

WHY DIDN'T YOU TELL SOMEONE?

AUSTIN MACAULEY PUBLISHERS™

LONDON • CAMBRIDGE • NEW YORK • SHARJAH

A CIP catalogue record for this title is available from the British Library.

ISBN 9781788782524 (Paperback)
ISBN 9781788782531 (Hardback)
ISBN 9781528955256 (ePub e-book)

www.austinmacauley.com

First Published (2019)
Austin Macauley Publishers Ltd
25 Canada Square
Canary Wharf
London
E14 5LQ

Chapter One

Why didn't you tell someone? Although, over the years these five words had rattled around in my own mind, this was the first time someone else had said them to me. Looking around the room I was sat in, it was full of children's toys and books; I always remember a picture on the wall that was crooked, although it annoyed me, I just sat and stared at it. There were comics on the small table in front of the big comfy sofa I was sat on. Rosie and Jim rag dolls, I recognised, these two colourful characters were favourites of my two young daughters, I remembered the many times we sat and watched Rosie and Jim videos over and over again, I sat on that big comfy sofa and smiled as I hummed the theme tune in my head. Here I was 24 years of age, sat in the child protection suite in my local police station feeling scared, very scared. This is a retelling of my experiences. My timelines are not always correct. I do not always remember the dates correctly. Names have been changed to protect anonymity.

Sargent Sally Henderson, whilst a very unassuming lady, had a calm and soothing persona, she put me at ease immediately. She wore a grey skirt and jacket, very business-like, you could pass her in the street and be totally unaware of the horrors this lady has heard over the years. I sat and fumbled with my car keys too scared to look up and look at her, I was afraid she would think me ignorant, truth was I was both scared and ashamed. Would she judge me? Would she snigger to herself?

My heart was pounding, my palms were sweating, how could I possibly tell anyone the horrors that I had hidden away in me for nearly 20 years? Why was I sat here? Get up and go home, I kept telling myself. Home, my comfort, my safety, my sanctuary. This room was alien to me, I felt uneasy, but Sally was great, she got me a drink and started chatting about my day at work, perhaps it was her training coaxing me to start talking, but I like to feel she was interested.

I had a very busy day at work that day. I was a driver for Royal Mail at that point for about seven years, to this day I miss that job, I miss the people, I miss the not-having-the-pressure my current job brings, my van, my customers; compared to work today, it was bliss. I stated to Sally that I could not believe I was here, after all these years it was my chance to unlock my inner demons, release this pent-up anger I had suppressed for so many years. How do I start, what do I say. Again, Sally reassured me everything was OK, take your time. I guessed it was easier to start with what had brought me to that place that night. Twenty years of nightmares bottled up inside me was about to be brought to the surface, I was so, so anxious.

Chapter Two

Less than a week ago, a Sunday evening, in fact, still warm enough to have the living room window open. Me and my wife were watching *Heartbeat*, prime time Sunday evening viewing. It was summer 1993, 8pm it would start, prior to this we would be beavering around getting school uniform sorted for Monday morning for my two young children, well, Carol sorted it, it was my job to polish the shoes and read the bedtime stories. Sometimes, during a story to my two girls Carol would shout up, "Heartbeat 5 minutes," the stories sometimes got very short. So, there we were watching TV when the phone rang. Who is that I would say, as if Carol was going to use telekinetic powers to tell me, it was my dad. My heart started to beat at that very moment, I knew something was wrong as my dad never phoned, not because we didn't get on, quite the opposite, in fact, but Dad was not the phone using type so I knew it had to be for something important.

"Your mum has been assaulted," I froze on the phone, before Dad told me the details of what had happened I knew what was going to follow. Deep down I knew what he was going to say, I don't know why, but I just knew. My worst fears were confirmed when Dad told me that my uncle and his allegedly poorly wife had visited my parents' house that evening so that she could argue with my mum about alleged allegations that my uncle had abused my brother as a small child. As soon as my dad told me that Ann, my Uncle's wife, had hit my mother the red mist came down, I shouted down the phone, "I am on my way."

I rang my brother straight away and just said, "There is trouble at Mum and Dad's, meet me there as soon as you can."

9

I grabbed my car keys and left. My parents lived just a couple of minutes away and as I screeched to a stop, my brother pulled up right behind me, we bolted from our cars and ran up the garden path, the sight of blood and broken glass on the front door caused me to panic even more.

As we rushed in, both Mum and Dad were in the kitchen, I could still smell the remnants of Sunday lunch wafting through the house. Mum was sat at the kitchen table, visibly shaking, I started shouting, "What the hell has gone on?" The adrenalin was pumping through me like a torrent of water. Dad told us that they just arrived at the door, Ann started screaming and shouting at Mum, Dad seemed clueless about the whole affair, he literally picked Ann up when she started to throw punches and pushed her out of the hallway that she was in after they opened the front door, when she was out, he slammed it behind her. As soon as the door locked in frame, Dad said there was a loud crash and Ann's hand came through a glass pane in the front door, she was screaming like a banshee. This explained the broken glass and blood on the front pathway. My parents' neighbour, seeing this mad woman and the way she was acting, rang the police and shouted this to the mad woman to go away, this is most likely why they left so quickly. Amidst all the trembling chatter from both Mum and Dad, I looked at my brother and said, "Let's go and sort this out," we ran from the house and into my brother's car and sped away, destination; uncle's home.

Chapter Three

My brother's car, which once seemed to be his pride and joy, was very untidy inside, it had work tools strewn all over the back seat; as he sped along, a screwdriver rolled out from under the seat and into my foot, I stared down at it and wondered what I was going to do and say when we arrived at his flat, to say I felt anxious was an understatement. My brother pulled up on a side road close to the block of flats, we got out of the car and walked across a grassed area to the entrance road to the rear of the flats that leads into a communal car park. We immediately saw a group of people gathered around a few yards ahead of us; as we got closer, we noticed Ann, my Uncle's wife lying on the grass as white as a ghost with blood pouring from a wound on her wrist. I imagined her punching her fist through Mum and Dad's front door and how painful it must have been, I remember looking right at her and shouting, "I hope you fucking bleed to death, you mad bitch." At first sight of me and my brother, my Uncle ran from his ailing wife to the safety of his flat, slamming the door behind him, it sounded as if he threw a hundred bolts.

I knocked the door at one point thinking I may knock it clean out of its hinges, shouting at him to open the door and talk to us. It seemed like an eternity, but I heard the clatter of bolts again and slowly the front door to this red-bricked council flat opened. Before I noticed him there, we were greeted by the smell of stale tobacco and fried food; it was quite repellent, then there he was, this monster from my childhood standing there in front of me, looking small, weak, dirty and pathetic, a small balding Irish man with rotten teeth and what hair he had was stained with nicotine; for once, I felt brave. As we stood outside Egan's front door, apart from the horrible smell wafting from inside his flat, occasionally the wind would blow through the hall and stairs and along the open walkway to his door carrying a stale smell of urine. As a Postman, it was an all too familiar smell within council flat stairwells, one could only assume it was used as a public convenience by passing revellers. Another thing I noticed was just how small Egan was. This guy didn't have much going for him in life really, he was pig-ugly, but due to some form of medical condition he was short, not a dwarf, but just short. This is the man that seemed like a giant when I was younger, in fact my entire life I likened him to the giant on the front cover of a ladybird book from childhood called *Jack and the Beanstalk*, but he was a giant no more. I am not sure who was more scared at that point, my brother or Egan, who was now being towered over. I could feel my heart pounding and trickles of sweat down my back, I could feel myself asking him in my head, *Why*, but I couldn't speak the words.

I was very calm when eventually I spoke, it seemed like ages but in reality was just a few seconds I guess. "What the fuck went on tonight?" I shouted. "Why did that mad bitch wife of yours hit my mother?"

I could see his mind working, trying to find an answer, he came back with, "You know why!"

I screamed at him, "Yes, I know why but I want you to tell me."

My anger was swelling inside with every breath he took, then as casual as you like, he said, "Because of what I did when you were boys."

This was the point that my anger exploded, I was angry but felt in control, though obviously wasn't, as I reached to the back of my trousers and produced a small mallet that I had picked up from the floor of my brother's car when I got out. I believed I had no intention of using it when I picked it up, it was as if some other force had told me to take it. Egan looked so pathetic and scared, but quite scary that didn't seem to reach my compassionate side, I raised the mallet up like He-Man raising his sword, this would have been the life changing moment for me, my mind was blank; I had nothing there to argue against, as if my sense of reasoning, my ability to know right from wrong had gone. As the mallet started to edge forward, it was snatched from my hand by Ray, my brother, I felt as if a spell had been broken and I was back in the room, total loss of control is a scary thing.

This is the point we left, we heard what we wanted, I was still kind of shocked, I was back in my brother's XR2, it could have been so much different, it could have been the back of a police car. That was the night that I almost killed a man, not metaphorically, but physically. My whole life could have changed for the worst that very night. On the journey back to my parents', I had visions of Egan lying in his doorway with this large hammer embedded in his skull, dead, dead, dead. As we pulled up outside our parents' home, I noticed a police car speed up behind us, we got out of the car and went indoors. *Someone had seen me with the hammer,* was all I was now thinking, *this is going to get serious,* I began to panic. Mum was still upset sat at the kitchen table, I hugged her, then the door was knocked, it was a heavy knock, and we mean business-type knock. Dad came into the kitchen with two young police officers, a man and a woman. I was waiting for the grilling to start about the mallet, but the young WPC started with Ray and Colin, I presume. She knew who we were! Then it unfolded that these were the officers who attended Mum and Dad, called by the concerned neighbour, they arrived just after we darted from there to Egan's home. Dad worried about what may unfold at Egan's, sent them there after us. I was safe.

Chapter Four

"Right," she said, the young WPC was bringing all that training to the forefront, what has happened here this evening. I think at that point everyone went to say something, but Ray just came out with it, "My uncle abused me as a boy." The kitchen was stunned with silence, the look on the young WPC was of shock, where in her training was this chapter?

Ray looked alone and vulnerable, this was my time, "It wasn't just you, it was me too," I cried. Stunned silence again. The room was charged with emotion, Mum was upset, Dad was shocked, the two police officers looked blank, I looked at Ray, him at me, we hugged and cried.

The two police officers came into their own, "You guys need to make statements about this." The events of the evening then unfolded and were taken down by the officers. On them leaving, they told me and Ray we would be contacted by specialist officers to make statements about the abuse, we thanked them and they left. This is one of the few times I ever saw my dad upset, many years later when he was in the later stages of Parkinson's, he used to get weepy, but this was an unfamiliar sight.

That was the night of the cold realisation that two boys were being abused for many years in that house, unknown to each other what was going on, unknown to our parents what was going on. Clever abusers don't just grab a child off the street and molest them. No clever abusers work systematically. They isolate their victim; build a world where the child becomes convinced that no one will believe them. They blur the lines between right and wrong. And that is the true, twisted genius.

I recall something my mum said that night, "If I had known what was going on, I would have killed him." This seemed to anger Ray, and it wasn't until later I was to find out why. There were hugs and kisses, and me and Ray left. We hugged each other, I think both knowing that there was a lot of uncertainty ahead, we both got into our cars and went home.

When I returned home, Carol was waiting, she knew something serious had happened, I broke down and spilled my inner most secrets to her, this was the first time I had ever told anyone. I was 25 years old and telling her things from my darkened past that to me were as fresh as they started. She said nothing, what do you say to something like that, but words were not needed; I knew she understood me and was there for me, just the warmth from the hug was all I needed to know that everything was going to be OK, no matter what the future was about to bring. A couple of days later, the call came from the police, Sargent Henderson from the Child Protection Unit asking me to meet with her and give a statement, not about recent events but events from 20 years ago. I was about to tell on Egan, could I do that? After all these years could I, or did I want to go through with this? Dragging all this up after all these years was going to be hard, could I do it, I knew for any kind of peace in my life I knew I had to, besides, I owed it to my brother too to unload this burden we had been carrying forever.

Chapter Five

So here we were, me and Ray in a police station about to unload 20 years of bottled-up anger, frustration, shame and guilt, we were about to tell someone for the first time the horrors we endured as children at the hands of Egan. I was very comfy sat on the big sofa in the interview room, Sally had made me a mug of tea, it was time. I think the first words I uttered were, where do I begin, when was the start point, I closed my eyes took a deep breath and began. I think my first child hood memory that I can recall is sitting on a large white and orange sofa which was being carried by friends and family of my parents as they moved into their first house, this was to be our family home, having moved from a small flat just around the corner. I think at this point I was about two and Ray three, the health and safety brigade would have had a field day with that move, but it went without any trouble. I think in the early days at our new house both Egan and my gran lived with us awaiting a place of their own. I don't remember much of this time other than waking at night sometimes to use the loo and always seeing a light on downstairs, I used to creep quietly down to peek to see who was down there, more often than not it was my gran sat at the kitchen table, playing cards. It was only years later that Mum told me she used to wait up for Egan when he used to go out, often she was up most of the night.

Mantaray House was 1960s' design block of council flats where they both lived for about a year I think, when they eventually moved out of our house. I always remember this flat to be quite cold and sparse, and I can still picture my gran sat in an armchair with a table in front of her playing patience, me and Ray would often go there after school whilst our parents were working, I have little memory of times in this flat other than having a sleepover one night, why I can't remember, but it went without event, other than going into the bathroom in the morning to see Egan being sick in the sink. Me and Ray used to play at the rear of the flats on our bikes, it was fun, the day an old car got dumped, there was like Christmas, we used to play all the time in that car, maybe sub-consciously wishing we could just drive away, in later years I know Ray would have wished this more as Mantaray House had bad memories for him at the hands of Egan, at the time I was safe and didn't know what was happening or what was to come as time went on.

There were so many unpleasant memories churning about in my mind, I was unsure of the order of some of the events, Sally reassured me this wasn't too important at this point, just start from where you remember. It was a Sunday afternoon, I knew that this was the first time Egan came to stay at our home, he lived in Ireland in a caravan with my elderly grandmother, they were not Romany's, I think the caravan was a temporary solution until a house was found for them. I remember my mum and dad were in the living room having eaten Sunday dinner, watching TV. Dad had his armchair, closest to the TV it was Dad's chair, pure and simple. I am sure every living room has one. My favourite spot was sitting on the floor leaning back on Dad's legs, this was my space, mind you after a hefty Sunday lunch it sometimes had its disadvantages from a windy perspective. There we were sat like any other Sunday afternoon, when there was a knock on the front door. Usually the calls were friends for me or Ray, so I jumped up and went to the door, the silhouette gave no clues really as it wasn't a tall figure, but it wasn't Mike or Boo, my mates, from the estate. I opened the door and saw Uncle Sean standing there, with an array of bags and a tatty-case, looking a little dishevelled, to say the least. I came back into the living room and looked at Mum and said, "Uncle Sean is here."

Mum looked bemused and said, "Don't be daft, he's in Ireland."

He came in behind me and said, "Hello." Egan had landed, at that point I was quite excited, Uncle Sean had come to stay, he was like a big kid really, lots of fun and I was glad he was here, little did I know what was to come.

Our new home was a three-bedroom council house which in the early '70s' was deemed a nice area, the same cannot be said today sadly. The layout upstairs was traditional, three bedrooms, two big and one small. The small room was always known as the spare room as it was used by no one, but I do recall it had an old bed in there with a spring base and mahogany headboard and a rather lumpy mattress, it had a design that reminded me of a pair of Dad's pyjamas, there was also a small bedside locker, that was it, really. This was to be Egan's sanctuary for his stay. Mum was puzzled as to why he turned up, he should have been at home looking after their elderly, frail mother, but he convinced Mum that she was being taken care of by friends, I am certain Mum never really believed this, and she was later to be proved right. The photo was taken many years later when Mum and Dad moved out, I guess the metal covers on the windows were to stop thieves breaking in and stealing the central heating, the top right window was my bedroom. Just a normal house in a normal road, but a house that hid dark secrets.

As days and weeks were to pass, the one thing I do remember quite clearly was that Egan's bedroom smelt horrible, he was a smoker and a drinker and hygiene didn't come high on his list of things in life. Being a nosey child, when he wasn't in the house, I used to ferret around in his room, not looking for anything in particular just being nosey, this was the first time I had ever seen a magazine which had pictures of naked men and women. I didn't know what to make of it, to be honest, there were several of them, and over the coming weeks I looked at them several times, curiosity perhaps. Under the bed were lots of empty wine bottles, empty of wine that is, but full of wee. How dirty and how lazy as the toilet was about ten feet away from his room.

One day whilst looking at the magazines, Egan came into the room, I didn't know he was in, I was in big trouble for sure. Egan sounded funny, he had a wobbly voice and smelled of beer. He sat on the bed and asked did I like the magazines, I think I shrugged my shoulders, I didn't know whether I liked them or not really. Egan's next question had me stumped, "Do they make you hard?" I always remember it and never knew at the time what he meant. He was sat on the bed next to me and picked up another magazine and started to peer through the pages, he then stood up and undid his belt, a large brown leather belt with a large buckle, he then unzipped his trousers, pulled them and his pants down and stood there in front of me, fully exposed. I remember thinking this was naughty and I got up to leave, he moved in front of the door as if to block my exit, he was now rubbing his willy, what a strange name for it, but I was young and that's what it was called. I remember him breathing heavily and pulling funny faces, then he moved closer to the bed where I was still sat, all of a sudden the front of my t-shirt and chin was covered in a white sticky stuff, I was shocked, what just happened. Egan told me to go to the bathroom and clean it off. "It's our secret," he said, he closed the door behind me and I went to the bathroom to clean off semen, I was five years old. This was the first of many such incidences, but worse was still to come many months later.

Chapter Six

Sally asked if I was OK and if I wanted another drink, "A cup of tea would be great," I replied. I couldn't believe what I had just said, I had never told anyone about these things before, it felt scary but at the same time I felt a sense of relief at having told someone. From then on, I really couldn't stop talking, it seemed to just flow, I think I told Sally I likened it to fizzing up a bottle of pop and taking the cap off and the contents just spilling out at super-fast speed. Talking openly about my abuse led me to remembering things that I had forgotten, this was it, time to sweep it all out and hopefully move on. One of the things that I did remember was Egan's fascination for recording devices of the day. He used to have these big reel-to-reel tape-recorders and would often set them up around the house and just record chit chat, me and Ray used to love talking into the old bacolite microphone, we used to giggle when we heard our voices being played back, Egan later had a cine camera, again we used to act the clown in front of it, we were young children, after all. We never thought for a moment that such equipment would be used for anything other than capturing the past. Many, many years later I was proved wrong.

Some months after Egan moved in with us for reasons unknown to me till very much later in life, Egan moved out of the small bedroom and Mum told me he was going to be sharing with me in the bigger room. I kind of guessed that as Ray was older he was now going to be getting a room of his own, it was fun sharing with my big bro, although on occasions I did rather torment him, but he was my big brother and I loved him. When Egan was not doing the horrible things, he was a funny uncle, very childlike himself, staying up late and telling stories, ghost stories especially. In mine and Ray's bedroom there were two single beds either side of the room with a dark wooden chest of drawers in the middle, I remember bashing my eye on those drawers when me and Ray were jumping from bed to bed, daft thing to do, and it hurt. The beds were very different, one being a posh new divan, very comfy, the other being mine was an old style rickety bed, I guess that's the perks of being a big brother, you get the better things. When Egan moved into my room, I thought I would get the posh bed, but Egan had other ideas and claimed it immediately.

Another of the more sickening events that haunted me was, in my mind, one that showed Egan to be the vile creature that he is in quite a nasty way. I remembered one evening being a little under the weather, feeling quite sick, so Mum put me to bed, Egan said as I was poorly I could have the posh bed, that was cool, it had candy stripe cotton sheets that were super warm, I think I went to sleep almost straight away. I was awoken some time later with Egan in the bed with me, I felt that my pyjamas bottoms were off; I knew I had them on when I got into bed, he had obviously taken them off. He told me he was going to teach me how to French kiss, I had no idea what he meant and then he began to stick his tongue in mouth, I hated it, his breath was vile, it smelled of the ashtray. I was for the first time scared of what was happening, this special game that he had named, these moments of abuse were becoming more and more scary to me. He was totally unaware that this young boy was scared, he didn't care about me, just himself and his evil ways. He then made me perform a sexual act on him, I knew it was wrong, he pushed my head down onto him, he smelt unclean, he jerked forward and made me sick in an instant. I burst out crying, he obviously started to panic, I cried louder despite his persistent shushing. Mum came into the bedroom, I had been sick on the bed, before I could speak Egan told her that I had woken him up being sick, I could see Mum was annoyed with me for getting her up, she cleaned the mess up and went back to bed. I felt alone and frightened, Egan was asleep; I was too scared to close my eyes.

Egan became bolder with his actions, another time he had me in his bed on a Sunday lunchtime whilst my mum and dad were preparing the Sunday lunch, I remember my brother sticking his head around the door shouting to Egan dinner was ready, he held my head under the blankets, I hoped Ray had seen me, but he didn't. He also used to make me have a wee in front of him, he had what I remember to be some kind of colour/paint chart type card and used to tell me he had to check the colour of my wee in case I had cancer. I knew cancer was bad and I was scared, scared of dying, Egan was a grown-up and knew these things, as a 5-year-old what else would you think.

Chapter Seven

Sally asked if I wanted to take a pause, but I declined, I had to get it out, I thought if I paused I might forget something, hardly likely when these nightmares have been haunting me for 20 years. Then she said it, bang right out of the blue, I think I have been dreading this question ever being asked, yet it was so simple. "Why didn't you tell someone?" This did make me pause, I had been asking myself this very same question my whole life and the truth was, I had no answer.

To this day, aged 43, I still don't why I didn't tell someone. The first time Egan started the abuse I knew it was wrong, from a very early age it's an in-built thing I am sure that makes us aware of what's right and wrong. He didn't threaten me, but yet I was too scared to tell, it was a culture, that like it or not, existed in the 1970s, that adults are believed over children. My behaviour, I know had all the tell-tale signs of a child in turmoil, I over-ate, I was poorly behaved at school when I did attend, I know the school inspector came to the house on more than one occasion.

At the school me and my brother went to at this time my parents were contacted as I was accused of being a bully, one thing for certain in life today is the fact I despise bullies, I remember a poor young girl, maybe the same age as me but very petite for her age was the subject of my vile tongue. I was not a physical bully but used to torment and tease her verbally until she cried, how wicked was that. I hate myself for it to this day. Nicola Atkins I am so, so sorry. My parents were never really interested in our school career; I think they thought of school as somewhere for your children to go so you could go to work, I am sure they were not alone in this way of thinking.

Mr Brown, the Head Master of the school summoned my parents for a meeting, they didn't attend, but instead sent Egan. I remember him coming to the school that day, he looked stupid. He wore a blue safari jacket that had a belt around the waist, a shirt and tie, he was trying so hard to look smart, but failed dismally. He went into the head's office, I dread to think of the lies he may have told that day on why my behaviour was poor, I knew after this meeting telling someone at school was no longer an option. Let me tell you what the 1970s was like. I heard my first talk on stranger danger at school, at the age of 6 in 1975 but no one told me. No one told me that you were far more likely to be a victim of a family member, a family friend, someone known to you. And when you did realise that those advances, those touches, the things he did to you and asked you to do weren't right, you realised he had created a world where you just would not be believed. And he made you believe it was all your fault, not his. My fate at the hands of this monster seemed sealed.

When I was seven, I remember being in Mrs Pearson's class at school, I remember her all of a sudden shouting at me, "Why are you wincing and pulling that face, aren't you listening to me, you stupid boy?" Next thing I remember was her slapping me across the face, the pain and shock of that did nothing, "Concentrate!" she yelled, "That minute of day-dreaming is gone, you will never get that minute back." The class was silent, I felt all eyes on me, perhaps I should have cried, I think my tears had dried up long ago, perhaps I was numb to pain, perhaps I deserved it. I sat quietly oblivious to the lesson, still thinking of the events of the day before. Junior school wasn't always like that, Mrs B-W and her great stories and her love of music, particularly the Beatles, they were often my escape. I still think of that lovely lady when I hear a song from that Scouse quartet, or by the smell of Dentyne chewing gum, isn't it funny how certain things cement themselves in your memory. I was home with Mum and Egan, I guess Dad was working and Ray was out somewhere. Mum had a slight drinking problem around about this time, as her mum had died back in Ireland, no thanks to Egan as it transpired when he arrived on that Sunday afternoon he had in fact left her in that cold dark caravan with no money and no food, ill health didn't help and she passed away. Mum blamed Egan for her death, but still allowed him to live with us whilst he found his own place.

Chapter Eight

Mum was partial to sherry and used to drink it in copious amounts, that afternoon she upped and walked out to the warehouse up the road to buy more. As she went out the front door, I made my way up to my bedroom as I didn't want to stay in the living room on my own with Egan. Perhaps I should have just followed Mum out, but she was volatile to say the least when she was drinking. I knelt on the bed and watched her walk up the road, missing her and longing for her to come back quickly. Almost immediately he was there in the room, he pulled me away from the window, I switched off at that point as I knew what was going to happen. He took me to a small area in the bedroom by the door, he stood me facing the wall, he pulled my trousers and pants down, he then left the room, I didn't flinch, I concentrated on the wallpaper, it had pictures of cottages and water mills on it, I fixated on the cottage and imagined me in there, safe. I felt a greasy squelchy feeling, he was rubbing a bar of soap around my bum. Egan was stood right behind me, he was slipping his willy between my legs, I hated the squelchy feeling, I screamed out, it hurt lots, I cried but still wouldn't turn around, *Who lived in the water mill?* I kept asking myself. Egan finished what he was doing and left the room, I heard the taps in the bathroom running, I didn't move until he told me to pull my trousers up, he went downstairs, I sat on my bed and cried. I heard Mum come back, I hoped she would come up and find me, I waited and waited. She never came. My own uncle had raped me, that still feels difficult to say even today, he stole my childhood in one act of wretched violence.

I guess there is always yin and yang in life, and my life was no exception. I had the evil uncle who was Egan, then there was my Uncle Terry. Uncle Terry was Mum's twin sister's husband, he was the nicest person in the world, a proper, honest, genuine man, me and Ray loved him. I think as children we both held so high the good things in life, Christmas was a particular favourite time of year, all the good that came with it soon outweighed all the bad that Egan did to us. It wasn't just the presents, although that was great, it was the feeling of the loving side of family life, I think this is why we are such advocates to Christmas to this very day. I think I can still remember every present I got during the years of abuse; 1975, I had a red Raleigh Chopper, Ray had a purple one, we were the envy of the street, I loved that bike and went everywhere on it. I remember my race 'n' chase, it was like Scalextric, it was awesome, I still have it to this day. Uncle Terry and Auntie Tolly as we called her couldn't have children of their own so me and Ray were often spoilt. Mum and Dad gave us all they could and we loved them for that, they both worked hard, Dad was a factory worker for nearly 30 years and Mum was a cleaner all her life, and only gave up eight years ago due to poor health. It is fair to say Uncle Terry was good stuff, but tragically he died aged 35 of a brain tumour, me and Ray were distraught, this smashing, decent man had been taken away from us and Egan remained. At that very early age, I questioned the very religion we had rammed down our throats as children, if there was a God, why take Uncle Terry who was good, and leave Egan who was evil. I so longed for Egan to have died that day, death to me back then was simple; you went to heaven or went to hell. I knew Uncle Terry went to heaven and he would never have to see Egan again, even when Egan died as he would never make it to heaven.

This photo was taken by Uncle Terry, that's Ray and Auntie Tolly on the left, and me and Mum on the right. This was a happy day, not long after Ray fell in the pond behind, it was funny, what was funnier was that he went home dressed in a string vest and pants of Uncle Terry's. Behind our smiley faces we hid such secrets, secrets that no child should ever have to hide, things that no child should ever have to endure. This was a happy day indeed.

I recall another time, I knew it was a Saturday morning as Tiswas was on; I, like most kids my age loved this show, the chaos, the mess, the fun, it was brilliant, perhaps another escape outlet. Anyhow, there I was watching Tiswas eating some sweets that Auntie Tolly had given to me, she was a regular visitor on a Saturday morning as she used to have her hair done at a ladies' hair salon just down the road from our house, and she always brought me and Ray treats. Mum had asked Egan to go and get her a bottle of sherry, for whatever reason he went to the off licence across at the shopping precinct across the park and asked me to go with him, I said no, but Mum told me to go, so off we went.

Prior to going to the off licence, Egan took a detour to, as he put it, a friend's place, we walked towards some flats, I recognised them as the flat where Egan's friend lived was close to Uncle Terry and Auntie Tolly's flat, this is where I met Burt, Egan's friend, or as later I discovered they were more than just friends. Egan had a key to the flat as he let himself in, Burt smelled of imperial leather talcum powder, he had white hair and gold, rimmed glasses, he was an old man probably about 70. Egan then made me stand in the hallway, pulled down my trousers and pants and told me to just stand there and not move, I was scared, why were we here. I stood there, I didn't move, I didn't even question why, Egan and Burt disappeared into one of the rooms, I heard shuffling and clicking, but no voices, I seemed to be there for ages, then Egan reappeared. We left the flat and made our way to the off licence, I was puzzled but relieved that he had left me alone, this was one of a couple of similar visits to Burt's; it was only many years later the realisation was I was being photographed and recorded. We left the off licence with one bottle of VP sherry, but we didn't go home, Egan decided another detour was needed.

We made our way to the block of flats where Egan and my gran had lived, Egan went to the flat opposite where he had lived to see an old neighbour, I remember this woman answering the door, she had a ginger beehive hairstyle, we went in, she made him a drink and they started chatting, there was a young boy around my age there, he didn't say much, but then neither did I. I ended up being sent out the back to play on my own, so off I went thinking nothing of it, again many years later there was the scary thought that this boy was alone with Egan, even though his mother was there it's possible this poor lad may have suffered abuse, I hope that's not the case. When Egan finally left we then walked into town, my memories are a little vague of where we went next, but we stopped at various places, including houses and a few pubs. We eventually ended up in a telephone box on the site of the Waitrose store where I listened to this drunken creature talking to the Samaritans claiming he was going to commit suicide, I was stood in the box with him as I only had shorts and t-shirt on and I was shivering with the cold, it was just after midnight, we had been gone for over 12 hours. I didn't even know what suicide was, it was this beast that introduced me to it. When he eventually emerged from the phone box, he told me to make my own way home and he just walked off. There I was about seven, freezing cold, still carrying a bottle of sherry trying to remember the way home. When I eventually knocked on the front door around 12.30, Mum was frantic, she hugged me and asked where on earth I had been, I told her all the places we went to, she was very angry with Egan. She made me a sandwich as I hadn't eaten all day, St Ivel Gold was a new butter, it tasted lovely. It was this that enabled the police to date this event.

Chapter Nine

The following morning, we were greeted with the news that Egan had taken an overdose, this was one of the three attempts that I remember whilst he lived with us, all pathetic attempts as he survived them all. As a result of this, he ended up being referred to a mental hospital called Coney Hill. This place had an awful stigma to it and everyone referred to it as a loony bin, worst still the private ambulance that used to collect him would stop outside our house around the same time as the school bus picked us up, very embarrassing. Egan would stroll out of the house like a schoolboy, hop on the bus and off he would go. It was at Coney Hill that he met his wife Ann, that just about sums them up I guess, equally inadequate. They both ended up renting a flat in town together, he moved out, my nightmare ended then, I was about ten years old.

I think it was just before midnight when we had finished at the police station, I think we had been there about six hours. I felt relieved, as if a ton weight had been lifted from me, I thanked Sally about a hundred times I think, she was a rock that night. My brother had given his statement to Anthony Black; he became a friend to us and supported us throughout the coming months which were to prove stressful to say the least. I hugged my big brother that night and didn't want to let him go, we never spoke about our experiences, we didn't need to, we had both suffered at Egan's hands, we didn't need to go into detail. This was the night I found out that many years ago my brother told my mother that Egan was abusing him. This was the time Ray was sharing the room with Egan, Ray went missing for a whole day after he told Mum fearing the fallout from her telling Dad and Egan being bounced down the street, he needn't have feared as Mum never told Dad and I was then moved into share with Egan. This was the result of Ray telling someone, that someone failed him and me as a result, and to this day Ray and Mum have a very distant relationship, and I know Ray felt guilty about me now sharing with Egan and being his next target, but Egan was clever and abused us both without either or knowing for many years.

We were contacted a week or so later by Anthony and Sally, the CPS had looked over the case and said there was sufficient evidence to bring charges. Egan was arrested, and no surprise, denied everything. We weren't surprised by this at all, *Why would he admit anything, self-preservation had kicked in,* I thought. Not only did he deny all the charges but he tried to paint our family as some form of sexual deviants, the lies were truly awful, just how evil could this man be. My naïve side always hoped that he would just admit to what he had done and we could move on, tell us why he did it? Do paedophiles really know why they cause so much hurt? Do they care? Are they just wired wrong from birth? What could possibly make a man do such a thing, to this day we all never know the answer to that one. My take on these people has never changed, the way I see it is, if you have a rouge dog that is a danger to people, you have it put down, enough said. Egan was released on bail and charged with several counts of rape, indecent assault, buggery, the list went on. Now we had to wait for it to go to court, the thought of that was an absolute nightmare.

Chapter Ten

A few months went by and the court case was upon us, I had dreaded this moment for so long, the thought of having to stand in a Crown Court and bare my soul to people I have never seen or met before, the thought of having to bare my soul to people I didn't know and had never met before was a bitter pill to swallow. The first morning in court, I had this overwhelming sense of guilt. I kept telling myself if Egan gets found guilty he could go to prison. I was so angry for feeling this way, but I just couldn't help it, I was worried what might happen to him, due to him being a beast how he would be treated in prison. Even all those years later, he still had some kind of hold on me, but I reached inside and found that inner strength and battled on. Me and Ray were called in and out of court and kept apart whilst giving evidence, it was an emotional time for us both. Mine and Ray's wife Kathy were in the public gallery for the whole two weeks, but left when we came in to give evidence, I couldn't handle her being there, had I have looked at her I may have lost it, although I did breakdown several times, but the whole time I was in the courtroom, Egan did not look at me once.

Towards the end of the trial, disaster struck. Due to the jury not being able to reach a decision, and when asked by Judge Tabor QC whether they would be able to, they replied no, so the case was dismissed. But Judge Tabor stated due to the heinous nature of the crimes, there had to be a re-trial. After all that, we had to wait for months and have to do it all over again, we were devastated. Egan and that side of the family who supported him saw this as a victory, it was hard to stomach. I think it was about six months before we had to go back and do it all again, it seemed harder as the raw emotion of the first trial didn't seem to be there. I was worried that perhaps I might not be able to appear genuine in court as I had said my piece before, it was like having a rehearsal beforehand. We did it all again, even though Egan's barrister was only doing his job, I hated him for the way he tried to spin things, but it's his job. The verdict came through, eight years unanimous verdict. We had been vindicated, time to draw a line and move on, or so we thought.

Whilst the court case was going on, I threw myself into a business venture with a friend; as we were both keen movie buffs, we decided to open up our own video rental shop. Around about the time Egan was sentenced, we opened the doors to Movie Zone, it was a hard slog to get it there but we did it. We knew it wouldn't make us millionaires but it was the fact we were doing something we wanted to do, besides, it took my mind off other things. I remember one afternoon, I was working in the shop when I noticed it was busy with people just looking but not renting. It turned out that two prostitutes had rented the flat above the shop and the clientele, so to speak, were using the shop as a waiting room. As it happens, we got to know the girls, they used to pop in and buy old films to watch, in-between shifts I guess. To be fair, they were nice people, we all have our own reasons and our own stories, who was I to judge. I think it was just under a year after the shop opened, I was in there one afternoon when Anthony Black came in, "What a surprise," I said to him. I could see by his expression he came baring bad news, he came behind the counter and we had a chat. The long and short of it was Egan had been released from prison after winning an appeal, I was stunned. All that stress and heartache for nothing, his appeal was granted on a technicality on the judges' summing-up of the case, because he didn't state clearly enough that the jury should take into consideration the offences were historic, the conviction was quashed. He walked free, claiming his release was due to lies we told. The anger consumed me, I went out of way too often, and drank heavily, I was fuelled with hatred and had lost all focus, I was falling apart. One evening, I sat outside his flat for hours with a huge kitchen knife, I contemplated confronting him and imagined driving the knife into his heart and ending this whole saga, I cried and thankfully just went home.

Chapter Eleven

Why didn't you tell someone? That was still plaguing me, if I had, I wouldn't be here feeling like this right now. When Egan moved out of the family home, I thought my nightmare had finished, little did I know it was to continue throughout my life? After he had gone, it was around the time for getting ready for secondary school, there was no way I could tell anyone now as the embarrassment factor had now set in. People would know what went on, I would be treated like a leper. Back in those days 'Bum Boy' was the buzz phrase, I couldn't have coped with it, so that part of my life was locked away until that Sunday evening. The pressure of living with it was at times unbearable, it made me hard and insensitive towards the very people who loved me most.

Carol, my wife, I kind of knew at school, or knew of her, we didn't mix with the same friends, she was a year older than me. My brother, Ray, was in her year at school and was dating Carol's sister through school, Kath was a year younger than me. If you think that is confusing, I ended up dating Carol a year after leaving school, we married in 1991, Ray and Kath in 1995. When me and Carol got together first, I was so worried about how a relationship would be, would I be haunted by ghosts that would affect me. Those ghosts were there but Carol turned out to be my rock; the connection was solid, I had found my penguin. We enjoyed all the things new relationships bring, we had our ups and downs but always had each other. We had a really fun weekend in Blackpool with friends in 1988, those friends sadly divorced very messily some years later. Some weeks after the Blackpool weekend,

Carol found out she was pregnant. I was stunned, and found this hard to deal with. I dealt with it very badly indeed.

At no point in my life did I ever see myself having children, it just never entered my head. When I found out I was going to be a dad, I was filled with fear and total dread, how could someone like me have children. How with my history could I do that, what if I was going to abuse my child? I had read a book about child abuse over the years and it was a sad reality that some abused people go on to be abusers. I was scared that people may look at me strangely if they knew my past and questioned the way I changed a nappy or such everyday parental jobs, the paranoia at one stage was suffocating. I knew it wasn't in me to inflict that kind of pain even on my worst enemy, but the fear was there, the fear of the unknown I guess. My way of thinking is anyone who has been abused knows how truly terrible it is, they know how it destroys part of you forever, there is no time-limit on it, but only a truly evil person would ever want to put anyone else through that. I reckon I was the opposite and worried about my children all the time, not saying other parents don't, but even to this day when they are both in their 20s, I worry when they go out, I do the 3am pickups, and to be honest, I would have it no other way. My children have given me every happiness, they are beautiful, intelligent, grounded young woman and I love them more than life itself.

Chapter Twelve

Part of me never recovered from the fact Egan had been released from prison, I was angry that the system had let us down, I felt we had been betrayed, but worst of all, it was the fact it felt as if people maybe hadn't believed us. I couldn't really keep my life on an even course from that point. I went out more often than normal looking for something to ease my pain. My solace wasn't to be at the bottom of glass but in the arms of other women, many, many, I'm ashamed to admit I lost count of how many and who they were. I used these women and thought nothing of it, I didn't set out to hurt people, but it was inevitable I would, and I did, a lot of hurt stays with me from that time from the outfall from my behaviour. I had a loving family and the love of a great woman yet abused her trust and seemed to go on a one-man-mission of self-destruction. I guess we are designed to be curious, to want things we don't have, and when everything seems to be going well, we often stir up drama – perhaps to remind ourselves that we are capable of being devilish or dangerous or interesting. But you can be interesting and dangerous with your partner – it just depends on how you define those terms. Find ways to have fun. Find ways to wipe the slate clean. The worst part about an affair is not while you're in it and trampling over people and feelings – no, you are much too caught up physically and emotionally for that. It's when it ends, when the truth is unveiled, when your affair partner doesn't choose you, or you don't choose them, when you return to your old life and realise that it is, has, and perhaps always was broken, and that you and only you can be left to fix it. It's the effects you must deal with, the scars you must heal, and the emotions you must work through.

At no time was I looking for a replacement for my wife, I wasn't looking for love, part of me felt I had to prove something to myself, what I do not know, as stupid as that sounds, truthfully I was looking for something to numb out the horrible things I had racing around in my head. I loved my wife but at times didn't even feel guilty about what I was doing, I hurt so many people with lies and deceit it totally consumed me for years. This may seem a pathetic excuse but this was how it was for me, it became an addiction I couldn't control. Like all addictions they have a price, mine was to lose the trust of Carol. I think too much had happened for her to forgive me, and I don't blame her for that, the most damaging aspect of mis-placed trust is the trauma to loved ones' hearts and souls from being betrayed by the people that they love and trust.

Towards the end of the 90's I felt as if I needed a radical change in my life, I had been an employee of Royal Mail for nearly 14 years at this point so I thought new job, move house and a fresh start to the new millennium. Work wise, I didn't really know what to do as I had no real skills other than working with people, it was purely by chance that I ended up joining the prison service. Even today I don't know why I chose this of all jobs, perhaps naively I thought I had something to offer, perhaps I could help make a change. It was a long laborious recruiting process, but there I was off to college about to embark on a new career, it was an exciting time but also one filled with trepidation. I always had the worry of coming into contact with child sex offenders, but the prison I applied to was a non-sex-offender establishment, these types of prisoners are normally held in units that cater just for them, but much to my dismay, this would ultimately change. I have a lot of prison stories to tell, which will soon be put to blog, some very funny, very real, everyday stories of the men and women of HMP Service.

Chapter Thirteen

2006 was a bad year for me, my dad who had been suffering from Parkinson's disease for a couple of years had started to deteriorate very quickly. Isn't it a strange thing, the instant panic you get when the phone rings at 2 am? I fumbled around for the phone on the bedside cabinet, on the end of it was my mum in a state of panic. "Col, your dad has fallen over and I can't get him up." I was dressed and at my folks' place within minutes, my poor dad was flat on his back, distressed and unable to move. Due to the Parkinson's, Dad was as flexible as a plank of wood, but I managed to get him into bed, he had a cut to his head where he hit the door frame when he fell, I got him comfortable and after an hour went back home, I couldn't sleep at all. First thing I was back and decided to get the doctor out, within an hour Dad was in hospital, for the GP said it was a bit of R&R and a change of medication, the following weeks were to be the worst ever.

It was Sunday lunchtime and we were just in the process of sitting down to Sunday lunch, it was the hospital telling me Dad had taken a turn for the worst and I should come quickly and prepare for the worst. When we arrived, I thought we were too late, Dad had pipes and tubes everywhere and what seemed to be dozens of nurses and doctors working on him. The staff stabilised him but he was very poorly, I stayed with him afraid to leave really, it was at that moment after reading through his notes I noticed he had not eaten for nearly nine days, I was shocked with the amount of entries in his file stating, "Food refused." I can't remember being so incensed by something, I screamed and shouted at NHS management on the fact my dad had nearly died due to malnutrition, their apologies seemed vague and insincere so I thought for all people like my dad I would take this further. I went to the local press, the national press which then led to radio coverage which further led to Age Concern contacting me for my story, which to them was all too familiar. A week or so later, I was contacted by the BBC and invited to participate in a programme about the issue of how elderly people are treated in hospitals, it was a real eye opener, I interviewed ministers, doctors, nurses and visited hospitals who had managed to change the way they care for elderly patients when it comes to food, I now realise how much work goes into such programmes, it was draining.

Thanks to a considerate boss at the time, I took a period of time off work to care for my dad whilst he was in the hospital, I felt I had lost faith in the hospital he was in, I came to the hospital at 8am and stayed for at least 12 hours until he was settled for the night, the NHS hierarchy hated me being there, the nurses loved it, they were brilliant and applauded my cause. Within a few days, Dad was a lot fitter and sat up in bed and chatting, when I asked him why he had refused food for all those days he told me he didn't, they would bring in his tray of food and leave it, he was too poorly to feed himself, this got put down as food refused. It still saddens me to hear of such stories in the news five years down the line; the promises of politicians were of the piecrust type, easily made, easily broken. Dad's Parkinson's took a turn for the worse in early 2007 and he passed away, I was distraught and to this day still miss him dearly.

This is a favourite photo of mine taken just a year before he died, a fantastic fella who has left a big gap in my life that's for certain, but hey Pops, I know we will meet up again one day.

It was about a year after Dad died, about 2008, that the prison I worked in became an establishment that would now hold and deal with child sex offenders, amongst other rather unpleasant individuals. I knew I would struggle, but felt trapped with nobody to turn to, the day loomed for the influx of around 300 vulnerable prisoners as they are tagged, I wanted to shout and scream at somebody and tell them how unfair it was that I now had to deal with people like my uncle on a daily basis. Staff were not consulted or trained to cope with it, there were tough times ahead.

Chapter Fourteen

Everything was running like clockwork, they were arriving myself and my work mates were doing the initial processing, it was fine, no dramas until one afternoon. I was talking to a prisoner who was a child sex offender explaining what we were doing with regards to his property, due to the nature of his offence he was not allowed photos of children, I explained why quite clearly, his response was one that shook me to the core, "I didn't fuck my kids," he calmly stated. He didn't seem to see any wrong in the response he had just given me, none whatsoever. I felt a deep rage booming inside me, I was scared of what could happen, thankfully a colleague was close by and walked me to a back office to calm down. I knew at that moment I had issues with this kind of person, and now I was going to be surrounded by them at work daily. I was so upset I had to leave work early, I went home and contemplated my next move, I had to tell work about my issues, that in itself terrified me.

I became very tired, withdrawn, and very moody as things really started to compound me, all those mixed emotions and frustrations were bubbling inside, I really felt that I couldn't cope with it all anymore so I was signed off with stress and anxiety later to be topped with bouts of depression. I decided to talk to the OT at work, Sue was to be my lifeline, I went to see her and told her everything, she was superb, and she listened and most importantly understood me. She referred me to Hilary, what a smashing lady she was, she too listened to me and helped me to deal with the past and try and move on from it, but whilst she helped for a while, I still had to face these monsters every single day. I guess it was towards the tail end of 2009 when I was seeing Hilary, they were really tough times. While driving home from Hilary's one afternoon, feeling quite emotional as it was a bit of tough session, I had a phone call from Anthony Black, he dealt me a blow that winded me, I had to pull off the motorway and sat in stunned disbelief with news he had just given me, I was truly wrecked with it.

I was sat in a motorway service station staring blankly at an advertisement billboard, I can't remember what was on it but it was colourful, "There is no easy way to tell you," said Anthony, "Egan has been arrested for child sex offences." Again, they were historic acts dating back to the late '90s against a lad me and Ray did not know, but Egan used to watch whilst his mum was at work. I felt sick to my stomach and struggled to listen to anymore that Anthony was saying. How could this be happening, I was finding things difficult because of my years of abuse and the clientele I was now dealing with at work, I had just found the courage to seek help through work and on the very day I had a counselling session for my childhood abuse, I receive this news. Anthony went on to ask to meet with me and Ray as he had a question to ask us, we made arrangements to see him a few days later.

Me and Ray went to the police station and met Anthony, he took us into an interview room, we had a cuppa and a bit of catch-up and then he asked us if we would allow our statements which we gave at Egan's trial in 1994 to be read out in court. He explained to us that the law now allowed bad character evidence to be used in such cases, it shows a propensity for such behaviour which a jury can take into account. I was very uncertain about it to begin with, I was unsure I could handle all this again, but me and Ray chatted and thought we had to help this unknown lad hopefully get the justice we didn't, so we agreed. Before we left, Ray pulled from a bag he had brought with him five or six old reel tapes, at least half were boxed, I remember seeing Kodak written on two of the boxes. Ray told us that he had found these some years ago in my parents' attic when they moved out of our old family home, he stated that they had been carefully placed between some beams. I had flashbacks of the many times I saw Egan going into the attic, even at this point it had not dawned on me what the tapes contained. Anthony looked a little stunned as he shuffled through the tapes, four were audio and two were cine films, for a brief moment I thought, *Wow, these could contain us as children being silly like we used too.* Then Anthony warned us they may contain something a little more sinister, we were floored with that. But things were to take an unexpected turn for the worst for us.

After speaking with Sue and her being aware of how difficult I was finding things at work now. The reality facing me now was that if Egan was convicted at this trial there was a real chance that he would come to the very prison I worked in, I was terrified of this, so I had to inform other people, some of those other people being managers. It was awful telling other people at work, I felt ashamed and perhaps I would now be seen in their eyes as unfit to carrying on with my job, Jean my union rep was great, I told her as she is one of the few people I trust at work, she was fantastic and offered a shoulder when I needed one. I think work were unsure as to what to do with me so I found myself being offered a job within the prison but without any prisoner contact. Basically, I became a bit of an office dweller, now whilst this was very busy, I found the work very, very tedious, but the office was another place to meet new people, people who I often passed by without much more than a polite hello, there were mainly women in the office and I found myself drawn into the middle of lots of bitching and sniping, it was very bizarre, but kind of fun too. I knew this new position wouldn't be a permanent fixture, but whilst the court case in 2010 was in full swing, it was an easier place to be without being face-to-face with prisoners, I really could not have handled that at that time. I managed just over two years in this office-based job and I got to a point where I began to hate it, it was a draining place with too many strong characters fighting for something that just wasn't there. I left there in April 2012 and was basically thrown back to the wolves, it was a nightmare.

Chapter Fifteen

It was around about this time that I attended a school reunion, I must admit to being slightly hesitant about it to begin with, but as time went on, I wondered what it would be like to meet up with people I hadn't seen for over 25 years. I made the decision to go with my dearest and oldest friend Ali, I was anxious, excited nervous even about meeting up with old school friends, but there was no need, it was great fun, but? There she was, that certain one, your first crush, your first real thing for girls, my heart melted at the sight of her, I was that lovesick spotty kid from school, all them feelings were there yet again. I guess there are good reasons why school reunions are not good ideas, I have read about happy and sad endings to such events, I was no exception to this. Me and H chatted, we danced, we kissed, we fell in love. We had a torrid few months ahead, fun, laughter, tears, sadness and hurt, so much hurt, something happened that shook us and will stay with us forever, I think as much as I loved H, we couldn't recover from that. It was a sad time, with everything else, this was unbearable, I am upset writing and thinking about it, so will end it there.

Our statements were given to the court as part of the case now against Egan, we knew we had done the right thing, now we could sit back and see what happens, or so we thought. A week or so later Anthony contacted us yet again and said whilst the judge in this new case was happy for the statements to be used, he would only allow it if we went back to court and read them ourselves, which really meant going through the whole court process for a third time. This was like a kick in the stomach for us, yet again we had to rake all of our past up and face this creature again, but again, we knew we had to go through it as although we didn't know the person involved in this case, we had heard he was in a bad way and in a very dark place, we had been there and in all essence still were there, we had to try and get some closure hopefully once and for all, but things in my world were never going to be that simple. I think it was around this time we found out that the tapes Ray had found had been analysed by experts, I think four of the tapes were useless, they had degraded over time, but the other two were shocking, so bad I refused to listen to them or read the transcripts taken from them, Ray confirmed the voices on the tape. Egan had recorded some of the abuse for his own sick gratification. I had flashbacks again to the times at Burt's flat when I stood there naked and heard clicking and shuffling noises, Jesus, had I been filmed and recorded? The times I cried when he did the things he did, did he film me? Egan was more evil than I ever really thought, how could he have done this to us.

The day of the trial seemed to arrive so quickly, I think I was more worried and scared this time than before, I was now 42 years of age, but part of me was still that small 5-year-old boy. There were times when I used to think I could go back in time and tell that small boy that everything would be OK, it would soon be over, that would have been true of the physical abuse, but the mental scars would be there forever. Me and Ray were sat in a waiting room at the court, nervously talking about everyday things when Anthony Black came into see us and give his support, although he wasn't the investigating officer in this new case, he wanted to be there for us, and that was a big help. We never got to meet the victim in this case, but the investigating officer on the case that brought the case against Egan this far came into tell us this guy was eternally grateful for what we had done, she said he too was scared and anxious, we passed on our best wishes to this nameless guy and just said, "Be brave, it takes a brave person to get this far." As the days went by, we sat in that room whilst people took their turn in the witness box, for us it was like that horrible wait in the dentist's waiting room, one day when it was our turn to start giving evidence, Egan feigned an illness so the court was adjourned, we had to go home, but we were soon back. A court official came into the waiting room, "Ray Haskins please." Ray got up and followed the man out, I was now alone. I had been told that I would not be able to talk to Ray again until I had given my evidence, Ray was called in at 10 am, I didn't see him again for the rest of the day.

The local paper had been reporting Egan's trial from the onset, they knew me and Ray were involved somehow, although they weren't allowed to name us as we had anonymity, they made reference to Egan being on trial in 1994, I remember they reported on it back then too. Well, here I was again sat in the court waiting room, I didn't even remember the drive to it, within minutes of being there, that same court clerk dressed in his long black cape came in and announced, "Colin Haskins," why he said this I don't know as I was the only person in there, but I guess that's how it works. We walked along a cold, stony corridor which had many big wooden doors along the way, then we stopped outside one, Court Room 3 was pained in gold letters on this huge door, he opened it and in we went.

Chapter Sixteen

My heart was beating so fast, I was sweating; I reached for my hankie to wipe my brow, the court looked so much smaller than I remembered, but it was full of people, people I didn't know. The jury were to my right, then there was the judge, the place just seemed to be packed with people, obviously all there for a purpose, then I spotted him, there he was, there was Egan sat just over to my left, he looked small and unkempt, above all, he looked old. I went through the formalities, swearing in, confirming who I was etcetera, then it began. Mr Fenny QC for the prosecution was a real nice guy, he met with me and Ray earlier in the week and explained what was going to happen, but we seemed old hands at this case. He asked me lots of questions about my experiences with Egan, my toes were hurting where I was cringing when answering, I felt so embarrassed. Then Mr O'Brien, the defence barrister grilled me, this was worse than I could remember it being, I was made to feel like a liar, a fake, my family was painted as dysfunctional and what angered me most was the fact that they tried to paint my dad in a bad light, nothing was further than the truth. I looked over at Egan trying to catch his gaze so he could see how angry I was, he didn't look my way once, I felt destroyed by the cross examination, I looked at the jury once and saw a young woman crying, I couldn't look again, I spent most of the time looking at my shoes, it was a tough time and something I would be in no hurry to repeat. When I was finished being questioned, the judge thanked me and wished me well, I turned and left and took one final look at the jury, the young woman there smiled, I looked away and left the court room, that was over at last.

I met with Ray outside the court and we went home, we had done our part and did not want to wait around for anything, we didn't say much in the car, but decided to stop at a pub on the way home to have a pint. We sat there, looked at each other, sipped on our drinks and that was it, we just talked and talked about the two weeks we had just endured again at court, I think we were glad we had helped the unknown chap and were thinking more of him than the outcome of the trial, whatever that was to be. We left the pub feeling good, but so, so tired. Egan's fate was now in the hands of those 12 jurors, I couldn't help but think of that young woman who was upset, I hoped she would be OK. I think it was a day or so later, I had a call from the female policewoman who was in charge of this new case, guilty on all charges she proclaimed. She was quite excited to be the bearer of good news, I thanked her for the news and her help throughout the trial and clicked my mobile off and just sat in my living room absorbing what I had just heard, I wasn't elated and didn't scream and shout, I had again a sense of vindication, we had been believed, those 12 members of the jury had heard our stories and believed us, that brings such a sense of relief. We could now try to rebuild our lives and move on, this to this day proves to be difficult, but for now we could rest knowing justice had been done. Egan was going to jail; he couldn't hurt us anymore.

The court case was finally over and the right result had been reached for all, so it was time for us to move on with life. Work had been pretty good to me up until this point, now that Egan had gone to prison, they kind of switched off the caring employer side and were anxious for me to get back to normal, the post I had in the office was now being axed so I was left to make the decision to move back to normal duties, but the thought of working with paedophiles and sex offenders wasn't something I was looking forward to, my pleas to slide into a job that gave me a gradual return back were ignored and basically I was just thrown back in the deep end, I resented them for this. I started back on normal officer duties in April 2012 and have basically tried to stay focused ever since, it has been extremely difficult in an ever-changing job which to a person without my history would struggle, every day is hard and it has become very tiring just being me, the guy who always has a smile on his face, who likes to act the clown, but inside feels like screaming, it is so tough.

About a year after being convicted, I was contacted at work by Anthony Black with the news that Egan had been granted leave for appeal, although I think it was expected, it hit me for six. How dare he even think of doing this, he was 100% guilty of the crimes and yet again was trying to play the hard done by and innocent victim. To be honest, this is a familiar trait with most prisoners, in particular sex offenders, they don't believe what they have done is wrong, and I guess it's a self-preservation instinct to protect themselves no matter what. Egan went to the appeal courts in London in 2011 and the basis of the appeal was the historic evidence that was given by me and Ray, his legal team stated this was at a detriment to his case. Can you believe that crap? Thankfully to my relief the residing appeal court judge threw the appeal out and sent Egan back to prison to serve his sentence, at last common sense prevailed, time to move on, even the police were pleased with this outcome.

Chapter Seventeen

I have learnt quite a few things over the years with regards to sexual abuse and the main thing being, survivors of sexual abuse live their lives in the face of massive shame. Survivors face shame that they "allowed themselves" to be demeaned and weakened, I questioned myself over this time and again over the years, again coming back to that same old question, "Why didn't you tell someone?" Over the last year, I have tried my best to cope with things on every level, work is still an on-going struggle for me, there are times I just find it hard to cope with certain prisoners, thankfully my professionalism keeps me in check, but I have come close to snapping at times and this does worry me. I am more than aware that people have to move on from such traumatic events, but when faced daily with people who constantly remind you of the horrible things you endured is difficult, but I am still having therapy and am on medication to help, but this in itself makes me angry as I still feel like a victim all these years later.

Sue, my very dear friend, who I first confided in at work has always been there for me. She was a victim of the public sector cuts and left the service during 2012, and thankfully moved on to better things. Sue contacted me when the whole Jimmy Savile saga started in the news. When this story first broke, I quivered. I knew what was to come. And come it did. Story after tragic story, being told by adults, who inside are still children, terrified of a man now dead. You see, when you think about the things you have kept locked away, you're not a rational grown-up. In that moment, you are back where you were, a vulnerable, frightened child. It was good to talk to her as I felt I couldn't escape the whole child abuse nightmare, work was always a constant reminder, watching the news when home was the same, I feel suffocated at times, it seems to surround me. I decided it was time to chat again with my GP, I am lucky I have a good relationship with Dr Flynn, he helped me through this in the '90s, he is a great bloke. We talked over the issues I was facing, the way I was still feeling, he thought talking to a professional again might help, so he referred me to a unit in my hometown.

Mental health? Wow, how ignorant am I when it comes to this subject. Dr Flynn referred me to a CPN to have a chat about my life and how I was feeling. I was mortified at the thought, I wasn't mad, I kept telling myself. I sat in the car park of Challing's Lodge, staring at this new building, scared to go in, not due to what I wanted to talk about, but the stigma attached to going here frightened me. I kept thinking back to Egan and his visits to Coney Hill. "Oh my God," I kept repeating, "why am I here." I know I have made big steps in my life and this was just another step to make, so in I went. I sat in a small waiting area for Chris, the lady I was seeing, to call me through. There was a woman also waiting who in my ignorance I classed as a loon as she was sat talking to herself, this again made me scared of where I was. I didn't have time to get up and go as Chris was there, she lead me to her room which was very relaxing, two big chairs in front of a window which overlooked a very pretty garden. Her first question to me was, "How do you feel about being here at Challing's Lodge?"

My response was immediate, "I don't think I should be here, I am not mad, only nutter's come here," I sadly claimed. Chris smiled and declared she had heard this response a million times before. We had a great chat after that, my ignorance towards mental health, I must admit, has changed somewhat, everyone has their own story after all. I have been referred for further assessments and still awaiting that to come through, I was prescribed medication to help calm me down and help me chill a little, I have been on it for around two months now and must admit to feeling a lot more relaxed. I will update as and when this moves forward. In my other stuff tab, there are some of the major things that affect children who have suffered child abuse; it is quite shocking and very sad.

Christmas 2012 has been and gone, and what a great time we had at home, despite only having Christmas Day off the rest was spoiled by work, my employer appears to be the Grinch when it comes to allowing staff time off at what is a very special time of year to me. 2012 just seems to have whizzed by, I think I perhaps say the same thing every year, but time seems to be galloping along. Today is New Year's Eve and whilst my daughters are getting ready to go out and party, me and Carol are having a quiet evening with a friend, my days of New Year partying and revelling seemed to have long since gone, I am beginning to sound like my dad at times. Today at work was an OK day to begin with, but during the afternoon things took a slight turn which ended in me almost exploding, one of the very situations that I dread. A prisoner was talking to some colleagues regarding an article he had published in a newspaper for prisoners, he offered the paper to me to read his letter, I read the article and became incensed with rage, I sat clutching the paper with white knuckles, I couldn't have been more angry if I had tried. The letter was basically one sex offender supporting other sex offenders, he declared how outraged he was that historic sexual abuse cases were ever heard and there should be a statute of limitation on such cases. It's just pathetic wannabes who are jumping on the band wagon, looking for compensation, if people endure this type of stuff, speak up or shut up, these rants were based around the Jimmy Saville allegations, but all such cases are equally as ridiculous he went on to say... I feel angry even now later today just thinking about it. How do I move on from it all with this crap in front of me every single day... Argggghhhhhh!!!!!!!

Well, today was a strange day indeed, first week of Jan 2013 and a meeting was held at work by senior managers which was to inform us of the closure of six prisons and the reduction in prisoner places in another three. As a result of these closures, there is the very sad news that many of my professional colleagues around the country will be cast aside like an old rag, thanks and goodbye is pretty much the basics of it. This whole debacle is due to government convincing the public that they have to find more cost effective ways to run prisons, prisons by their very nature are a powder keg at times, places that are full of the type of people that nightmares are made of, it's impossible to do this on the cheap without serious consequence to both prisoners and staff, shame on you coalition, shame on you. One of the prisons that has been announced for closure is where Egan is being held, these prisons are due to close in the next two months, the reality for me is that Egan could land in the prison I work in any day now. I think if I had people to express my concerns to, they would be met with contempt now due to impending job losses, so once again I fear I am going to have to suffer in silence.

Chapter Eighteen

While the physical pain fades in time, the scars of child abuse never fade. Children are never the same again after an abuser has entered their lives; they lose not only the innocence of childhood, but also the chance at a normal future. One cannot erase the memories of abuse, they live in conscious and the subconscious, invading every aspect of one's life. Child abuse victims are given a life sentence, forced to live in the shadows of their abusers. It has been a strange week at work, the announcement of seven prison closures has caused a strange excitement with staff, the chance to take voluntary redundancy, this day and age it seems odd people looking to dump a job, but it really speaks volumes to me. I have been working the past few weeks in a prison workshop for vulnerable prisoners, predominately sex offenders, this shop seems to be filled with needy, whining creatures, four in particular feel a need to talk to me, although being professional at all times, I give the impression I am listening, but I am so not interested in them, their problems, there issues or anything. One in particular feels the need to try and impress me with his apparent wealth and fortune, his affluent and supportive family and the many businesses they own. He has lead me to believe he has been imprisoned unjustly due to drug related offences, it didn't take me long to find out he was a rapist, very nasty one at that, but just another example of these creatures trying to convince themselves of how hard done by they are. If only he knew just how little I think of him, how much I detest him in fact, one of these days I think I may be just a little truthful, it's brewing, that's for certain.

Today I went to see Chris at Channing's Lodge, I had less trepidation about this visit than the last one a few months ago. I arrived a little early and sat in the waiting area browsing the web on my mobile phone, a middle-aged couple came in and immediately I realised they had mental health issues shall we say, last time there were similar folks in there and it made me cringe, not today, who was I to judge them, we all have our own stories after all. They were quite childlike in there chat about their journey on the bus to Channing's, it made me smile, in a warm way, not a patronising one. Chris came out and called me through, a big beaming smile and warm welcome, we went into a room to have a chat. Unlike last time, things were really positive, I have been on the anti-depressants for a few months now and to be honest, they have lifted me from my knees and given me the focus I needed to deal with everything around me, suddenly things seem a little easier to bare. We had a chat and the good news for me was I no longer have to see Chris, this is a positive step for me, happy days indeed.

Chapter Nineteen

I have been asked by a few people recently where does the nickname Ollie come from? Well, it's a daft story really, but when at secondary school I was a little rotund shall we say, and a lad I became friends with, a lad called Steve Salmon, he was the total opposite of being rake-thin. Then came a lad called 'Bell', a total dick who I had no time for to be fair, but the nickname came from him, I was fat, Steve was thin, Stan and Ollie, as simple as that. When I joined the Prison Service I ditched the nickname as I wanted to leave it behind, only recently a couple of close friends from work have used it, old school mates no me by nothing else. A sad fact being Steve is currently in prison, sentenced about a year or so ago for sexual offences against an underage girl, that came as a real shock, although we never really kept in contact much after school, we did have some laughs back then, I guess you never know how folks will turn out in later life. I don't really see much of the old gang, some of them drifted off the radar many years ago, some seemed to nose-dive into a life of drinks and drugs, that I found hard to swallow when I met up with another good school friend a few years back, 'Morph' as he was known, was the same age as me, but his lifestyle had aged him by ten years or more, that was a shock. I guess there is also a reason why you don't see some people, purely because you just don't want to. Ali Fraser, he was my best friend through school and still to this day we keep in contact, we live close and often have a catch-up over a coffee, he is a top bloke, a real nice fella, we shared many good times as we grew up. Ali didn't know anything about the years of abuse when it was happening even though we were mates at the time, but he knows now and has been a good ally. Even though I don't see the old gang from school, I hope they are happy and content in life no matter what they are doing.

Today, 25th Jan 2013 has been tinged with sadness to be fair, I had a phone call from my wife at work today which upset me a little, but news I kind of knew was coming. When growing up, me and Ray had a handful of friends who we still keep in contact with today, Ali being one and another was Marty, he was, he is a nice guy, slightly jaded outlook on life perhaps, but not a bad man. Back in September 2012, Marty texted me whilst I was away in Cumbria, taking a break with Carol. We were in the middle of Lake Windermere on a boat when the message arrived, Marty was in trouble, there was no signal to enable me to ring him right back, but I did as soon as we hit dry land. Marty had fallen foul at work, he has worked in retail since leaving school and for the past ten years has worked for a major chain in the town, to cut a long story short, he has been stealing from that store and selling items on eBay. I was gob smacked, but what was done was done, when I was back from holiday, I found a solicitor for him to use, I couldn't believe how naïve he was to the whole thing. Today Marty was sent to prison, that was the call from Carol, whilst I knew it would happen, it still shook me, I feel sad for my friend, I immediately thought of school-day times when despite my secrets life seemed carefree, it's funny really we just don't know what is around the corner, we just don't always know the people we call friends, but despite his wrong doing, Marty is still a friend and I just hope he can cope with prison, stay strong Marty.

Chapter Twenty

Sunday 27th January, my baby daughter's 21st birthday, God, where has the time gone, I remember holding her for the very first time, she was so small, so precious, I thought I might break her. I used to talk to both of my girls before they were born, Carol would be lying on the bed, or sat on the sofa, I used to put my head against her tummy to hear them, feel them kick, I used to talk to them, daft things most likely, but it was my bonding. There she was, this small bundle of life, my heart melted, I cried when she was born, I couldn't help it, it just happened. My years as a Prison Officer have made me perhaps a little more over-protective of my girls, I see the most ordinary looking men every day that have committed crimes that would leave you cold. Watching your children grow is one of best experiences one could ever be part of. It's not only children who grow, we as parents do too, and as much as we watch to see what our children do with their lives, they are watching us to see what we do with ours. I can't tell my children to reach for the sun. All I can do is try to reach for it, myself. I think I am still trying to reach it to be honest, but hey, life is no race I guess.

I was supervising vulnerable prisoners in the chapel today, I questioned the very nerve of them being in church knowing the evil things some of them had done, it makes me feel cold to the core. Could God really accept these people, could he forgive them for the wickedness they had done? I prayed to God when I was a little boy, I prayed He would save me, take me from the hands of Egan. He never came. As I got older, me and religion kind of parted company, that was tough for me as religion was a big part of my upbringing. I couldn't stop thinking of Marty, my friend, today, I wondered how he was coping with prison, I know him and know he will be struggling, I spoke with his wife today and she is in pieces as are their children. I will do what I can to help them out, after all, that's what friends are for, right? Well bed beckons, an early start tomorrow in the house of sin, I am thinking of Marty, good night friend.

I don't know if I am 'normal' anymore. I'm always asking 'Would normal people feel like this?' I feel so overwhelmed by certain things at times. I try to keep my head above water but I kind of expect a big wave to break over me at any minute. I used to be so organised. Now, I live in a state of chaos half the time. The medication I am on is having effects that I am beginning to worry about, I feel quite carefree about most things right now, whilst this is quite liberating and kind of exciting, but is it a false state of mind, what happens when the tablets stop? If I am honest, I wonder whether I would be here right now if it wasn't for anti-depressants. That sounds quite sad to say, but then maybe it's partly due to me trying to move on too. I had yet another laborious conversation with a prisoner today, yet another sex offender, more whining about not getting his own way, he sounded like some spoilt child. In my head, I was screaming at this creature to f**k off and leave me alone. I have managed to upset the big boss too this week, simple mistake on my part, which was corrected in an instant, but this was not good enough for this anal retentive buffoon who now thinks I cannot count, I wish I could say I was slightly concerned what he thinks, he is a bully and gives the air of being an unpleasant man, if he thinks he scares me he is so, so mistaken, I have seen really nasty, unpleasant and scary things in my life, he doesn't come close.

Wednesday, 30th January 2013. Today I went out to see a good friend of mine who is at home recovering from bouts of chemo and radiotherapy. Phil was diagnosed with cancer last year. Cancer? What a vile, crappy disease this is. It creeps up on people and attempts to take away all physical abilities. But my friend Phil is testament that it cannot touch the mind, it cannot touch the heart, and it cannot touch the soul. I have felt a little down the past few days, then I spent a few hours with Phil today and came away and felt as if I had absorbed some of his positive energy, I left feeling happy, feeling positive, he is by far one of the bravest men I have known. Fate is a strange thing, I am a firm believer in it, perhaps fate had a hand at making our friendship a little stronger, after all we can never have enough good friends, I thank fate for that. One of my favourite films of all time is *It's a Wonderful Life*, it is such a feel good film, one quote in that film sticks with me, "Remember, no man is a failure who has friends." Enough said.

Sunday, 3rd February 2013. Well, the past few days have been very tiring, the weekend was so long in coming. Thursday, last week, was very eventful at work, there I was in my fixed post-work shop when a prisoner collapsed more or less in front of me, we moved him to a small classroom within the work shop, he had a suspected heart attack. I went through the usual procedures and within a few minutes the cavalry arrived in the form of other colleagues and nurses from the healthcare unit. I had been talking to this prisoner all day, the conversation revolved around him and his issues, as they always do with VP prisoners, I had no interest in any of his babbling whatsoever. He came to me later in the day and complained he felt unwell, I wasn't really interested as I felt it was a ploy to gain sympathy for his earlier ramblings over personal issues. None the less, I watched him over the next few minutes and my concern did grow as he looked rather poorly.

The nurses were administering treatment and asked for an ambulance to be called, this was serious. One of the nurses came out of the classroom and said that he was asking for me, *Why on earth would he want me*, I thought. I went into the classroom and looked at him, he beckoned me to come closer, I did, what happened next scared me. He asked me to contact his partner in the event he dies, he was shaking and looked awful, at that moment I felt quite sorry for this guy, that bothered me, but at the same time reassured me I still had a compassionate side. Compassion for the kind of people who wouldn't know compassion if it jumped up and slapped them in the face, *How much compassion did he show his victims,* I thought? But then fear grows out of the things we think; it lives in our minds. Compassion grows out of the things we are, and lives in our hearts. Whilst I detest men like this and the despicable things they do, he was in need and my very nature would not allow me to turn my back on him, for I am a decent man with a good heart I guess. I accompanied him to the hospital with a few other work mates and sat by his bedside, handcuffed to him for the rest of the evening. As the evening progressed and he was checked over by doctors, the staff with him resorted to prison officer humour, it was funny, even the prisoner was in fits of laughter at times. I think for a short moment there was a sense of normality for this prisoner, perhaps this could have been a glimpse of what could have been, a trip beyond the four walls he has known as home for so long, who knows. He was discharged the next day and told to take things easy. The weekend passed without event for me really, I was glad to have some me time, feet up with a cuppa and a film, happy days indeed.

Chapter Twenty-One

Well yet another birthday came and went yesterday, another year older, but really no wiser, or maybe I am and just don't see it fully. Birthdays used to be an exciting time when younger, party food and presents, but as you get older, you just can't be bothered with it all, well I can't that's for sure. A couple of things dawned on me yesterday, firstly I am pretty sure my marriage is over, things just haven't been right over the past few weeks, it's the small things you notice, I think we may have just reached a juncture where it really is make or break, we just seemed to have drifted apart, I am sure I have just put Carol through too much and enough is enough, only time will tell I guess, but I do love her and hope she will stand by me, I also realised I might be old before my time, I spent my birthday afternoon in the cinema watching a really funny but moving British film, I was the youngest person in the screening, a lot of blue rinsers sat around me, it was great. My mum popped up to see me with a card; I could see she was a bit down so asked her what was wrong. When she stopped staring around the room, I could tell it was something I probably didn't want to hear, my mum has a habit of doing daft things that annoy me, things often need my intervention to correct afterwards, but not this time. "Egan's wife has died," she blurted out. She may as well told me what she was having for tea for what it meant to me. Why did she think I would be bothered, she's dead, so what. Mum was having a guilt trip, that Catholic guilt thing, utter bollox. Egan's wife was the one that started this whole saga with the assault on Mum 20 years ago, it's not nice to speak ill of the dead, so I won't, but neither will I shed a tear or a minute of time on the woman. Another thing is that my weight which was on the downward spiral has started to slip back on. I am sure the anti-depressants may have something to do with it. I don't want to slip back into old ways, I want to shed the weight and things back on track, I am back at the doctor's next week so will see what he says, still trying to stay focused.

Monday, 22 April 2013

Well, here I am sat at home feeling numb, my head is aching so much it feels it will split in two! Today, I rang in work and reported myself as unfit for duty, I just felt I couldn't cope, couldn't bear to deal with prisoners today. I am now working on a VP wing, vulnerable prisoners, a mix of sex offenders and inadequate prisoners incapable of coping on mainstream wings. Whilst I have no time or patience with such people, the wing is made a more pleasant place due to the staff, there are a mix of old and new, but a real good bunch which makes it easier for me. I have just had a long weekend away from work which was blissful, but a mixture of having a wisdom tooth out which was no fun, and a constant thumping head and a note which had been put through Mum's door for me which was a charming childlike garbled rant from "a friend of Anne's", Egan's wife, the mad woman who back in the '90s started this whole saga off by assaulting Mum, which basically pushes the blame for her death at my feet. It transpires she committed suicide, whilst I want to say I couldn't care less; there is a part of me that feels sorry for her. She too in a weird way is a victim of Egan; she was dependant on him for everything, so when he was sentenced I guess she was too. She is without doubt to me a vile creature, but she's dead! She couldn't cope alone, I couldn't help think she died alone and sad. My old friend, stress has been hovering this weekend, this was all he needed to grab on to and call on his friend depression, once again these two have a hold of me, they have cloaked me with their darkness and right now I feel I am at their mercy. Depression is hard work, it consumes you if you let it, it turns the rational into the irrational, you can't make sense of even the simple things in life, it is not a good mix in prison, with prisoners with issues of their own. I had to step out, I have to get my head straight, I will no doubt receive flak from the big boss when I return, but he is the least of my problems right now. I am seeing my doctor tomorrow, he knows my history and seeing him will be a relief in itself, I feel like a victim today and not a survivor, I am tired and fuzzy, I feel the need to sleep for a long time...

I think I may have ended the last paragraph rather poorly, a good friend of mine read the updated part above and came to see me thinking I was in such a dark place I may do something stupid. I am grateful for friends like this who care enough to contact me to ensure I am OK, Facebook is a place I check into daily really to see the updates friends leave, again my last update was cause for friends to check I was OK, just those messages are a big lift when feeling low, I thank all my friends for this. One in four people suffer from some sort of mental health problem in their lifetime yet we don't talk about it. Part of that is the shame inherent in the illness, you feel bad enough about yourself without everyone knowing how much you're struggling. However, this stigma which involves keeping your illness as a shameful secret is only going to make things harder. The more I've been open about what I went through, the more I realise just how common these problems are. The recent Time to Change campaign has been a big step forward in mental health awareness and tackling stigma. It's hard to talk about these things and one of the reasons I did, and still do in some respects, find it difficult is the thought that if people knew about my illness it would change their perspective of me. I would no longer be this lovely, fun person but instead a weird, depressive type. Mental illness can affect anyone and I've come to realise that depression can go together with any personality traits; it's an illness not a personality in itself. So when people learn that you've been depressed, they may well be surprised – but likely they will have respect for you for battling through this difficult illness.

The people that don't understand mental illness are often given either isolated medical symptoms or sensationalised stories in the media. The people that do understand, because they or someone close to them has gone through mental illness, don't talk about it out of shame. It's only by talking about it that we can tackle misunderstanding and discrimination. This in itself is so tough, I wouldn't know where to start with friends from work. Working in a prison brings its own problems, the very people that are in our custody are the kind of people who suffer from mental health problems, not the custodians, the good guys, surely we don't suffer such things. As I write this I can think of people I work with, good people who would find it hard to believe that I suffer from depression, the funny guy, Ollie the one who makes them laugh, the clown, the confidant, the one they trust enough when they need a quiet word, but I do. I have faced many things in my life, faced up to demons from my past, persevered through the courts to seek justice, and yet I am not brave enough to open up about my depression.

Chapter Twenty-Two

I was very reluctant to go on anti-depressants, feeling I should be able to cope without them. This is ridiculous – imagine if a diabetic was insistent on beating their condition without insulin. However, it's a surprisingly common reaction, I dreaded the thought, but eventually accepted that it may help me, pride and shame being a huge factor in this. To begin with, I didn't really notice they had any effect, but as the weeks rolled on, I began to become calmer and found I could just chill. Stupidly, I just decided a month ago to just stop taking them, that was a big mistake and helped lead to my current situation which resulted in me taking time off work, something I do not do lightly, but lack of medication and the news that I had received were just too much to cope with and I needed to step out and clear my head. I am back on my medication and things are starting to calm a little, I am trying to not worry about how vulnerable I feel I am making myself with my boss, but I guess I can deal with that when I return to work.

Well, it has been a few months since I reported back in, and a few things have happened that have I guess angered me and again reinforced my distaste at the creatures I work with. Myself and a colleague had the unlucky task of searching a prisoner and his cell, it is fair to say things didn't quite go to plan. The prisoner concerned is quite impaired to say the least, one might say prison isn't where he should be, but it is and that is just how it is. We took the prisoner to his cell and started the process of a full search, he was not happy with this at all, and no amount of explaining from us seemed to have any bearing on the matter. He became aggressive, but due to his low intellect and the fact we know his behaviour, we didn't take action to restrain him for his actions. Although, he objected and ranted and raved about what we were doing, we proceeded as planned and thought no more about it that was till later in the day we heard something that shook me to the core. The prisoner we had searched had thought it clever to tell other prisoners and his mental health nurse that me and my work mate had sexually assaulted him in his cell, I froze with shock when I heard this, shock turned to anger and hatred for this vile low life creature. Due to the nature of this prisoner's complaint, he had to be interviewed by the duty governor, the potential fallout from these ludicrous allegations could have been we were suspended from duty and have to explain why to our families, what an awful position to be placed in. The upshot of these events were that after interview the prisoner stated he had made up the allegations because he didn't want to be searched and also he wanted to be transferred out of the prison. These are the kind of scumbags we have in custody, who would sink so low as to do such things. My hatred for these people increased my tolerance levels decreased dramatically. The unit I work on at the moment, although full of such creatures, is made all the better for the superb staff, most who are younger than me, but they make me laugh listening to them it is fun to work with them, and my mate accused of the above has become a great ally in the work place.

My health is still a cause for concern for me, my daily medication seems to have increased, my weight is still a major issue and seems to be going up instead of down, the anti-depressants have had a major impact on trying to get my weight down. I saw my GP last week to chat about blood test results, as a result I am being sent to the hospital for tests to rule out cancer. The very mention of the word cancer just clouds your thinking, although it is unlikely according to my doctor, I have to say I am a little worried. On top of this, I was due to have a major operation for another matter at the end of the year, lady luck is definitely not with me right now, still only time will tell, I will report back in with news as and when.

Well, here I am again, with good news. After drinking copious amounts of what tasted like drain cleaner, then having the loo as a fixed post for the past 24 hours which resulted in having a bottom that of a baboon I had my tests at the hospital. I had a camera put down my throat to check things, I also had to have a camera put in other places too, I was so wound up about that I had to have a sedative, which almost knocked me out. As much as I hated the whole process, but knew it had to be done, they were checking for cancerous growths and other nasties, but thankfully they found nothing. What a huge weight this is off my mind, I couldn't be happier. I still have another operation looming later in the year, but now this clear that should go without any problems. I do feel very tired today, an accumulation of things, medical stuff, work, particularly the long shifts and monotony the job brings. The clientele are still a tough audience at times for me, some days are better than others, but I am getting there. Happy days folks.

Chapter Twenty-Three

November 14th, 2013. Well, here I am again feeling a bit crap to be fair, I had a really strange day at work, it started off OK but went downhill rather rapidly, and not due to prisoners. I got onto the unit at lunchtime and whilst the beasts were locked up a group of us had a daily dose of clagg, a card game made up by bored prison officers on nights or so I have always been lead to believe. As the lunch hour diminished and the rest of the staff came back from there bouts at the gym and feverishly wolfed down there low fat lunches, it was almost time to unlock when one of the lads, Sloppy came into where we were playing clagg, a few of the clagg boys are also keen golfers, they started talking about making dates for playing golf. I jokingly stated I never get invited on the golf days, I have never played golf in my life but in jest stated I was a budding Tiger Woods. I was shocked with Sloppy's outburst, albeit it was said in fun, prisoners officers humour is rather warped at times, he stated, "We don't allow fat c**ts to play with us," he reiterated it time and again, I know it wasn't meant and it was just Sloppy's way of having fun, but it cut me to the quick. It sat with me all afternoon, and yet again I felt like a victim, it reminded me of school bullies, I couldn't shake it off, but all that aside, I wouldn't have Sloppy any other way, he is a fantastic fella, and if he ever read this, I wouldn't want him to be any different towards me, I would hate that, it's just how he is, any other day I would have just laughed it off, bad day I guess. I feel better this morning as I am not in work, but my weight is baring heavy on my mind this morning, I know I am still comfort-eating, it's my coping mechanism. I am off work this weekend so will relax and get my head around things, I keep telling myself it will all be ok, and I am sure it will be, it could be that I feel down as the dark nights come to early, the short days, I hate them they are so depressing. Christmas is looming, I remember reading somewhere once that the festivities we know as Christmas, not the religious side of it, were brought in to ease the burden and depression of the poor during the long winter months, I understand that. I have battled with all of this for many, many years, whilst I am doing my best to move on I know this will follow me to my grave, I just hope that isn't any time soon and hopefully peace will find me first.

30 January 2014

Well, it's been a while since I reported back in, Christmas has been and gone again, it was a strange Christmas this year, I was working all of Christmas Day. My Christmas spent in the company of some of life's most despicable people, the day was made better by the great staff that I work alongside, the day went without event, dinner consisted of a buffet that we all chipped in with, that and a game of clagg it wasn't too bad at all I guess. What made my day was when I got home and found that Carol and my daughters hadn't opened any of their presents, they told me we were going to celebrate our Christmas Day on Boxing Day, that really put a smile on my face, and that is exactly what we did. I mentioned in my blog that I had an operation looming towards the end of the year; well the date came through 15th January 2014, that has now been and gone.

Chapter Twenty-Four

For the past two years I have been seeing specialists at hospital regarding my weight, the process involved yet more counselling, something that I am so familiar with nowadays. I have had a weight problem since day 1 really, one of the things that came out when I received counselling with Hilary and Sarah at the hospital was I used food as a coping mechanism. As a young child, I used food to mask how scared and unhappy I was, this stayed with me throughout my life. I have been overweight all my life, but hitting my 40s it started to affect my health, I was diagnosed with type 2 diabetes, I suffer gastro problems, pains in my feet and knees, I just started to feel old before my time. I think I have tried every diet under the sun, all the fad diets, the miracle fixes, everything, but to no avail. After lots of therapy, lots of talks and skills sessions I have now embarked on a whole new radical lifestyle change in order to shift the weight I need to shift. Food was my drug of choice, food was my crutch to lean on, it was always there, easy to get and always satisfying, when I was down I believed food helped me to forget the bad things in my life, it never did, like alcohol dependant people it only masks the problems. I feel positive for the first time in many years, it is the first part of a new journey for me, but I am happy to be on it. Wish me well friends…

27 June 2014

Well folks, I thought it time to report back in and let you know how I am doing, lots of changes in the last six months. Firstly, I am six tones lighter than I was back in January, and I have never felt better. My eating habits have changed only in that I eat far less, my portions are normal, I no longer crave the crap I once did, I do treat myself with nice things occasionally as opposed to just eating junk at every opportunity, its working for me. I took on a rescue dog too called Skipper, he is a Cocker Spaniel and is nearly 12 years old, he and Doug my Sprocker Spaniel who is now 18 months get on famously, the exercise I now get is great, I walk them for miles and miles and enjoy every minute of it. The joy those dogs have brought me is immeasurable, I think you only know it if you are a dog owner, it's amazing. On another positive note, the wing I work on with sex offenders has now re-rolled to mainstream prisoners, although they are very different to deal with the fact I haven't got those constant reminders around at work now is a big relief. I think I can now start putting things back on track, I am healthy, kinda happy right now so it is onward and upward.

11 August 2014

Well, what a sad, sad day, I was listening to the news on the radio whilst lying in bed waiting for my early morning alarm when I hear about the death of Robin Williams, AKA Mork, Mrs Doubtfire to name just a few of his screen personas. I must admit to being extremely saddened by the news, it was on my mind all day. Now I don't know Robin Williams personally, of course I don't, but I grew up watching this man, he appeared on *Happy Days* if memory serves me right, this being a cool programme to watch in the very early '80s, from this Mork and Mindy, this had to be my most favourite childhood TV show, it was brilliant. But there was a sad side to Robin, and that was depression. Here is a man you would think had everything, fame, fortune, the life only ordinary people could dream of, but it was tainted by my old friend's presence, depression. The dark cloak that hangs around you and suffocates you, when you are so far down it's like drowning, you can't function properly, nothing makes sense, you can't control the way you feel no matter how hard you try. I feel so sorry for Robin, he just couldn't shake off the heavy, dark shroud, I wish I could have helped a fellow sufferer I really do. The media have been reporting all sorts of stories, but let me say this, Robin Williams did not die from suicide and the sick people in this world saying it's his own selfish fault do not understand how serious depression is, you do not choose to take your own life. Depression paralyses you from making any rational choices. If someone dies from cancer, you don't say, they died from a pulmonary embolism (which can be the cause of death related to cancer). You say, cancer killed them.

Robin Williams 1957–2014

Robin died from DEPRESSION, not suicide. Suicide is the unfortunate final result in the illness.

Look around the office today, the gym, the street, your own home – one in four people in the UK suffer a form of depression the person next to you could be suffering right this moment with the same thoughts going through their mind as did Robin's moments before he took his life to free himself from the illness.

One in four means someone in your family is likely to suffer from this horrible illness. What can you do today to help? No more playing small. Spread the awareness.

RIP. Robin. Genie, you're free!

Chapter Twenty-Five

7 November 2014

Oh God, I am feeling so, so weird this past few weeks, a mixture of being tired, completely fed up and pissed off with my life and I am not sure as to why really. My life has changed quite a bit with my 6 stone weight loss, but although it has changed to me I feel as if hasn't, not sure if I am making sense really. I think what I am trying to say is, I feel no different, I have been overweight all my life and now all of a sudden I am a normal weight, yet I don't feel any different, I still see the fat bloke in the mirror, in the shop windows when I walk by, I hate what I see. Things at home are different too, me and my wife just seem so distant, we get on, but not in a way a married couple should, there is no passion, no intimacy, no spark, no communication, it feels just awful. I am just tired of all of it, I haven't felt so low in a long, long time, that old dark cloak of depression seems to have wrapped around me like once more and I can't seem to shake it off, who do I talk to, where do I turn, I have never felt so lonely. It's a kind of tired that sleep can't fix. I am the big fella as they say at work now and again, all it takes is a smile, one of my cheeky laughs to hide my injured soul, and nobody will ever see just how broken I am.

How can you feel loved, when you feel empty inside? How can you be heard, when no one listens? How can you feel there is purpose, when you are lost? How can you love, when you don't feel loved? How can you speak, when you have no voice? How can you feel important, when you always comes last? How can you keep going, when there is no end? How can you keep trying, when there is nothing left? How can you long for, when you are just tired out? WELCOME TO MY LIFE.

It's really sad how one day I'll seem to have everything going right then the next day I'll lose everything so fast. No one wants to hear my problems so I keep it all inside, I can handle it after all, can't I?? My wife, my partner of nearly 30 years, she is sat the other end of the sofa here, totally oblivious to what I am writing here on my blog, I tell her nothing, she asks nothing, we can't talk about anything like this, I find her the most difficult person to talk too, and I really do not know why, perhaps she would listen and understand me, sometimes I feel so angry towards her for no reason I know of I just can't open up, it's utter madness I know. Sometimes I think I forget how to feel, then I log on to this and tap away these things that are on my mind, it helps me I guess to off load, hopefully you guys who wade through my drivel may see some sense in that. Sometimes all I want is for someone to look me in the eye, ask me if I am OK then hug me tightly and say, "I know you are not." I guess my biggest fear is the people who are my friends will one day see me the way I see myself. I feel I can't do this anymore. Pretend that everything's great. Act like there's nothing to hate. Wipe away every tear. Run away from my fears. Talk like everything's okay. Live like there's nothing wrong with today. I feel lonely every single day of my life, but I am too ashamed to admit it to the people I love. I will endeavour to fight the good fight with depression. Till next time folks.

4 December 2014

Well, here we have another Christmas galloping towards us, I am at a loss as to where the time went. The past few months have been hard for me, I have had my old demons to deal with, and these have been enflamed with recent events involving my eldest daughter. One Saturday night, late summer, she was with friends enjoying a night out with friends, as youngsters do, they took their party mood from town to one of their friends' homes to continue, girls having fun, as simple as that. Even though both my daughter have grown into fine young women the worry head remains when they are out and about, my job makes me nervous when they are out, I see the evil people behind the most heinous of crimes. I always say to them when they are out, travel with friends never alone, and if you need a life home then ring, many a time I have been on the taxi run in the early hours. Well this night she left her friend's house and decided to walk home, a 20-minute walk I guess, and besides it was a warm summer evening/morning. Just five minutes into her walk home, she was grabbed from behind and dragged into a garden of a large house. "Do as you are told and you won't get hurt," her attacker snarled. She fought with this creature, little did he know she is training in martial arts, something I frowned about when she started it. She managed to get this vile man in a headlock using her legs, in a panic he punched out several times striking her in the face, as he got up to run she kicked him in the face, hopefully breaking his nose. She fled to the homeowner's door and raised the alarm.

Chapter Twenty-Six

Every parent's nightmare, I was screaming with anger inside when I heard what had happened, I wanted to sit in the road where it happened hoping I would find the scum bag, my anger consumed me and scared me to be honest, if I had of caught him, I dread to think what I may have done. The morning after the incident, my daughter came downstairs, I was stunned, her face was so swollen and bruised, I couldn't help but cry. My daughter was very resilient, unlike me anger raged through me, I wanted justice, I wanted to hurt the man responsible for this, I still do. Weeks and weeks passed and then a phone call saying they had caught a local man. Churchdown-man-charged-connection-attempted-rape. This piece of shit was now in custody and facing Crown Court, yet again our family through no fault of ours will have to go through the court process and face a nasty sexual predator. This man, Mark Raymond Willis is in prison awaiting trial, I want him to pay dearly for what he has done, and who knows I may meet up with him one day…

11 February 2015

Well, yet another Christmas came and went, it was a strange affair this time around, it just seemed to be there upon us before we knew about it, and work does have that nasty habit of spoiling home life. Me and my dear wife had another upset, I had foolishly let my guard down and almost broke my marriage for being nothing short of stupid, an innocent friendly chat with a fellow dog walker in the park almost turned into an illicit affair. Did I want it? Not in the slightest. Did I do anything? No, I did not. I was so down and away with it, this complete stranger was an ear to listen to my sad ramblings, but this lady was no stranger to sadness herself and was perhaps as lost as I felt at that moment. Thankfully, I saw sense and realised everything I ever wanted was right here at home, it always was and always will be, the love of a good woman is such an intoxicating thing and I almost lost sight of that, never again, it's fair to say the woman who I have spent almost 30 years of my life with is the woman I want to spend the next 30 plus years with.

4 March 2015

Well, here I am again in a bit of a mess, a mind mess to be precise. That's the easiest way to describe it really, I have taken a week off work, a few days ago I just felt so tired, cranky and just physically spent it was untrue. It was all the tell-tale signs of depression, an all too familiar scene for me. I have been signed off work for a couple of weeks, the prison environment doesn't need me when I am feeling low, my tolerance levels aren't up to it. The unit I work has gone through some major changes, to be fair the whole job has changed so much of late which makes it more difficult to be around at times. I have as before come through my black dog day unscathed, my friends and family are key to this. During my time off work what with nights, rest days and leave, I applied for a new job, selling motorcycles, and surprisingly to me after a few interviews I was offered the job. Whilst I was excited at the thought of a new career, there was this niggling doubt throughout the whole process whether I was doing the right thing. Excitement is a powerful thing, it can and does jade reality slightly, or it has done for me. The thought of leaving my job as a Prison Officer fills me with dread, did I really want to quit this job that at times I thought I hated. The truthful answer is, NO I don't. I have realised that I have been doing the job so long, that firstly I am quite good at it, and secondly in a macabre way I enjoy it. I enjoy the company of my colleagues, and I guess the challenges of the clientele, do make for an interesting job. Perhaps, I have had one of those epiphany moments where you realise what you have is what you want really. Well, I am looking to change my outlook that is for sure, I want off the medication, and get my life back on track, put the past in the past and move on and start enjoying the things I have in life and be thankful for them. Happy days indeed.

The Boogeyman

The Boogeyman comes late at night.
So stay under the covers, tuck them in tight.
Close your eyes, pretend to sleep,
Even though you hear him creep.
If your eyes stay shut so tight,
You can make it through another night.
Just let him play his twisted games,
In time my child, he'll go away.

Breathe deep and even, don't say a word.
Keep your calm, little child.
After he leaves, tuck the covers back in,
Put it out of your mind, forget about him.

Go to sleep, proud you did not scream,
Tell yourself it was just a bad dream.
Wake up and wash with water that scalds.
Keep your secrets, build your walls.

Sit down to breakfast, take your place.
After all, you never saw his face.
Remind yourself it was just a fable,
And that's not him sat at the table.

Ollie

The Typist's
A–Z
Edith Mackay

Pitman

PITMAN BOOKS LIMITED
128 Long Acre, London WC2E 9AN

Associated Companies
Pitman Publishing Pty Ltd, Melbourne
Pitman Publishing New Zealand Ltd, Wellington

© Edith Mackay 1983

First published in Great Britain 1983

British Library Cataloguing in Publication Data
Mackay, Edith
    The Typist's A–Z—(Pitman Office Guides)
    1. Typewriting
    I. Title
    652.3   Z49

Text set in 10/11 pt Linotron 202 Ehrhardt, printed and bound
in Great Britain at The Pitman Press, Bath

ISBN 0 273 01930 9

Contents

iv   Contents

Preface

Today more than ever, expert typewriting is a vitally important skill, an essential qualification of every secretary and personal assistant. Yet every typist is at times faced with something new that causes hesitation. It may be how to type something, how to express something, or what a whole new concept is about. This book is designed to provide the answer, or point the way to it.

With so diverse a subject, it is difficult to carry in one's head all the information needed to perform every task well. In this handy, up-to-date reference source there are instructions, hints, and practical illustrations on a very wide range of topics — as well as explanations as to *why* things are done as they are, since understanding is half the battle of mastery and retention.

Numerous typists are returning to work after a lengthy spell away: they understandably feel rusty and in need of help to get back quickly into the swing of things. This comprehensive guide — which takes in new developments in office equipment and procedures — will at once serve as a refresher course and a confidence booster.

Written with all these needs in mind, *The Typist's A–Z* is offered as a source of information and ideas to practising typists at all levels, and to those students aiming for the top.

EM 1983

Acknowledgments

My grateful thanks go to the publishing and production staff at Pitman, whose expertise has in no small measure contributed to the outcome of this book: especially Pam Wickham and Janet Murphy.

Abbreviations

With open punctuation these are not followed by a stop. Compare the two lists below.

Open punctuation	Full punctuation
Please come at 7 pm <u>not</u> 8 pm.	Please come at 7 p.m. <u>not</u> 8 p.m.
Mr T S Waters BSc works here.	Mr. T. S. Waters, B.Sc., works here.
PS I flew on an MEA plane.	P.S. I flew on an M.E.A. plane.
Ann is a BBC announcer.	Ann is a B.B.C. announcer.
He arrives at 1800 hrs not 1900 hrs.	He arrives at 1800 hrs. not 1900 hrs.
Pets, eg dogs and cats, are banned.	Pets, e.g. dogs and cats, are banned.
NB Raincoats, etc, are needed.	N.B. Raincoats, etc., are needed.
Augustus ruled from 31 BC to 14 AD.	Augustus ruled from 31 B.C. to 14 A.D.
A Scot, viz Ian Bell, won the title.	A Scot, viz. Ian Bell, won the title.

Full stops are always omitted in acronyms (abbreviations which are pronounced as a word instead of letter by letter), eg NATO, UNICEF.

See also Open, full and optional punctuation, pp 126–7

Recognised and drafting abbreviations

Recognised abbreviations like ie, eg, etc, viz, NB, PS *always* appear in abbreviated form. Drafting abbreviations, used for speed, like wd, shd, Yrs ffy, or the writer's 'personal shorthand' may be commonly used. In context the meaning should always be clear. Drafting abbreviations can be used in clean drafts unless the originator instructs otherwise (eg to gauge page length), but in final typing they must appear in full.

   Note   In-house documents sometimes retain abbreviations which would be spelt out in external use.

List of abbreviations

Decorations, Honours, Educational and Professional qualifications: see pp 181–6
Foreign words, phrases, abbreviations: see pp 61–4
Weights and measures: see pp 118–20

AA	Automobile Association
AAA	Amateur Athletics Association
ABCC	Association of British Chambers of Commerce
ABTA	Association of British Travel Agents
AC	alternating current
A/c	account
ACAS	Advisory Conciliation and Arbitration Service
ACGB	Arts Council of Great Britain
ADC	Aide-de-camp; advice of duration and charge (telephone)
AEA	Atomic Energy Authority
AEU	Amalgamated Engineering Union
AGM	Annual General Meeting
Ald	Alderman
ALGOL	acronym contracted from 'algorithmic language' (computing)
AMA	Assistant Masters Association
amp	ampere
AN	advice note
anon	anonymous
AOB	any other business
AP	Associated Press
APEX	Association of Professional, Executive, Clerical and Computer Staffs
AQ	achievement quotient
AR	all risks (marine insurance)
ASLEF	Associated Society of Locomotive Engineers and Firemen
ASLIB	Association of Special Libraries and Information Bureaux
ATC	Air Training Corps
ATV	Associated Television
AUEW	Amalgamated Union of Engineering Workers
AUT	Association of University Teachers
BA	British Airways
BAA	British Airports Authority
BACIE	British Association for Commercial and Industrial Education
BALPA	British Airline Pilots Association
BASIC	acronym from 'beginner's all-purpose symbolic instruction code' (computing)
BBC	British Broadcasting Corporation
BC	before Christ
b/d	brought down
BDA	British Dental Association
B/E	bill of exchange
BEC	Business Education Council
Beds	Bedfordshire

BETA	Business Equipment Trades Association
b/f	brought forward
B/L	bill of lading
BMA	British Medical Association
BR	British Rail
B/S	balance sheet; bill of sale
BSA	Building Societies Association
BSC	British Steel Corporation
BSI	British Standards Institution
BST	British summer time
Bt	Baronet
Btu	British thermal unit
Bucks	Buckinghamshire
BUPA	British United Provident Association
C	Centigrade (Celsius)
CAA	Civil Aviation Authority
CAB	Citizens Advice Bureau
Cambs	Cambridgeshire
CAP	Common Agricultural Policy (EEC)
Cards	Cardiganshire
CAT	College of Advanced Technology
CBI	Confederation of British Industry
c/d	carried down
CEGB	Central Electricity Generating Board
CEng	Chartered Engineer
CET	Central European Time
c/f	carried forward
CI	Channel Islands
CID	Criminal Investigation Department; Council of Industrial Design
CIF	cost, insurance and freight
C/N	credit note
CNAA	Council for National Academic Awards
c/o	care of
COBOL	'common business orientated language' (computing)
COD	cash on delivery
C of E	Church of England
COHSE	Confederation of Health Service Employees
COI	Central Office of Information
CRO	Criminal Records Office
CSC	Civil Service Commission
CSU	Civil Service Union
CTT	capital transfer tax
CWO	cash with order
DC	direct current
d/d	days after date; delivered docks

DD	direct debit
deb	debenture
DEP	Department of Employment
dept	department
DES	Department of Education and Science
DHSS	Department of Health and Social Services
div	dividend
DM	Deutschmark
D/N	debit note
do	ditto (the same)
DO	delivery order
DOE	Department of the Environment
DP	data processing
Dr	debit; debtor; doctor
DTI	Department of Trade and Industry
D/W	dock warrant
E & OE	errors and omissions excepted
ECE	Economic Commission for Europe
ECGD	Export Credits Guarantee Department
ECSC	European Coal & Steel Community
EDP	electronic data processing
EEC	European Economic Community
EFTA	European Free Trade Association
EMA	European Monetary Agreement
enc	enclosure
EOC	Equal Opportunities Commission
ERII	Elizabeth Regina II (Queen Elizabeth II)
ERNIE	'electronic random number indicator equipment' (premium bonds)
Exon	of Exeter
F	Fahrenheit
FAO	Food & Agriculture Organisation
FO	Foreign Office
fo	folio (plural ff)
FOB	free on board
FOC	free of charge
FOQ	free on quay
FOR	free on rail
FORTRAN	'formula translation' (computing)
FOS	free on ship
fr (or f)	franc(s)
FTI	Financial Times index
GATT	General Agreement on Tariffs and Trade
GHQ	General Headquarters
Glam	Glamorganshire
GLC	Greater London Council

4 Abbreviations

Glos	Gloucestershire
GMC	General Medical Council
GMT	Greenwich mean time
GMWU	General and Municipal Workers Union
GP	general practitioner (medicine)
Hants	Hampshire
HE	His Excellency (an ambassador)
Herts	Hertfordshire
HF	high frequency
HM	His (Her) Majesty
HMI	Her Majesty's Inspector (education)
HMSO	Her Majesty's Stationery Office
hon	honourable; honorary
HP	hire purchase; horsepower
HQ	headquarters
Hunts	Huntingdonshire
IATA	International Air Transport Association
IBA	Independent Broadcasting Authority
ICI	Imperial Chemical Industries
ICJ	International Court of Justice
IDD	international direct dialling (telephone)
ILEA	Inner London Education Authority
ILO	International Labour Organisation
IMF	International Monetary Fund
Inc	Incorporated
IOM	Isle of Man
IOU	I owe you
IOW	Isle of Wight
IPS	international paper sizes
IQ	intelligence quotient
IRO	International Refugee Organisation
ISBN	International Standard Book Number
ISO	International Standards Organisation
ITA	Independent Television Authority
ITB	Industrial Training Board
ITU	International Telecommunications Union
J/A	joint account
KLM	Royal Dutch Airlines
Lancs	Lancashire
lat	latitude
lc	lower case (small letters); letter of credit
LCCI	London Chamber of Commerce and Industry
LF	low frequency
Lincs	Lincolnshire

long	longitude
LSE	London School of Economics
LTA	Lawn Tennis Association
Ltd	limited (liability)
LV	luncheon voucher
M	Monsieur (French)
MC	Master of Ceremonies
MCC	Marylebone Cricket Club
MICR	magnetic ink character recognition
Middx	Middlesex
Mlle	Mademoiselle (French)
MLR	minimum lending rate
Mme	Madame (French)
MO	Medical Officer; money order
MOD	Ministry of Defence
MODEM	acronym from 'modulator-demodulator' (computing)
MOH	Medical Officer of Health
Mon	Monmouthshire
Mont	Montgomeryshire
MP	Member of Parliament; Military Police
mpg	miles per gallon
mph	miles per hour
MRC	Medical Research Council
ms	manuscript (plural mss)
MSC	Manpower Services Commission
NAAFI	Navy, Army and Air Force Institute
NALGO	National Association of Local Government Officers
NAS	National Association of School Masters
NATFHE	National Association of Teachers in Further & Higher Education
NATO	North Atlantic Treaty Organisation
NCB	National Coal Board
NCCL	National Council for Civil Liberties
NCO	non-commissioned officer
NCR	no carbon required
NEB	National Enterprise Board
NEDC	National Economic Development Council
NERC	National Environment Research Council
NFER	National Foundation for Educational Research
NFU	National Farmers Union
NHBRC	National House-Builders' Registration Council (or Certificate)
NHS	National Health Service
NI	National Insurance
no	number

NOP	National Opinion Poll
Northants	Northamptonshire
Northumb	Northumberland
Notts	Nottinghamshire
NP	Notary Public
NR	no risk (insurance)
NRDC	National Research Development Corporation
NTDA	National Trade Development Association
NUGMW	National Union of General & Municipal Workers
NUJ	National Union of Journalists
NUM	National Union of Mineworkers
NUPE	National Union of Public Employees
NUR	National Union of Railwaymen
NUS	National Union of Students
NUT	National Union of Teachers
O&M	organisation and methods
OAP	old age pension or pensioner
OCTU	Officer Cadet Training Unit
O/D	overdraft
OECD	Organisation for Economic Cooperation and Development
OED	Oxford English Dictionary
OFT	Office of Fair Trading
OHMS	On Her Majesty's Service
OPEC	Organisation of Petroleum Exporting Countries
OR	owner's risk
OS	Ordnance Survey
OTC	Officers Training Corps
Oxon	Oxford
p	page (plural pp)
pa	per annum
PA	Press Association; Publishers Association
PABX	private automatic branch exchange
Pan Am	Pan-American Airways
P and O	Peninsular and Oriental (Steamship Co)
P&P	postage and packing
PAYE	pay as you earn (income tax)
PC	Privy Councillor; Police Constable; petty cash
PEI	Pitman Examinations Institute
P/L	profit and loss
PLA	Port of London Authority
PLC	public limited company
PM	Prime Minister
PMBX	private manual branch exchange
PN	promissory note
PO	Post Office; postal order

POD	pay on delivery
POP	Post Office preferred (envelope size)
PPS	Parliamentary Private Secretary
PRO	Public Relations Officer; Public Record Office
PROM	programmable read-only memory (computing)
PSDip	Private Secretary's Diploma
PTA	Parent/Teacher Association
QB	Queen's Bench (division of the High Court)
QC	Queen's Counsel (barrister)
RA	Royal Academy (or Academician)
RAC	Royal Automobile Club
RADA	Royal Academy of Dramatic Art
RAM	random access memory (computing)
R&D	research and development
R/D	refer to drawer (cheques)
RDC	Rural District Council
re	with reference to
rm	ream (of paper)
ROM	read only memory (computing)
RP	reply paid
RPI	retail price index
SAA	South African Airways
SABENA	Belgian national airline
sae	stamped addressed envelope
Salop	Shropshire
SAS	Scandinavian Airlines System
SAV	stock at valuation
SAYE	save as you earn
SCOTBEC	Scottish Business Education Council
SDP	Social Democratic Party
SE	Stock Exchange
SHAPE	Supreme Headquarters Allied Powers Europe
S/N	shipping note
SNP	Scottish National Party
SO	standing order (banking)
soc	society
SOGAT	Society of Graphical and Allied Trades
SOR	sale or return
SOS	distress signal ('save our souls')
SPQR	Senatus Populusque Romanus (the Senate and People of Rome)
SRN	State Registered Nurse
SSAFA	Soldiers', Sailors' and Airmen's Families Association
Staffs	Staffordshire
STD	subscriber trunk dialling

STUC	Scottish Trades Union Congress
STV	Scottish Television
TB	trial balance (accounting)
TEC	Technical Education Council
TGWU	Transport and General Workers Union
TOPS	training opportunities scheme
trs	transpose
TUC	Trades Union Congress
UDC	urban district council
UFO	unidentified flying object
UGC	University Grants Committee
UHF	ultra high frequency
UN	United Nations
UNCTAD	United Nations Commission for Trade and Development
UNESCO	United Nations Educational, Scientific & Cultural Organisation
UNICEF	United Nations Children's Fund
UNIDO	United Nations Industrial Development Organisation
UNO	United Nations Organisation
UNRRA	United Nations Relief & Rehabilitation Administration
UP	United Press
UPU	Universal Postal Union
USDAW	Union of Shop, Distributive and Allied Workers
USSR	Union of Soviet Socialist Republics
VAT	value added tax
VDU	visual display unit
VHF	very high frequency
VIP	very important person
VLF	very low frequency
WEA	Workers Educational Association
wef	with effect from
WHO	World Health Organisation
WI	West Indies; Women's Institute
Wilts	Wiltshire
WMO	World Meteorological Organisation
WNP	Welsh Nationalist Party
Worcs	Worcestershire
WP	word processing; without prejudice (legal)
YHA	Youth Hostels Association
YMCA	Young Men's Christian Association
Yorks	Yorkshire
YWCA	Young Women's Christian Association

Accounts and financial statements

It is helpful to have a basic knowledge of accounts when typing them; this clarifies general format and the correct positioning of related items with sub-totals and totals, etc.

Companies present their full financial position in a set of 'final accounts': the **trading account** (showing gross profit before deduction of sales expenses and overheads); the **profit and loss account** (showing net profit before tax); and the **balance sheet** (setting out all assets and liabilities). Thus, the accounts show current performance, while the balance sheet indicates the company's underlying strength — to withstand short-term losses for the sake of investment, expansion, and so on.

Various other financial statements are produced as and when required: comparisons and analyses of results, cash flow statements, budget forecasts, etc, all of which are invaluable aids to efficient business management.

Much accounting material is produced by computer, but typewritten presentation is still used for selected purposes in even the largest companies. The layout and typing method are similar to tabulation with money columns.

Layout

- **Full-page statements** Centred horizontally and vertically on the page. As a general rule, the blank spaces between columns of figures should be equal, but the space between the descriptive column and the first figure column may be wider.
- **Statements within continuous copy** May be blocked at the left-margin *or* start five spaces to the right of it *or* be centred to the typing line. Vertical placement requires equal space above and below. It may end the page if there is room for a bottom margin, otherwise it should start on the next page.
- **Two-column layout** (traditional) With the balance sheet, the left-hand column shows liabilities (what is *owed*) and the right-column shows assets (what is *owned*). With the income and expenditure account, income items are listed in one column and expenditure items in the other. The column totals are 'balanced' on the same level, at the bottom.

```
                    HOME SECURITY BUILDING SOCIETY

                            Balance Sheet
                          as at 31 May 19--

LIABILITIES              £'000    ASSETS                    £'000

Investors' shares       777,416  Mortgages                688,437
Investors' deposits      31,824  Investments and cash     168,170
Taxation and                     Fixed assets               7,169
  other liabilities      21,589  Other assets                 314
Deferred taxation         2,457
General reserve          30,804
                        _____                          _____
                       £864,090                          £864,090
                       ========                          ========
```

Balance sheet: two-column layout

```
                    HOME SECURITY BUILDING SOCIETY

             Income and Expenditure Account for year ended
                            31 May 19--

INCOME                   £'000    EXPENDITURE               £'000

Interest on mortgages    95,306  Interest on shares and
                                   deposits                 76,686
Interest on investments
  and bank deposits      16,573  Income tax on interest     21,733
Other income              1,697  Management expenses         8,185
                                 Branch security screens        48
                                 Depreciation of fixed
                                   assets                      259
                                 Mortgage losses                 8
                                 Excess of income over
                                   expenditure               6,657
                        _____                          _____
                       £113,576                          £113,576
                       ========                          ========
```

Income and expenditure account: two-column layout

Wide paper and a long-carriage typewriter are often required
for typing accounts. Alternatively, separate sheets of paper can
be used for each column and then taped together. Great care is
needed to ensure that the columns are aligned correctly, with
well balanced margins. It is best to type the side with more items
first, and make pencil guidemarks on the second sheet for the
positions of the heading, the first item in the column and the
total.

● **Vertical layout** Many firms now present all accounts in
  vertical style, ie *all* the items are listed one under the other.
  For example, in the balance sheet all the assets appear first,
  followed by all the liabilities, with the balance struck below
  that.

- **Typing layout**   Various styles are possible, however there is the advantage of speed in maximum use of blocking.

CENTURION OIL COMPANY LIMITED

Balance Sheet at 31 December 1982

	Notes	31 December 1982 £million		31 December 1981 £million	
Property, plant, and equipment	12	19,000		15,139	
Less Depreciation, depletion and amortization	12	5,831	13,169	5,153	9,986
Investments in associated companies	11		794		599
Long-term receivables and deferred charges	14		457 14,420		516 11,101
Current assets:					
Inventories of oil, coal, chemicals and metals	15	4,847		3,214	
Inventories of materials		334 5,181		285 3,499	
Accounts receivable	16	4,747		3,871	
Short-term government and other securities	17	644		364	
Cash and short-term deposits		1,859 12,431		1,974 9,708	
Current liabilities:					
Accounts payable and accrued liabilities	18	5,576		4,749	
Income tax payable		1,074		572	
Short-term debt	18	1,108		697	
Long-term debt due within one year	21	225		210	
Capitalized lease obligations due within one year	22	42		39	
Dividends payable to Royal Belgian and Pegasus Transport		344 8,369		513 6,780	
Excess of current assets over current liabilities			4,062		2,928
Total assets less current liabilities			18,482		14,029

Keith Anderson)
Derek R Brown) Directors

Balance sheet: vertical layout

Typing method

- *Columns of money figures*   As in tabulation, correct alignment of figures is essential (see p 121). Ensure that *all* figures, sub-totals and totals are in the correct horizontal and vertical position; only then can the trained eye take in the financial picture at a glance.

12 Accounts and financial statements

- *Accurate copying and proof-reading* This is vital. Check additions and subtractions, but consult the originator about discrepancies — there may be a faulty figure in the sum. Never guess or change figures without reference to the originator.
- *Order of items* The order of presentation can be significant; preserve this strictly.
- *Addition and subtraction* Where successive items are added or subtracted and the resulting amount carried to the next column as a sub-total, this figure may be aligned with the last item of addition or subtraction *or* dropped to the next lower line. Follow copy.
- *Loss (minus) figures* These are shown in red by the use of bi-chrome ribbon (effective only on top copy), *or* typed within brackets, *or* enclosed in a box.
- *Comparative figures* Published accounts often include the previous year's figures for comparison. In print these may be in a second colour; in type they should be clearly headed and separated.
- *Notes on accounts* Published accounts include 'notes' explaining items like depreciation of fixed assets, current and deferred taxation, directors' emoluments, and investments. Some of this information is required by law. The notes may appear as numbered footnotes. If they are very long and numerous they may be presented on a separate sheet(s); follow the same system when typing them.
- *Short-cut method* As with tabulations, when the typist is pressed for time or when typing a draft, horizontal spacing may be adequately judged by eye (see p 167).

See also Business transactions pp 19–22

Alphabetical indexing

- Arrange in order of surname, followed by initial(s) and/or forename(s).

  Adams, R T
  Armour, Brian

- When surnames are the same, the *initials of forenames* determine the order (other letters of forenames are disregarded).

  Williams, A B
  Williams, Andrew D
  Williams, Alex E
  Williams, A F

- If a person's name is included in the name of a firm, place it in the order: surname, forename, and then remainder.

  Brown, Walter Engineering

- Where two or more names are included, the *first* name determines the indexing order.

  Stimpson Lock & Vince

- With hyphenated names, index according to the first name.

  Baldwin-Davies, Mrs R

- For impersonal names, index according to the part that distinguishes it from others.

  Education Officers, Society of Fuel, Institute of Publishers Association

- Surnames beginning with Mac, Mc, or M' are *all* treated as if spelt Mac.

  Macdonald, A
  McLeish, D
  M'Namara, W

- Surnames beginning with St are treated as if spelt Saint.

  Sainsbury, A J
  St John Rivers, B
  Sairs, L B

- Short before long (*or* nothing before something).

  Watt, V
  Watts, A

Rearrangement in alphabetical order

The following method is quick and reliable:

1 On a sheet of paper, write the first name on the list in a suitable position, eg Browning near the top of the sheet, James near the middle, Watson near the bottom. Follow the surname with initial(s) etc.
2 Continue down the list in the same way, fitting in each name in alphabetical order.
3 If any surnames recur, position them according to initial(s).
4 On completion, count the names on both lists to ensure they agree.
5 As you type names, use a ruler to mark your position on the list.
6 When the list is typed, count the names again as a final check.

This method can be applied to any task requiring rearrangement of material, eg price order, date order, etc.

Apostrophe

1 Shows possession: it is placed before s in the singular, after s in the plural.

```
The boy's coat was ragged.  (singular)
The boys' coats hung in neat rows.  (plural)
```

With plurals not ending in s, place apostrophe in front of the s.

```
The women's faces were haggard.
The children's cots were all blue.
The mice's tails were unusually long.
```

Names and words ending in s can take a second s; many people consider this awkward and omit it.

```
Keats' poetry or Keats's poetry
The headmistress' study or the headmistress's study
```

With compound words, the last part takes the apostrophe.

```
My sister-in-law's house
The Serjeant-at-arms' summons
```

Avoid the double possessive.

```
The house of Mrs Brown's sister not Mrs Brown's sister's house
```

2 Shows the omission of a letter or letters in an expression.

```
haven't, wouldn't, couldn't, can't
```

3 Used optionally in decades.

```
The flower-power ethic of the Sixties (or 'Sixties) lives on.
```

4 Used optionally in the plurals of figures and abbreviations.

```
She is in her 50s (or 50's) but looks much younger.
Twenty MPs (or MP's) abstained in the vital vote.
```

Note The possessive pronoun 'its' has no apostrophe.

```
It's a long time now since its inception.
```

Audio-typewriting

The ability to type quickly from recorded dictation is an increasingly valuable skill, and may be an alternative to shorthand or additional to it. The main advantage of audio-typewriting is that executives may dictate at any time that suits them, which makes for an even flow of transcription and speedy work turnround.

Description of skill

The expert audio-typist types almost continuously, seldom having just to listen. She starts by listening to a phrase or sentence, stops dictation (with foot control), and transcribes it. *Before finishing*, she restarts dictation (with foot control) and takes in another group of words: it is virtually one merged operation. Experience enables her to stop and restart the machine so that long sentences are broken into meaningful phrases for typing. Transcription is verbatim (word for word). *Understanding* is important for accurate transcription and for the correct insertion of commas (which are not normally dictated). Knowledge of homophones helps avoid confusion between like-sounding words. The length of the transcription may be gauged by the length of the dictation — this will be shown on the index slip.

Backing sheet

A plastic or stout-paper backing sheet should be used when typing on a single sheet, to prevent pitting of the platen. Backing sheets with a folded end keep edges straight when feeding in several carbons. It is useful to mark the backing sheet showing one inch margins, and the centre lines (horizontal and vertical) of the paper. Lines must be heavy enough to show through the typing paper. If both A4 and A5 sizes are frequently used, it is helpful to have such a backing sheet for each size.

Bar charts

Bar charts (also known as histograms) provide visual representation of a wide range of statistical data. They are frequently prepared for discussion at business meetings, often incorporated in typewritten reports. An expert typist is expected to cope with them.

There are two axes — a horizontal base line, joined at right angles by a left-hand vertical line (the x axis and y axis respectively). Measured points along the x axis (reading from left to right) indicate the independent variable, eg time period: scale points along the y axis (reading upwards) indicate the dependent or measured variable, eg the value or number of sales.

Several sets of related data (for home/export sales, different departments, etc) can be shown on the same chart, for at-a-glance comparison. The different data is shown in different ways, accompanied by a key. Sometimes the bars are shaded with different colours, but this is effective only on a top copy. More often a combination of white space, lines (horizontal, vertical and oblique), dots, and shading is used. The different groups of data are best separated by a space, as in the example below.

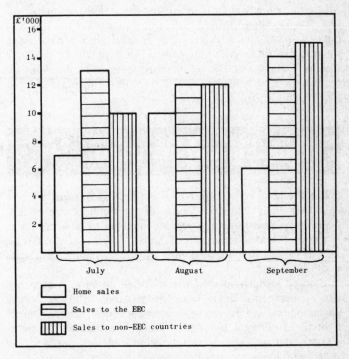

Alternatively, the information could be shown on a **component bar chart**. A single bar for each month would show its overall total and the bar would be divided into its component parts, explained by a key.

Yet again, one might choose to use a **percentage bar chart**. This is similar to a component bar chart but the vertical axis indicates percentages, each bar rising to 100. Each bar is therefore akin to a pie chart.

Data presented by bar chart can often be alternatively shown by line graph, pie chart, or tabulation.

Bills of quantities

When a building or engineering project has been designed and planned by an architect or engineer, a bill of quantities is drawn up by a quantity surveyor. It analyses the work item by item, the standards to be adhered to, and the materials to be used. A copy of the bill of quantities is sent to interested contractors who price it, item by item, taking account of the cost of materials, labour and overheads involved: the total price arrived at becomes the 'tender figure'. Usually the work is given to the contractor who submits the lowest tender.

The trades and items are listed on the bill in the order in which the work will be carried out. Long bills of quantities, however, are often divided into separate units for the different trades. Specially ruled A4 paper is used with vertical lines running the full length of the paper. Tab stops should be set for the start of columns. Bills of quantities present no problems for the experienced typist: they are a form of tabulation, rendered easy by the pre-ruled pages.

Blocking and centring

When the blocked style of layout was first used, many thought *everything* should be blocked, both for speed and for consistency: centring and insetting only with indented paragraphs. However, others preferred to retain some features from the 'centred' style, and there was much questioning as to how far the two styles might be mixed.

Blocked layout is now well established for most documents, but a liberal attitude is taken to deviations which *aid rapid communication and reference* — centring headings, insetting 'high-lighted' matter and footnotes, placing the date at the right-margin, and so on. Judicious variation combines the merits of speed with greater prominence for key features.

Yet a consistent method of layout and style is an important aid to efficiency in any organisation. Most therefore have their own 'house style' (see pp 69–70).

Brackets

These enclose in parenthesis:
● a part of a sentence which stands apart from the main flow

```
Publishing our accounts in April (previously it
was January) has several advantages.

Mr Brown explained the point at length (and
Mr Black did so briefly), but the Committee
remained mystified.
```

● a reference

```
This is clearly stated (Section IV, iii, page 129).
```

● any interpolation

```
Dogs (and cats for that matter) make good pets.
```

Sentence construction may require a comma (or a semi-colon, etc) after the closing bracket. Sometimes dashes or commas are used as alternatives to brackets (see p 71).

Square brackets

Where no special keys are available, combination characters (see pp 29–31) have to be used. Square brackets are used:
● for brackets within brackets, in the outer or the inner position

```
The Committee (meeting Tuesdays, Thursdays and
/except in January/ Fridays for three-hour
sessions) cannot keep up with the work.
```

● in reports to show comments added by the writer

```
The reporter wrote that last winter was the coldest ever
/this was not borne out by the records/ but that less
damage was done than in other recent years.
```

The enclosed words are not part of the newspaper report, but are added by the writer commenting on it.
● in quoted matter to indicate corrections, comments etc, not in the original.

Business transactions

These can pass through many documented stages — enquiry, quotation, order, advice note, delivery note, invoice, debit (or credit) note, statement of account. There is a wide variety of styles and layouts — but once the standard pattern is understood, there should be no difficulty in dealing with the variations found in different offices. (Many firms now use computers to handle such transactional information.)

E & OE (errors and omissions excepted) on a form means that the supplier reserves the right to rectify any errors or omissions that come to light.

VAT (value added tax) A trader who supplies taxable goods must be VAT registered and issue a tax invoice. Certain goods (eg books, food) are VAT exempt.

Two specimen invoices (one VAT exempt, the other VAT chargeable), a specimen credit note and a statement of account are shown below and on the following pages. Since the VAT rate is subject to fluctuation, it is shown in the examples as 10 per cent.

	INVOICE		No 2486

International Book Company Limited
86–90 Kings Parade
CHESTER CH3 2BQ

Sold to: Smart Bros
46 High Street
OXFORD OX3 3BQ

Date: 18 April 19--

Terms: Net 30 days

Quantity	Description	Unit cost	Amount
		£	£
20	The Wines of Europe - T Prince (Fanfare)	4.50	90.00
15	Wales and Its Castles - D White (Long)	6.50	97.50
10	Good Grooming - S Shaw (Everest)	8.25	82.50
12	Silent Waters - A Browning (Sanderson)	4.20	50.40
			£320.40

Invoice

Southern Furnishings (Wholesale)

80–82 Christchurch Road

BOURNEMOUTH BH6 3OT

VAT Registration No. 431 2871 63   **Date:** 10 October 19--

Sold to: Jennings & Harlow
86 Castle Road
SOUTHAMPTON SO3 4PL

Your Order No. F 198   **Terms:** Net one month

Tax point	Type of supply	Description	Unit cost	Amount	VAT rate	VAT amount
			£	£		£
(date as	Sale	2 Armchairs No 632	85.00	170.00	10%	17.00
above)	"	2 Sideboards No 248	300.00	600.00	"	60.00
	"	2 Desks No 143	150.00	300.00	"	30.00
	"	2 Bookcases No 325	112.00	224.00	"	22.40
		Total Goods		1,294.00		129.40
		Total VAT		129.40		
		Total Amount Due		£1,423.40		

CREDIT NOTE

International Book Company Limited   No C 963
86-90 Kings Parade
CHESTER CH3 2BQ

To: Aztec Book Co Ltd   Date: 18 April 19--
18 Meadow Lane
DERBY DR4 3XV

Reason for Credit	Quantity and Description	Unit cost	Amount
		£	£
Goods returned (faulty)	2 Dressmaking for Style - G Grace (Everest)	6.00	12.00
Goods damaged - 50% reduction	4 Gardening for All - C Davis (Long)	7.00	14.00
	Total Amount Credited		£26.00

Business transactions 21

STATEMENT

International Book Company Limited
86-90 Kings Parade
CHESTER CH3 2BQ

To: Smart Bros
46 High Street
OXFORD OX3 2BQ

Date: 30 April 19--

Fo 102

Terms: Net 30 days

Date	Ref		Debit	Credit	Balance
19--			£	£	£
31 March		Balance			205.87
4 April	2106	Goods	186.20		392.07
10 "	2487	"	75.80		467.87
18 "	2763	"	320.40		788.27
18 "	C 962	Returns		17.70	770.57
20 "		Cheque		205.87	564.70
25 "	2968	Goods	54.60		619.30

Carbon copying

For immediacy and cheapness, this is still a much used means of
making one or two copies of a document (though some offices
use only copying machines). The main disadvantage is that it is
slow and fiddly to correct every copy (by erasure or correcting
fluid) in order to produce an exact replica of the top copy.

Carbonised side

Wrong side of
carbon paper

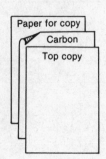

Paper for copy

Carbon

Top copy

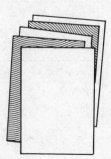

Use and storage

1 Insert the papers carefully into the typewriter to prevent
creasing. If they feed unevenly, ask the mechanic to check
the feed roll mechanism.
2 A backing sheet with a folded end keeps the edges straight
and helps insertion. Also, use the paper release when

inserting, so that when it is returned the papers are all gripped together.

3 On a manual typewriter, use a sharp, even touch and clean typefaces for good results.

4 Obtain maximum use from your carbon paper by occasionally turning it top to bottom, and by cutting a thin strip from the top edge.

5 Store carbon paper in a cool place in a flat box.

Types

Standard (in general use) usually has a plastic coating, which is clean to handle and prevents curling.

Plastic film (long life) has a microporous plastic coating impregnated with quick-drying ink. It is crease and curl resistant. It is clean to handle, and copies are smudge-free. It can be used up to 200 times.

One-time is thin and cheap, for use once only. It is supplied with stencils and sets of forms.

Weights	*No of copies*	
Super heavyweight	1–2	
Heavyweight	1–3	The heavier the weight,
Standard weight	4–6	the fewer the copies, but
Manifold (lightweight)	7–10	the longer the life
Super manifold		
(extra lightweight)	11–15	

(Electric and electronic typewriters (with pressure control) produce more copies than manuals.)

Colours Black, blue, brown, green, purple and red. Some organisations use different colours for copies to different departments.

NCR (no carbon required) The reverse side of the top copy and the top side of the sheets below are specially treated. This is used particularly in form sets, where it saves handling time.

Cards

Problems of typing on a small area

1 *Thickness of card* Unless the card is thin enough to curve easily round the cylinder, it can be difficult to keep straight lines of type and uniform line-spacing. The plastic card clips help to hold the card firm; as will the paper grips if moved so that they grip the card.

2 *Typing at bottom* The use of a backing sheet helps the typewriter to grip the card long enough to prevent the last lines running off the straight.

3 *Very small card* For easier feed into the typewriter, tuck the top edge into a narrow fold along the top of a sheet of paper.

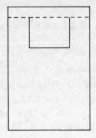

For a long run of small cards prepare a sheet of A4 paper (lined for ease of alignment) by cutting slits to hold the corners of four or six cards. Feed this into the typewriter to type cards speedily in series.

4 *Layout* Narrow margins (but not less than $\frac{1}{2}$ inch) and use of half line-spacing help make the best use of limited space.

5 *Carbon copies* Light and medium weight cards take at least one good carbon copy — as for a duplicate set of index cards. The file copy of a message on a business postcard is best taken on A5 flimsy.

Main uses of cards

Correspondence Cards may be used when the message is brief and not confidential; they save envelope handling. Businesses usually have their name, address, and telephone number printed across the top of the message side. When these are typed, a dividing line below them, right across the card, is effective. No salutation or complimentary close is required. Signature (or initials) at the end of the message is optional.

```
W & G BROWN, Coal Merchants
5 North Road, YORK  YO2 4AB                     Tel 0904 6893
──────────────────────────────────────────────────────────────

22 October 19--

Here is the information you asked for from our new price
list.

                                                    5 sacks
Price per 50 kg open sack        1-4 sacks          and over

                                     £                 £
OPEN FIRE SMOKELESS FUEL
Coalite                            6.75              6.54
Homefire                           7.15              6.96

HOUSE COAL
Cobbles                            5.51              5.39
Nuts                               5.25              5.13
```

Correspondence card

Indexing   To store skeleton information systematically, index cards are categorised and alphabetically or numerically filed by region, type of business, etc. Any set of index cards *must* be consistent in style and layout for speedy location of information.

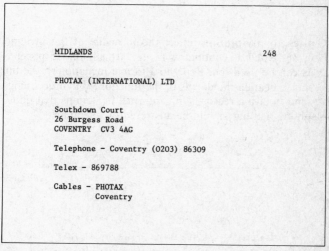

```
    MIDLANDS                                       248


    PHOTAX (INTERNATIONAL) LTD


    Southdown Court
    26 Burgess Road
    COVENTRY  CV3 4AG

    Telephone - Coventry (0203) 86309

    Telex - 869788

    Cables - PHOTAX
             Coventry
```

Index card

Invitations   For formal social functions printed cards are used, with space to insert the guest's name — but the typist should be familiar with common layouts. For less formal functions, the typist may have to type an original, and photocopy or duplicate the number required. Style of wording and layout depend on the formality of the occasion and the preference of the sender. They are usually in the third person with no salutation, complimentary close or signature. Invitation cards are normally sent in envelopes.

```
                   Mr and Mrs R Browning

              request the pleasure of the company of

              .........................................

              at the marriage of their daughter, Diana

                      to Mr Philip Gardiner

                   at St John's Church, Bath

              on Saturday, 21 March 19-- at 12 noon

                 and afterwards at the Regal Hotel


              26 Regency Court
              BATH  BA3 4CX                        RSVP
```

Formal invitation in centred style

Replies to invitations reflect the formality of the invitation. They are typed as continuous matter, usually on A5 paper but cards can be used too. Reply to a formal invitation in the third person, repeating the details of the function. When declining, it is polite to give a reason. Only informal invitations that quote a telephone number should be answered by telephone.

```
                                        64 Linden Crescent
                                        BATH  BA2 3GH

                                        10 February 19--

        Miss Elizabeth Morgan thanks Mr and Mrs Browning
        for their kind invitation to the wedding of their
        daughter, Diana, to Mr Philip Gardiner at St John's
        Church, Bath, at noon on 21 March 19-- and after-
        wards at the Regal Hotel.  She has much pleasure in
        accepting.
```

Reply to above invitation (**Note**: no salutation, complimentary close or signature)

26 Cards

```
        The Directors of INTERNATIONAL BRIDGES LTD

        request the company of

        ........................................

        at Cocktails and Dinner

        at the Greenacre Hotel, Seabourne

        on Friday 26 June at 1830 hrs

        following the West Harbour Bridge opening


        The Secretary
        International Bridges Ltd
        28 Wharf Walk, Seabourne  SO2 5AG    RSVP
```

Semi-formal invitation in blocked style

```
        ........................................

        John and Mary Clark invite you to their
        housewarming Cheese and Wine Party on
        Saturday 20 May at 7 30 pm.  (The house is
        on the corner of Queen's Avenue - which
        leads off Preston Road at the Clock
        Tower.)


        68 Kings Drive
        Longmore Estate
        NOTTINGHAM  NG3 2DX           Regrets only

        Tel: 6829
```

Informal invitation in blocked continuous prose; guest's name at top

Place cards   Place names for a dinner table are typed on small cards (usually A8) to fit into a slotted stand, or on A7, folded to stand free on the table. Ensure a clean fold by lightly scoring the reverse side with a metal blade. Conference seat reservations are typed likewise, on A7 size.

Standard (or form) cards One common use of these is to acknowledge a communication where the matter cannot be dealt with quickly. Such cards are printed or typed with spaces for typing in identifying details and a brief message. There are many other uses of standard cards (see p 164).

Travel information and short itineraries These can be typed on a card for convenient carrying in a wallet or handbag.

TRAIN TIMES

(Mon - Fri)

Wiseton	Morely	Morely	Wiseton
Dep	Arr	Dep	Arr
0703	0820	1710	1825
0720	0835	1720	1840
0740	0905	1745	1910
0750	0915	1800	1920

Miscellaneous information Information typed on cards includes: advertisements for notice-boards, speech points (headings with cues to guide a speaker), borrowed file dockets, follow-up reminders, etc. More durable than slips of paper, cards are useful for typing *any* brief or condensed information for frequent reference.

Centring

1 Horizontal

Always centre over the typing line. With equal margins, the centre point of the paper and of the typing line is the same.

Centring to the page (or over equal margins)

- *Backspacing method* (no counting) Move the printing point to the centre of the paper, and backspace once for each two characters (letters and spaces) in the line to be centred (ignore an odd letter at the end). When centring successive lines, set a tab stop at the centre point.

- *Arithmetical method*   Count the characters in the line to be centred, and subtract the total from the number of characters across the paper. Divide the answer by two for your starting position.
- *Mixed method*   Count the characters in the line to be centred. From the centre of the paper, backspace (or, using the carriage release lever, move the carriage back) half the number of characters in the line.

Centring over unequal margins

The backspacing method is the simplest. To find the centre of the typing line, add the numbers at which the right and left margins are set, and divide the answer by two. For example, using A4, elite, and margins at 25 and 93:

$25 + 93 = 118$ $118 \div 2 = 59$ (Centre of typing line is 59)

2   Vertical
Count the lines (of both type and space) to be vertically centred. Subtract this from the number of lines down the paper (1 inch = 6 lines in pica and elite), and divide the answer by two: this gives the number of blank lines above and below the centred typescript.

Combination characters and special signs

To increase the number of symbols produced by a typewriter, combination characters are formed from *two* characters. Special signs use existing keys for an alternative purpose.

Characters formed without raising or lowering paper

Caret sign	Type a solidus, backspace and underscore. (Used to show omission.)	$\angle$
Cent sign	Type small c, backspace and type solidus. (Used in various currencies.)	¢
Decimal point	Type full stop in its normal position.	6.5
Diaeresis, umlaut	Type required letter, backspace and type double quotation marks. (In English used to show that the second of two adjacent	naïve

	vowels is pronounced separately — this has virtually died out. In German the umlaut, indicating vowel sound change, is common.)	Düsseldorf
Ditto sign	Use double quotation marks. In blocked style typed under first letter of each repeated word. In centred style typed under centre of each repeated word.	"
Division sign	Type colon, backspace and type hyphen.	÷
Dollar sign	Type capital S, backspace and type solidus.	$
Exclamation mark	Type apostrophe, backspace and type full stop.	!
Feet, minutes	Use apostrophe.	12'
Inches, seconds	Use double quotation marks.	8"
Minus sign	Use hyphen with space before and after.	6 - 2
Multiplication sign	Use small x with space before and after.	6 x 2
Sloping fractions	Use solidus. Leave one space after whole number. Most typewriters have keys for common fractions. (See also p 172.)	6 3/5

Characters formed by raising or lowering paper

Use variable line-spacer, interliner, or (except in single spacing) the half-spacer. (Always return paper to typing line before continuing.)

Asterisk*	Lower paper, type small x, backspace and type hyphen. (On most typewriters an asterisk is provided on the top row.)	metals*
Brace	Type left or right bracket one under another.	)))
Cedilla	Type small c, backspace and type comma slightly below c. (Often used in French to give sound of 's' to a c.)	garçon
Dagger*	Lower paper, type capital I, backspace and type hyphen.	Notes†
Degrees	Lower paper and type lower case o.	15°
Double dagger*	Lower paper and type capital I. Backspace and type capital I slightly higher than the other.	query‡

30 Combination characters and special signs

Equals sign	Type hyphen, backspace and type second hyphen above first one. (Most typewriters have an 'equals' key.)	$=$
Per cent (per hundred)	Lower paper and type lower case o. Return paper to typing line and type solidus followed by lower case o. (Most typewriters have a 'per cent' key.)	$24^o/o$
Per mille (per thousand)	Lower paper and type lower case o. Return paper to typing line and type solidus followed by two lower case o's.	$2^o/oo$
Section mark	Type capital or small s and backspace. Slightly raise paper and type second capital or small s.	§ §
Square brackets	Type solidus, backspace and type underscore. Lower paper one line space (use half-spacer twice) and type underscore. For right-bracket, type solidus, backspace twice and type underscore. Then lower paper one space and type underscore.	⌐ ⌐
Subscripts	Characters typed below typing line.	H_2O
Superscripts	Characters typed above typing line.	$x = a^2b$

* See also footnotes pp 59–61

Note Plus sign and accents should be neatly inserted with matching-colour pen after the paper has been removed from the typewriter.

Compliments slip

This is usually A6 or $\frac{2}{3}$ A4. It is sent as a courtesy with an enclosure(s) instead of a covering letter when no substantial message is necessary. There will be space for a brief typewritten message (if required) over the signature (or initials) or typed name. Optionally, the addressee's name may be typed at the top left, and the date at the top-right or at the bottom.

Software Product Services Ltd

37 Rosebank Westfield Square Woking Surrey GU22 9QZ Telephone: 04862 68588

Here is the literature you requested: new price list will
follow (due from printer in about a week).

Dr Carole Bailey

With Compliments

Compliments slip

Continuous documents

Consistency in layout and style is essential throughout. Points to watch include paragraph style (which may be consistently different for sub-sections), open or full punctuation, line-spacing, and method of enumeration. Ensure that headings, sub-headings, and their sub-division headings are typed in different styles consistently. Unless it is house style to do so, do not type at the foot of the page (as a catchword) the first word(s) of the next page or PTO, Contd, etc. Note also the following:

1 **Margins**
- Top, bottom and side margins should be consistent on all pages.
- Dropped heads at the start of new chapters or sections should be uniform in depth.
- If the papers are to be fastened together down the side, leave an adequate 'binding' margin.
- If both sides of the paper are used either in the original or in the copies, the left and right margins must be reversed (a wide left-margin on the front becomes a wide *right*-margin on the back of the page). Page numbering is then best centred. Equal side margins avoid the need to reverse margins.

2 **Numbering pages**
The first page is not usually numbered. Subsequent pages use arabic numbers (2 3 4) but preliminary pages sometimes use small roman numerals (ii iii iv). Numbers may be at the top *or* bottom of the page *or* in the right-margin *or* at the centre (consistently). A consistent one or two lines of space must be left between text and page number. It is sometimes wise to include the *total* number of pages, eg 1 of 24, 2 of 24.

3 'Fit' (shared typing)

When a lengthy document is divided among several typists the different parts must fit together unobtrusively. The same size and style of typeface (pica, elite, etc), similar ribbons, and the same paper should be used. Each typist must closely observe instructions about all matters of style and layout. Where possible, each should be given complete chapters or sections to conceal any slight differences.

Copying and duplicating

Word processors and office copiers have led to much less use of duplicating methods requiring specially prepared ink and spirit masters. Word processors and office copiers can make as many high-quality copies as required both quickly and cheaply.

Typed master for multiple copies (camera-ready copy)

- Ensure the type is clean for sharp typescript.
- Use good-quality plastic ribbon for dense black print.
- Type on one side of paper only.
- Special care is needed for corrections, and erasers should not be used. Correction liquid can be effective for deletions and scarcely shows when expertly used — but it is seldom satisfactory to type on top of it. The best method is to paste the correction over the error: hold it up to the light to ensure that the overlay alignment is correct.
- Protect the completed master by keeping it in a folder.
- Never fasten pages together with pins, staples or paper-clips — these may leave marks which will show on copies.

Carbon copying

This is widely used for one or two copies of a letter or other document (see p 22).

Ink duplicating

The master is cut by typing, writing or drawing (with a special stylus) on a stencil. This has a perforated heading to attach it to the duplicator drum. A stencil 'set' includes a backing sheet and one-time carbon paper to help reading on the stencil as the master is prepared. For guidance, the stencil shows the typing area for different paper sizes and scales, and a vertical centre line.

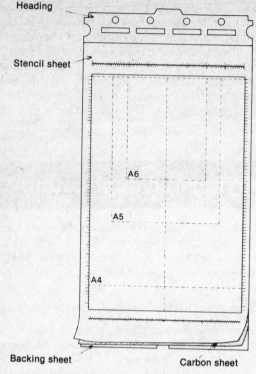

Heading

Stencil sheet

A6

A5

A4

Backing sheet

Carbon sheet

A stencil set

When typing a stencil, disengage the ribbon by moving to the stencil position — usually white. Clean typefaces are necessary for clear copies. With a manual typewriter, use a sharp, even touch. To correct errors, hold the stencil away from the carbon (eg with a pencil) and paint over the error with special correction fluid: when this is dry, type the correction. For a large error, remove the stencil from the typewriter, and cut out the incorrect section with a sharp blade: then 'graft' in part of another stencil, securing the edge with correction fluid: then type in the correction. Gummed paper strips may be used to delete sections not required for retyping.

When the stencil is fitted to the drum of the duplicator, ink penetrates the cut stencil and makes copies.

Note The electronic stencil-maker can copy drawings, photos, and printed or typed text ready for duplicating: a high-quality typed original is made on bond paper.

Spirit duplicating

A master is produced by typing, writing or drawing on special chromo paper contacting with hectograph carbon paper (the reverse image is transferred from the carbon to the shiny side of the master).

When typing the master, use clean typefaces and an even touch on manuals. To correct errors, draw the master forward to expose the reverse image. Remove the error with spirit eraser or with a sharp metal blade. Then, using a new strip of hectograph carbon, type the correction.

The master is then fitted to the drum. As each sheet of copy paper enters the machine it is lightly moistened with spirit and then pressed against the reverse-image master to produce readable copy.

Hectograph carbons are available in seven colours. As many colours as desired can be used on a single master by changing the colour of the carbon paper at the required position. It is therefore a useful method for multi-colour diagrams, etc, but only a limited number of copies can be made from a single master.

As with ink duplicators, masters can be prepared from typed or printed originals on a special copying machine.

Offset lithography duplicating

This method is based on the principle that oil and water are mutually repellent. Masters are prepared on special metal or paper plates coated with a greasy substance. Master plates are available in a variety of colours, but a separate master is needed for each colour; and each requires a separate run through the machine. The quality of the copies is very high, but the machines are relatively expensive, tricky to operate, and costly to maintain.

When typing the master, use the correct paper plate for the number of copies required. Clean typefaces are essential and, with manuals, use a sharp (but not heavy) touch. Corrections are made by lightly removing the surface ink with an offset (non-abrasive) eraser; use a special grease-free erasing liquid for deletions. Special pens, pencils, and crayons are obtainable for manuscript and for ruling lines.

Note   Masters are often produced from print or from a typed original (which must be of high quality, on bond paper) on a special plate-maker.

Correcting errors

Word processors (with electronic correction and amendment of script) avoid the need for erasing or covering up errors. The following techniques apply only to manual and electric type-writers.

Correcting after paper is removed from typewriter

1 Remove error with an eraser or correction liquid.
2 Reinsert paper into typewriter.
3 Using paper release lever, bring a 'thin' letter (such as i or l) exactly above printing point.
4 Use variable line spacer or interliner to level up typing line with alignment scale.
5 Disengage ribbon by moving it to 'stencil', and lightly tap first letter to check alignment and position.
6 If satisfactory, return ribbon position to black, backspace, and type correction.

Correcting by backward feed

This is used for errors on a sheet of typescript which is fastened to others at the top.
1 Erase or paint out error.
2 Insert a sheet of plain paper into typewriter in the normal way until about two inches appear above alignment scale.
3 Insert bottom of sheet for correction between plain paper and *front* of cylinder.
4 Turn cylinder backwards to point where correction is to be made: as soon as feed rollers grip paper to be corrected, remove plain paper.
5 After necessary paper adjustments, type correction.

Half-space correction

This is a useful method of word substitution if the correct word has only one character more ('squeezing') or less ('spreading') than the wrong one.
1 Remove incorrect word.
2 If new word is one character *longer*, move carriage to where *second* letter of old word was typed.
3 Hold down backspace key, type first letter of new word, then release backspace key.
4 Tap one space, hold down backspace key, type second letter and release backspace key.
5 Deal with each letter in same way.
The new word will appear with half a character space on either side.

If the new word is one character *shorter* than the old one, the procedure is the same except that the carriage should be moved at the start to the position of the *third* letter of the old word. The new word will appear with $1\frac{1}{2}$ character spaces on either side.

Half-space correction is simple when the typewriter has a special half-space key.

Correction signs for typescript and print

The following list of signs for amending manuscript or typescript is derived from the printers' code of symbols for correcting proofs (and is also used when correcting print). Some originators do not use them all, so be prepared for changes indicated in other ways.

The marginal sign, followed by an oblique sign — which acts as a division when there is more than one correction — should be written in the margin nearest to the error.

Marginal sign

lc/	Use lower case for capitals underlined, stroked through, or encircled
uc/	Use upper case for small letters underlined, stroked through, or encircled
stet/	Restore crossed-out word(s) underlined with a broken line
trs/	Transpose letters, words, or phrases marked ⌐⌐; these may be numbered in the draft to clarify changed order
NP/ (or) para/	Begin new paragraph at ⌐ or // in the text
run on/	Do not begin new paragraph at ⟶; run on with previous one
⌐	Delete letter(s) or word(s) struck through
words for insertion/	Insert additional matter in text at ʌ (caret sign)
#/	Insert a space at caret sign
close up/	Close up space where ⊂ is shown
⌐BINARY⌐	Unfamiliar or badly written word is repeated in capitals in the margin within a broken or unbroken line
caps/	Use capital letters where indicated
sp caps/	Use spaced capitals where indicated
init caps/	Use capital for the first letter of each word where indicated
eq #/	Equalise spacing where indicated
raise/	Raise matter as indicated by ⌐
lower/	Lower matter as indicated by ⌐
⌐	Move matter to right as indicated by ⌐
⌐	Move matter to left as indicated by ⌐
spell out/	Encircled abbreviation to be written in full, or figure(s) to be written in words

‖	Straighten margin or vertical alignment
⊙/	Insert full stop at the caret sign
,/	Insert comma at the caret sign
⊙/	Insert colon at the caret sign
;/	Insert semi-colon at the caret sign
?/	Insert question mark at the caret sign
!/	Insert exclamation mark at the caret sign
ᵞ	Insert apostrophe (or superscript figure or letter) at the caret sign
ᴧ	Insert subscript figure (or letter) at the caret sign
ᵞ ᵞ	Insert single quote(s) at the caret sign(s)
ᵞ ᵞ	Insert double quote(s) at the caret sign(s)
|-|	Insert hyphen at the caret sign
|—|	Insert dash at the caret sign
c/)/	Insert bracket(s) at the caret sign(s)

(circled handwritten note: TYPIST— names in alpha order please) When the originator wishes to give the typist a general instruction, this is written in the most effective position, and ballooned for clarity.

The following signs are used in printing:

underline/	Underline word(s) underlined in proof
ital/	Use italics for word(s) underlined
bold/	Use bold type for word(s) ⁓ ⁓marked ~~~~~~
×/	Improve the encircled f. ..ty character
wf/	Wrong fount; use correct one for the encircled character(s)
ꝺ/	Encircled letter is upside down; correct it
out see copy/	Word(s) omitted at caret sign to be included
rom/	Change encircled word(s) to roman type

Note Underlining _three times_ on a proof tells the printer to use capital letters (sometimes used in typewriting to call for _spaced capitals_). Underlining _twice_ tells the printer to use small capitals (in typewriting sometimes used for _closed capitals_).

Curriculum vitae

These Latin words (often abbreviated to CV) mean 'the course of one's life'. Curricula vitae vary in style; and what details are included depends on the CV's purpose. It must always be clearly and systematically set out to give the picture at a glance. Relevant information should be itemised, with suitable headings and dates, in chronological order.

```
CURRICULUM VITAE

NAME:                Mary Anderson (Miss)

ADDRESS:             68 Poplar Drive, Westdale, Middx  TW8 3AG

HOME TELEPHONE:      0895 27361

DATE OF BIRTH:       27 July 1959

AGE:                 24

NATIONALITY:         British
_____

EDUCATION AND        Mount Road Comprehensive School,     1971 - 1977
EDUCATIONAL          Twickenham
QUALIFICATIONS:
                     GCE O Level passes in: Art
                                            English
                                            French
                                            Geography
                                            German
                                            Mathematics

                     GCE A Level passes in: English
                                            French
                                            German

                     Marchmont Secretarial College,       Sept 1977 -
                     Twickenham                           July 1979

                     Royal Society of Arts certificates
                     obtained as follows:

                     Accounting Stage II
                     Audio-typing Stage III (Distinction)
                     Commerce Stage II
                     Office Practice Stage II
                     Shorthand (Pitman 2000) 120 wpm
                     Shorthand-typewriting Stage III
                     Typewriting Stage III

FULL-TIME            Secretary at Phoenix Department      Aug 1979 to
EMPLOYMENT:          Store, Twickenham                    present

PERSONAL             Art, literature, travelling
INTERESTS:

REFEREES:            1.  Mrs J Turner
                         Principal
                         Marchmont Secretarial College
                         Twickenham  TW6 9CB

                     2.  Mr J S Brown
                         Office Manager
                         Phoenix Department Store
                         Twickenham  TW9 4KM
```

Cut-off (or tear-off) slip

This is part of a form, circular letter, leaflet, or other advertising
material. It is, in fact, a small form and, for line-spacing,
method of typing lines, etc, should be treated as for forms (see
p 64).

Horizontal cut-off

- The cut-off ends one inch (2.5 cm) from the bottom of the
  paper. Leave any spare space *above* the cut-off.
- The cut-off portion should be separated from the matter
  above by a line of spaced or unspaced hyphens, dots, or

underscore (the cutting or tearing line), extending from edge to edge of the paper. At least one line of space should be left above and below this line. (Where there is room, some prefer equal top and bottom margins to the cut-off — ie six lines of space below the cutting line.)

- Find and pencil mark the starting line of the cut-off by counting the number of lines required for it (including top and bottom margins).
- The side margins in the cut-off need not be the same as those in the text above it.

Town End
Hillchester
HD3 4NQ

Telephone 2861

Diehard
Domestic
Equipment

Date as postmark

Dear Sir or Madam

A SOFT SOLUTION TO HARD PROBLEMS

At a time when all your household bills are rising, let us tell you of a way you can hit back! The answer is a water softener which can help with many hard problems. Here are some:

1 It cuts down the amount of soap, shampoo and detergent you need to buy.

2 Clothes come softer from the wash and last longer: this applies particularly to woollens.

3 Maintenance and service costs are reduced on appliances like dishwashers and washing machines which can be ruined by hard water.

4 Steam irons and kettles last longer for the same reason.

Complete and post at once the coupon below. By return we will send you a lot more information about water softeners.

Yours faithfully

D Adams

Marketing Manager

DIEHARD DOMESTIC EQUIPMENT, Town End, Hillchester HD3 4NQ

Name ....

Address ....

....

....

....

Circular letter with horizontal cut-off

40 Cut-off (or tear-off) slips

Corner cut-off

This is suitable only for brief information such as a name and address because its lines become progressively shorter.

- Remove the typed sheet from the typewriter, and work out by lines the amount of space required.
- Rule a light pencil line across a corner of paper at the appropriate position, measuring equal length along the bottom and side of the paper (making angles of 45°).
- Insert paper cornerwise into the typewriter and line up the pencilled line with the paper bail bar. Then type a line of spaced or unspaced hyphens, dots or underscore over the cutting-line.
- Complete typing of the cut-off.

```
                    EVEREADY   OFFICE   EQUIPMENT


Model 570 Automatic Mail Opener

                                 JOGGER - ensures no part of letter
                                          is cut
                                 HOPPER - accepts most sizes of
                                          envelope
                                 STACKER - receives opened envelopes


                                 Model 350 Envelope Filler and Sealer


COLLATOR - takes up to 5 insertions
FOLDER - takes 2 sizes of envelope
INSERTER - opens envelopes and feeds
           in enclosures
SEALER - ready for stamping
STAMPER - franks with pre-set
          postage, date, and
          personal slogan



At-a-Glance Control Aids

* WALL CHARTS
* YEAR PLANNERS
* SWIVEL or ROTARY BOARDS
* VISIBLE CARD and STRIP INDEXES
* COLOUR SIGNALS for speedy recognition

Our illustrated leaflet No 384 gives full details
of all the above

DON'T DELAY!

Send at once
```

To: EVEREADY OFFICE EQUIPMENT
132 Southampton Row, London WC2V 5QB
Please send illustrated leaflet No 384
Name _____
Address _____

Publicity material with corner cut-off

Display

This should be eye-catching and pleasing in appearance, with suitable emphasis on important parts, so that the meaning is conveyed immediately with the greatest impact. Where choice is allowed, choose the best paper size and 'shape' (landscape or portrait).

Preparing a layout

Study the copy and devise a line by line layout. Arrange the information in logical order, and divide lines at points that enable emphasis to be given where needed (some variation from the original wording and order may be necessary). Decide on typing style and line-spacing for each line to give it appropriate prominence: *too much* variety within a display can be self-defeating.

Here is an example of display layout and styling:

Please type the following as a notice for the staff notice-board

At 5 pm on May 8th the Walters Engineering Company Limited branch of the Clerical Association will hold a special meeting in the Recreation Room, dealing with pay policy. A full attendance is requested & members are particularly asked to read News Sheet 127, coming prepared to vote on its proposals.

```
        Walters Engineering Company Limited

             The Clerical Association

                    will hold a


      SPECIAL   MEETING   ON   PAY   POLICY


             in the Recreation Room

                on 8 May at 5 pm

       * Read in advance News Sheet No 127
          * Come prepared to vote on it

       P L E A S E   D O   A T T E N D !
```

Fully-centred style

Styling devices

Line 1	Initial capitals
Line 2	Initial capitals, underscored for emphasis
Line 3	Lower case
Line 4	Closed capitals, underscored; *two* spaces between words for added emphasis; extra space above and below this line to help it 'stand out'
Line 6	Date and time typed over a second time to make them 'bold'
Lines 7/8	'Pointers' used to draw attention to the signalled items (these could be typed with the red half of a bi-chrome ribbon — but this would be effective on the top copy only); single spacing to keep items together as a unit
Line 9	Spaced capitals, underscored for extra emphasis and to draw line together; exclamation mark strengthens call for attention

Blocked display

Displays are frequently blocked to save time. Work out the starting position for centring the longest line and begin all lines at this point.

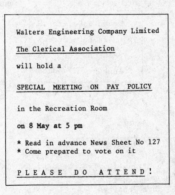

Walters Engineering Company Limited

The Clerical Association

will hold a

SPECIAL MEETING ON PAY POLICY

in the Recreation Room

on 8 May at 5 pm

* Read in advance News Sheet No 127
* Come prepared to vote on it

P L E A S E   D O   A T T E N D !

Fully-blocked style

(Before starting some full-page displays, it will help to indicate the horizontal and vertical centre of the page. Draw light pencil guidelines right down and across the page.)

Additional display features

Boxes to highlight key material. Enclosed typescript may be blocked or centred. Leave uniform space between the box and the typewritten matter round it. Boxes can be drawn by a ball-point pen held firmly in one of the holes to be found on either side of the printing-point. Use the carriage release for horizontal lines; turn the platen for vertical lines (using the variable line spacer to ensure neat corners).

Alternatively, horizontal lines may be made with the underscore and verticals added with a ruler and pen of matching colour. Boxes may also be drawn completely with ruler and pen, which is often the simplest and quickest way. (See also Ruling p 170.)

Any size of box may be drawn by reference to the paper bail scale for horizontals, and by measuring vertical space with the line-spacer. Sometimes it is simpler to type the matter for enclosure before adding the box.

Justified right-margin for lines of continuous copy within a display (see p 77). (A short last line is best centred.) It is sometimes effective to make several short lines *end* at the same point, eg an address at the foot of the display. Backspace for each line from the common ending point (using a tab stop).

This device can be used in several formats, illustrated below.

```
Brown & Goldsmith
24 Fore Street
BRADFORD  BD3 2AS
Telephone 0274 3689
```

```
           CAST
   (in order of appearance)

Mrs Jennings  Mary Downing
      Ellen  Jean Friar
Diana Gibbons  Frances Matthews
Alan·Gibbons  Peter Meredith
```

```
Programme of Films

24 January ............... Hamlet

21 February ... Annie Get Your Gun

20 March ........... Modern Times

24 April ................ Ben Hur

22 May ........ Gone With The Wind
```

(The heading Programme of Films could equally well be centred.)

```
                    VARIETY CONCERT

Merry Widow Selection      CHORUS          Franz Lehar

The Blue Danube       SILHOUETTE DANCERS   Johann Strauss

Primrose                LINDA SPEIRS       Ivor Novello

O Sole Mio              DAVID DIXON         Di Capua

Goodnight Vienna           CHORUS         George Posford
```

Measured space for the insertion of a photograph, diagram, etc, of given dimensions. Mark the four corners of the picture by pencil dots or angles, and allow equal space all round between the picture and any typewritten matter.

Ornamentation Some displays are given a typed border or other form of typed decoration (see p 131).

Some of the foregoing features are illustrated in the display on page 46. See also the programme displays, pp 146, 147.

```
                    CATERING   DE   LUXE


                         Are you giving


      A BANQUET?  A RECEPTION?  A CELEBRATION DINNER?

              A BUFFET LUNCHEON or SUPPER?

                    A COCKTAIL PARTY?


    In our promenade reception and dining rooms, we offer a

    first-class  service for any occasion.   Our cuisine is

    famed  throughout the county,  and our personal service

                  is of a standard to match.


       WE CAN ALSO CATER FOR ANY FUNCTION IN YOUR OWN HOME


              Send for our Illustrated Brochure

                            or

              Visit us to Discuss Your Needs


        CATERERS                  Cuisine Fantastique
       for a century                 Marine Parade
            to                          WEYMOUTH
    Clubs and Societies                   Dorset
        in Dorset              Telephone 0305 796812
```

Drafts

From a rough amended draft (manuscript or typescript) either a clean draft (for further consideration and amendment) *or* a final document is typed.

A *clean draft* should normally have double or treble spacing, with wide margins, for changes. No carbon copies are needed unless perhaps several people are to work on the draft. A clean draft may be called for *as in finished form* to gauge length or to assess display.

Tackling difficult manuscript copy

1 Study the handwriting. If some words are not clear, note the letter formation in easy words, and consider the context.
2 Mark all your clarifications boldly on the draft, in red ball-point pen — eg transpositions and re-numbering, ballooned insertions — to avoid oversight when typing at speed.
3 Ensure that you understand all the correction signs (see pp 37–8).
4 Distinguish between recognised and drafting abbreviations (see p 1) and type accordingly.
5 Correct obvious slips in grammar, spelling, punctuation, enumeration, etc, but where there are acceptable alternatives, the preference of the originator must prevail. Use a dictionary for doubtful words.
6 Look out for discrepancies and inconsistencies in figures, dates, names, etc. Check with the file if possible, otherwise *refer to the originator*.
7 If the manuscript is heavily amended and the equipment is available, it may be faster and safer to audio-type from your own dictation.

See also Footnotes pp 59–61

Electronic typewriters

Micro-processor controlled, these have revolutionised typewriter operation. Machines vary: the following list of features (in alphabetical order) is a general guide only.

- Automatic carrier return, centring, form preparation, right-margin justification, and underlining.
- Backspacing versatility, with express backtracking, or one character at a time, or in increments of $\frac{1}{60}''$.
- Bold typing facility for emphasis (automatic second printing is slightly to the side of the first).
- Corrections are simple. A thin window display panel enables the typist to detect and correct errors in the text before it is committed to paper or memory. Also, correction is easy within the last 100 or so words typed: as the printhead backtracks to the point of error, the lift-off or cover-up correction ribbon is automatically brought into operation. After correction, the RELOC key returns the printing-point in a split second to the last character typed.
- Impression control — useful when carbon copying.
- Lighter and more durable than manual or electric machines — far fewer moving parts.
- 'Memory' will automatically print out addresses, signature

block, short texts, etc, as well as reproduce page formats. Some machines have a memory of 8000 characters (1600 standard words). This built-in memory is 'volatile', ie it disappears when the machine is switched off unless the battery device is engaged — this powers the memory retention for up to 72 hours. A double disc drive can be connected to some machines to double the memory to 16 000 characters. Thus a list of names and addresses together with a standard letter could be entered into the memory and merged in print-out for a mail-shot, etc. At this sophisticated stage, electronic typewriters begin to enter the realm of word processor facilities.

- Paper (with up to 7 carbons) is automatically fed into the machine by pressing the paper-set key. The typing position from the top of the paper is programmable.
- Paper-end indicator (programmable).
- Repeat typing for all keys.
- Reverse-tone effect, ie white print against a black background. This is achieved by setting up a block of black with the film ribbon and then lifting off the appropriate characters with the lift-off correcting ribbon.
- Ribbon changes are quick and clean with the cassette system. Multi-strike film, correctable film, one-time film, or fabric ribbon are available in cassettes that can be quickly changed or replaced. Immediate correction-tape change-overs: cover-up for multi-strike film, lift-off for correctable film.
- Ruling facility — for both horizontal and vertical lines.
- Scientific, mathematical and foreign language text requiring special symbols or accents is easily undertaken by use of the appropriate daisy-wheel print element or (with IBM machines) golfball print-head.
- Subscripts and superscripts (inferior and superior characters) are simple. At the touch of a key, the paper advances or retracts in $\frac{1}{2}$-line increments.
- Tabulation is simplified by automatic column layout. The decimal control feature correctly aligns columns of decimals for fast statistical typing. Some machines have the ability to tabulate backwards as well as forwards.
- Timing device — the machine can be programmed to calculate and print out a typist's typing speed to within one-hundredth of a second.
- Touch, sound, and speed. Electronic typewriters have a very light but positive touch and a very quiet printing action. The typist cannot 'out-type' her machine since it is capable of 20 characters a second (240 words a minute). This speed of operation becomes significant when the electronic typewriter is connected (by insertion of a special interface) to a micro-computer for high-quality print out. When printing from stored text the machine operates bi-directionally, ie it prints

alternate lines *backwards* (from right to left) for speed.

- Typeface and pitch changeover. Each daisy-wheel print element is enclosed in a cassette. Different typefaces are available and can be changed over in seconds. The preferred pitch — from $\frac{1}{6}''$ $\frac{1}{10}''$ $\frac{1}{12}''$ $\frac{1}{15}''$ — is obtained at the touch of a key. This ability to select and mix different typefaces and pitches provides the typist with considerable flexibility.
- Warning red light and bleep sound. The former reminds typist that a certain mode is set (eg the shift lock); the latter signals various functions (eg approach of end of line).

Two-part electronics

Operating on the same principle as word processors (where the printer is not an integral part of the keyboard and display unit), these typewriters separate into two parts: a printer and a keyboard. The advantages are:

- easier reading of copy, with document holder on keyboard section and adjustable to suit typist
- better use of desk space
- typist freed from vibrations of printer

Ellipsis

Use three spaced or unspaced full stops to show that wording has been omitted — at the beginning, in the middle, or at the end of a sentence:

```
It states that footnotes are notes ". . . which it
is desirable to separate from the main text . . .
avoiding distraction from the flow of thought . . ."
```

Enumeration

Numbering of sections and sub-sections should follow a consistent method, drawing on figures, letters of the alphabet (upper and lower case) and roman numerals (large and small) eg figures (1 2 3) for main sections, small letters (a b c) for their sub-sections, and small roman numerals (i ii iii) for divisions of the sub-sections. Various combinations are possible.

Typing method

- Enumeration stands alone, is followed by a stop, or is enclosed in brackets
- It is typed at the left-margin *or* within the left-margin
- Consistent space (2–5) should be left between enumeration and the start of the text

- Figures and roman numerals should be consistently lined up to the right *or* left
- Consistent space should be left between numbered items; also above and below them

The all-numerical (or 'decimal' or point numbering) method uses only figures, always separated by a full stop. There is no full stop at the end.

```
C A L E D O N I A N    F L O O R I N G S    L T D

EXPORT PROMOTION STUDY

Table of Contents


Section                                        Page

1   INTRODUCTION                                 1

2   GENERAL BACKGROUND

    2.1  Home Market                             3

    2.2  European Market                         5

    2.3  World Market                           10

3   RAW MATERIAL PRICES

    3.1  Jute                                   14

    3.2  Cotton                                 16

    3.3  Other Fibres                           18

4   LABOUR AND WAGES

    4.1  Skilled Manpower Shortages             21

    4.2  Wages and Productivity

         4.2.1  Basic Wages                     24
```

Envelopes

1. The name and address are typed parallel to the longer side: each part is typed on a separate line.
2. The top margin should be *at least* 1½ inches (38 mm). It is preferable to start the first line half-way down. The name and address should be approximately centred horizontally. (These positions should be gauged by eye.)
3. The typed lines may be blocked or evenly indented in single, 1½, or double spacing, depending on preference and the size of envelope (single-spacing is most widely used).

4 The addressee's name must appear fully as in the copy. The choice of Mr or Esq must follow copy, as must abbreviation (or otherwise) of Co, &, Ltd, plc, Bros, etc.

5 The town should be typed in capitals (closed or spaced) with or without underscore.

6 The county is not underscored. (Except with certain large towns and cities — given in the Post Office Guide — the county should be included. Abbreviations for counties are included under Abbreviations pp 2–9.)

7 The entire envelope *may* be typed in closed capitals (this is usually a house style).

8 The additions Confidential, Personal, etc, should be typed at least one clear line-space above the name.

9 In UK addresses, the postcode is the last item typed and must not be punctuated. One or two spaces may be left between the two parts. Where the postcode is not on a separate line, it should be placed at least two and not more than six spaces from the previous word.

10 If the envelope is to be sent Registered or by Recorded Delivery, type Reg or RD at the top left-corner (over which a sticker will later be fixed).

11 Use adhesive labels for addressing envelopes too large to go in the typewriter.

Hyphenated place names   The hyphen is sometimes treated as optional: follow copy. Note that a preposition is *not* capitalised.

Weston-super-Mare	Weston super Mare
Stratford-on-Avon	Stratford on Avon
Newcastle-upon-Tyne	Newcastle upon Tyne

Deep envelope flaps   Open the flaps before feeding the envelope into the typewriter to prevent through marking.

Long envelope run

For speed:

a Suitably position the paper guide, and set the left-margin for the beginning of each line (blocked style).

b Place the stacked envelopes on your left.

c Insert the first envelope and bring it into typing position. Then insert another so that it rests on the paper-table.

d Type the first envelope. Then twirl the cylinder with your left hand: the motion will at once remove the typed envelope and bring forward the envelope resting on the paper-table.

e Remove the typed envelope with your right hand and place it face downwards to your right.

f Repeat this procedure until all the envelopes are completed.

All the addresses illustrated in the left column below have been typed in blocked style with open punctuation (the fastest method); in the right column all have full punctuation.

UK postcodes (for electronic sorting of mail)   The first part signifies the area within a town or region; the second part denotes a particular road.

```
PERSONAL

Mrs G Hawkins
27 Spring Street
BRIGHTON
Sussex  BN21 4AG
```

Postcode on same line as county

```
Personal

Mrs. G. Hawkins,

27 Spring Street,

BRIGHTON,

Sussex.

BN21 4AG
```

Postcode on separate line

USA and Australia   The postal number of the town (zipcode in the USA, postcode in Australia) is placed after the name of the State, to facilitate sorting.

```
Mr & Mrs T Andrews
69 Hillcrest Drive
Bartlesville
Oklahoma  74003
USA
```

```
Alcoa of Australia Ltd.,
320 Collins Street,
Melbourne,
Victoria, 3000.
Australia.
```

Post Office Boxes   These are widely used in countries and areas where there is no regular house to house delivery service. Customers are issued with keys to individually numbered boxes at the nearest post office. The correct PO Box Number is therefore a vital part of the address. (The name of the building or street is superfluous as far as delivery is concerned, and may be omitted.) Post Office Box Numbers are sometimes used in Britain, eg when a large response is expected to a newspaper advertisement.

```
Mr H D Rivanbai
Karume Avenue
PO Box 46578
Nairobi
Kenya
```

```
Recruitment Officer,
Civil Service Bureau,
P.O. Box 1068,
Bahrain,
Arabian Gulf.
```

The conventional manner of addressing envelopes varies in different countries, but an incoming letter, or another filed address for the same country, will normally be available. The main need is for careful copying of unfamiliar words. Some examples follow.

Germany Note the unusual order of items. The town follows the person's name, preceded on the same line by its postal number. Then comes the name of the street, with the number *after* it. Note: Herrn (to Mr); Frau (Mrs); Fräulein (Miss).

```
Herrn Bruno Vogel
4730 Ahlen
Hindenburgstrasse 25
Germany
```

France The word for street (rue) starts with a lower case letter. The number after Paris signifies the district. Note: M (Mr); Mme (Mrs); Mlle (Miss).

```
Mlle. J. Dupois,
25 rue Halévy,
Paris 9e,
France.
```

Spain The street number follows the name of the street. The number after Madrid signifies the district. Note: Señor (Mr); Señora (Mrs); Señorita (Miss).

```
Señor Rodolfo Villa
Calle de Fernando 16
Madrid 4
Spain
```

Italy The street number follows the street name. The postal number precedes the town, on the same line. Note: Signor (Mr); Signora (Mrs); Signorina (Miss).

```
Signor Paolo Pedini,
Via Della Scorfa 68,
00186 Rome,
Italy.
```

Folding paper for envelopes

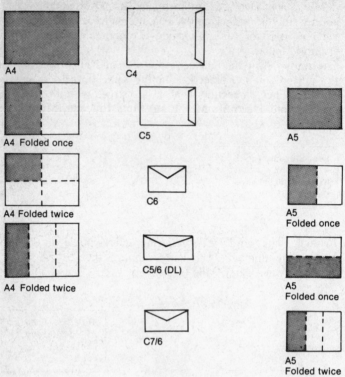

Types of envelope

Banker — opening on longer side (see last 3 above)

Pocket — opening on shorter side (first 2 above)

Window — name and address not typed on envelope: the paper is folded (with the help of fold marks) so that the inside name and address (typed within guide marks) are visible through a transparent 'window'. (Aperture envelopes are similar, but have an *uncovered* address panel.)

Quality As with correspondence paper, envelopes are available in a variety of qualities (bond, parchment, cream wove, airmail, etc) and tints so that envelope and paper can be matched.

Size	(*millimetres*)	(*approx inches*)
C4	324×229	$12\frac{3}{4} \times 9$
C5	229×162	$9 \times 6\frac{3}{8}$
C6	162×114	$6\frac{3}{8} \times 4\frac{1}{2}$
C5/6 (DL*)	220×110	$8\frac{5}{8} \times 4\frac{1}{4}$
C7/6	162×81	$6\frac{3}{8} \times 3\frac{1}{4}$

* DL stands for DIN lange. The standard and rational system of paper and envelope sizes now in general use (A sizes of paper, C sizes of envelopes) was originally drawn up by the Deutsche Industrie Normen (DIN) — German Industry Standards. Lange means long.

Post Office Preferred (POP) sizes The sizes of envelopes and cards are given below, and the Post Office has the power to restrict the lowest postage rates to these sizes only. Electronic sorting equipment is designed for them, and other sizes must be sorted by slower, more expensive methods.

POP range — envelopes and cards should be at least 140×90 mm (approx $5\frac{1}{2} \times 3\frac{1}{2}$ in) and not larger than 235×120 mm (approx $9\frac{1}{4} \times 4\frac{3}{4}$ in). The two most popular sizes for letters (C6 and DL) and A6 cards fall within these limits.

Expert typist

Watch an expert at work, and note the following:

1   The extreme rapidity and precision of the keying, using all the fingers, and the thumb for spacing. At each slight pause, the fingers naturally revert to the home row.

2   The utmost economy of every movement, particularly of the wrists and forearms. The deft handling of materials and correction of any errors.

3   The comfortable sitting position, with the back supported by the chair rest, and the feet flat on the floor for balance. The typist sits at the correct height and distance from the machine, neither crouching nor stretching. He or she is physically relaxed but mentally very alert.

4   The eyes are on the copy, with only fleeting glances at the typescript and keys. For audio-typing the eyes are on the transcript, checking for accuracy as the typist transcribes. Keying is *continuous* in either case.

5   The ability to make rapid decisions on paper size, margins, line-spacing and styling.

6   Typing from a difficult draft is expertly approached: the typist begins with a quick read through, marking in clarifications of words, figures, abbreviations, 'ballooned' matter, etc, where snags could arise when typing at speed.

7   Each page of the typescript presents a clean, well-balanced, 'expert' look.

This impressive professional performance is the result of sound learning and thoughtful practice.

Fingering

Use of all the fingers (with the thumb for spacing) is essential to touch typewriting. Each finger controls its own keys, moving upwards, downwards or across from the central position of the 'home' keys (a s d f // j k l ;). In this way, the typist learns to orientate himself or herself to the whole keyboard without the aid of sight.

Fingers over home keys

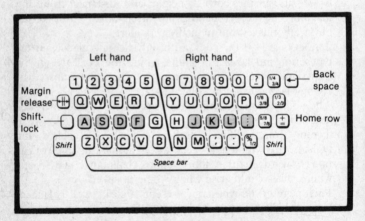

Division of keyboard into fingering units. (**Note**: strong index finger operates twice as many keys as others. Straight method of fingering is illustrated — keyboard is divided into oblique vertical rows)

Flow charts

These indicate the 'flow' or sequence of stages in an operation or procedure. Their simple visual presentation confirms a logical and effective order or shows up inefficiencies.

Uses They are an aid to decision-making in work study, organisation and methods, etc. They are also used in electronic data processing for designing and recording computer-based systems; and for computer programming. A diagrammatic explanation is more easily understood and remembered by learners than a verbal description.

Symbols Chart design varies, but the essence is that stages in an operation are separately stated, and joined in sequence by 'lines of flow'. Symbols — boxes, triangles, circles, diamonds, 'flowerpots', etc — signify different kinds of activity. The functional meaning of the symbols can vary, but a recognised code of symbols within a system assists the understanding of the chart.

Brief verbal descriptions are given within the symbols or close beside them. Longer notes, which would obscure the clear outline of the chart, are presented separately.

Not all flow charts use shaped symbols: boxes may suffice, or the wording by itself may stand clearly enough apart.

Lines of flow The different parts are connected by unbroken lines, which may run *in any direction*. Thus the chart may be made long, wide, or square, to suit the paper size. Connecting lines must clearly indicate by arrowheads (or numbers) the correct sequence of activities from start to finish. *Broken lines* are used to indicate anything other than progressive flow.

Hand preparation Charts with shaped symbols are best done by hand. A transparent template with cut-out shapes is useful for the fast drawing of uniform-sized symbols. These take only brief typewritten wording, but the amount required can usually be neatly fitted in by hand printing. Larger symbols could be drawn by hand to take most captions in suitably 'shaped' typescript — but this is seldom cost-effective. Usually the typist is only expected to type a chart with rectangular boxes.

Typing method Carefully analyse each draft to ensure that the chart is understood. Balance should be achieved wherever it is meaningful and practicable. Set tab stops for columns, and note the scale-point beyond which the type must not extend; alternatively, draw a light pencil vertical guide line at this point, by holding the pencil at the printing-point and turning the cylinder. Boxes need not line up horizontally unless there is a horizontal relationship between them.

With complex charts for camera or copier it may be faster to paste in certain parts.

Ruling is best done last, with a pencil (for preliminary ruling), a ball-point pen and a transparent ruler. For columns of boxes, take the widest line of type and, at an appropriate distance from it, draw two vertical pencil lines from top to bottom of the typed column. Then ink in each horizontal line, working from top to bottom. Ink over two verticals for each box. Mark the centre of the top box and the bottom box and, lining up the ruler, draw in all vertical connecting lines *in a single ruling*. Complete the ruling, draw in the arrowheads, and erase your pencil marks.

Final assessment Critical evaluation of the completed chart is important, to confirm that it is clear and accurate.

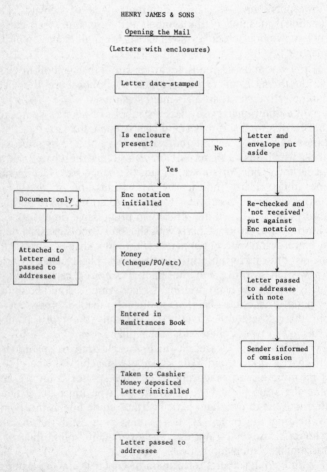

HENRY JAMES & SONS

Opening the Mail

(Letters with enclosures)

Simple flow chart: mixed centred and blocked style

Footnotes

Footnote symbols

Combination characters   When not more than three foot-notes appear at the foot of any page, footnote signs (asterisk, dagger, and double dagger) can be used.

* Asterisk — lower case x plus hyphen — if there is no asterisk key on top row
† Single dagger — upper case I plus hyphen
‡ Double dagger — upper case I plus raised I (or I plus equals sign)

Alternatively, asterisk keys *   ** and *** are simpler to type.

Figures or letters   Figures (1 2 3) or letters (a b c) standing alone or enclosed in brackets are often preferred; they *must* be used where there are more than three footnotes per page.

Indicating footnotes

a In the text — a sign, figure, or letter is raised with no space between it and the word it follows.
b At foot of the page etc — a sign, figure, or letter is typed in the normal position on the line. Leave one character-space between the sign and the footnote itself.

Typing footnotes

Typed documents   Footnotes appear at the foot of the page on which the reference occurs; or are grouped together at the end of sections or of the complete work. Single spacing is used, regardless of the line-spacing in the document.

Footnotes typed on same page as reference   Leave enough space at the foot of the page for the footnote(s) plus an adequate bottom margin. If the footnotes are very long they may run on to the following page. The footnotes are usually separated from the text by a line of underscore running the full width of the typing line or page: leave at least half a line-space above and below this line. The second and subsequent lines of the footnote are consistently aligned, starting under the footnote sign *or* under the first word of the footnote. Leave one line between successive footnotes.

Footnotes may run the full length of the typing line, *or* may be equally inset at left and right (ie centred).

Draft (where finally footnotes will be at foot of page)   Each footnote is typed, in single spacing, immediately after the line in which the reference occurs, and is separated from the text above and below by a line of space and an underscore from margin to margin; this helps the typist (in final typing) to assess the space to be left on

```
EXPENDITURE ESTIMATES

Recreation and Community Activities

                              1984/85      1984/85
                              Original     Revised
                              Estimate     Estimate

                              £            £

Playing Fields ...........    86,250       90,000

Tennis Courts ............    10,160       11,200

Swimming Baths* ..........    74,360       48,750

Play Centres .............    8,555        9,115

Community Centres‡ .......    75,346       77,890

Other Community Activities
and Facilities ...........    8,000        8,500


TOTAL                         £262,671     £245,455


* The building of the proposed new swimming pool
  in the Downland Community Centre has been
  postponed indefinitely.

‡ Including Senior Citizens Club.
```

Simple tabulation with footnotes

```
              AN INVITATION FROM GLOBAL PUBLISHERS[1]
                 80 Park Avenue, LONDON  WC2B 6AQ


    Last year we issued a general invitation to potential authors to submit
proposals for new books.  The response was encouraging and 2 of the titles
in our new Global booklist originated in this way.[2]
    Once again we should like to hear from lecturers and others interested
in writing.  We are particularly concerned with Business and Professional
Studies but, in principle, we shall be willing to consider any aspect of
vocational training.

1 Formed by the amalgamation of Western County Publishers and the Barking
  Educational Press in January of this year.

2 ESSAYS IN ECONOMICS by J P Greene and ADVANCED ACCOUNTING by R Black.
```

Short text with footnotes

60 Footnotes

the page for footnotes. (These can then be given their signs or numbers.) If there are two very close references, both footnotes are typed within the one pair of lines. This method is useful for theses, reports, etc, where footnotes are numerous and lengthy. (See example on p 179 under Theses.)

See also Typing for print pp 188–9.

Foreign language typing

A knowledge of the language makes this task easier; otherwise it is necessary to type letter by letter. If material is regularly typed in foreign languages, the relevant accent typefaces may be fitted to the machine, replacing seldom-used characters, eg fractions. Accents are fitted to 'dead' keys, so the carriage does not move forward when the accent key is struck; the accented letter is then struck without the need for backspacing. On an electronic typewriter a daisy-wheel print element with the required accents would be used.

If accent keys are not available, accents must be neatly inked in with a matching-coloured pen, after the typed page has been removed from the typewriter. (If accents are infrequent, mark their lines in the margin as you check the page in the machine.)

Frequently used accents in European languages are:

(acute)	´	Portuguese	$\tilde{a}$
(grave)	`	Norwegian,	$\mathring{\gamma}$
(circumflex)	^	Swedish	$\mathring{a}$
(cedilla)	ç	Danish ø now often	
(umlaut)	"	superseded by	$\ddot{o}$ or $ø$
Spanish tilde	$\tilde{n}$		

(The umlaut can be made by double quotation marks.)

If an accent is not clear in the copy or you are uncertain about it, pencil 'x' in the margin to remind the originator to deal with it.

Foreign words, phrases and abbreviations

(Abbreviations: Fr French, It Italian, L Latin, lit literally)

ab initio (ab init)	L	from the beginning
addendum (pl addenda)	L	thing(s) to be added
ad hoc	L	for this special purpose
ad infinitum	L	to infinity, indefinitely
ad interim	L	for the meantime

ad nauseam	L	to the point of disgust
ad referendum (ad ref)	L	for further consideration
ad valorem (ad val)	L	according to value
à la carte	Fr	according to menu
à la mode	Fr	fashionable
al fresco	It	in the open air
alter ego	L	one's second self
anno domini (AD)	L	in the year of our Lord
ante meridiem (am)	L	before noon
au fait (with)	Fr	well informed (about)
bête noire	Fr	pet aversion
bona fide	L	in good faith
carte blanche	Fr	freedom of action (lit, blank paper)
cause célèbre	Fr	a famous trial; a sensational controversy
circa (c)	L	about; approximately
compos mentis	L	of sound mind
confer (cf)	L	compare
coup d'état	Fr	sudden stroke of State policy
coup de grâce	Fr	a finishing stroke
cul de sac	Fr	a road closed at one end
curriculum vitae (CV)	L	course of one's life
de facto	L	in actual fact
de jure	L	by right
de rigueur	Fr	required by custom
en bloc	Fr	in the mass; all together
enfant terrible	Fr	precocious child; outspoken person
en masse	Fr	in the mass; all together
en passant	Fr	in passing; by the way
en route	Fr	on the way
entente cordiale	Fr	friendly understanding
erratum (pl errata)	L	error(s) in printing or writing
et alia (et al)	L	and the others
et cetera (etc)	L	and the rest
et sequentia (et seq)	L	and the following
ex cathedra	L	from Pope's throne, hence authoritatively
exempli gratia (eg)	L	for example
ex gratia	L	an act of favour (not of right)
ex officio	L	by virtue of office
fait accompli	Fr	an accomplished fact
faux pas	Fr	false step; blunder
femme fatale	Fr	dangerously attractive woman
force majeure	Fr	circumstances beyond one's control
habeas corpus	L	writ to produce prisoner in person and state reasons for detention.

ibidem (ib, ibid)	L	in the same place
idem (id)	L	the same; as mentioned before
id est (ie)	L	that is
in camera	L	privately; not in open court
in extenso	L	at full length
infra dig	L	beneath one's dignity
in loco parentis	L	in place of a parent
in situ	L	in position
inter alia	L	among other things
in toto	L	in full; wholly
intra vires	L	within the powers
in vacuo	L	in a vacuum; in no apparent context
ipso facto	L	by the fact itself
laissez faire	Fr	policy of non-intervention
le mot juste	Fr	word which fits context exactly
locum tenens	L	substitute; eg for a doctor
locus sigilli (LS)	L	the place of the seal (legal)
magnum opus	L	an author's chief work
modus operandi	L	method of working
modus vivendi	L	way of living
mutatis mutandis	L	necessary changes being made
nemine contradicente (nem con)	L	without opposition
nil desperandum	L	nothing is to be despaired of
noblesse oblige	Fr	rank imposes obligations
non sequitur	L	conclusion that does not follow logically
nota bene (NB)	L	note carefully
objet d'art	Fr	article of artistic value
par excellence	Fr	of the highest standard
per capita	L	for each person (lit, by heads)
per centum (per cent)	L	for every hundred
per procurationem (per pro, pp)	L	on behalf of
per se	L	in itself
persona grata	L	person in favour
persona non grata	L	person not in favour
pied-à-terre	Fr	temporary or part-time lodging
poste restante	Fr	section of post office where letters kept till called for
post meridiem (pm)	L	after noon
post mortem	L	after death
post scriptum (PS)	L	postscript
prima facie	L	at first sight
pro forma	L	as a matter of form
pro rata	L	in proportion
pro tempore (pro tem)	L	for the time being
quasi	L	seemingly

quid pro quo	L	one thing in compensation for another
quod vide (qv)	L	which see
raison d'être	Fr	reason for being
répondez s'il vous plaît (RSVP)	Fr	please reply
résumé	Fr	summary
savoir faire	Fr	knowledge of the world
sic	L	thus (within brackets in quoted matter shows original being faithfully reproduced even though incorrect)
sine die	L	indefinitely; without naming a day
sine qua non	L	an indispensable condition (lit, without which not)
sotto voce	It	in an undertone
status quo	L	the state in which things stand (or stood)
stet	L	let it stand
sub judice	L	under judicial consideration
sub poena	L	under penalty; writ commanding appearance in court
table d'hôte	Fr	set meal at fixed price (lit, host's table)
tête-à-tête	Fr	face to face; private conversation
ultra vires	L	beyond the powers or rights
verbatim	L	word for word
vice versa	L	the order being reversed
videlicet (viz)	L	namely
vis-à-vis	Fr	face to face
viva voce	L	orally
volte-face	L	complete change of attitude

Forms

Skilled typists may be required to design and type forms, or to complete them in type.

Devising the layout

Forms are used to obtain specific information in clear, standard format for current use and subsequent reference. Thus the layout and wording are crucial. Badly designed forms are inefficient: they may fail to elicit all the necessary facts, and may produce unwanted ones. So consider precisely what information is needed, taking account of the clerical processes through which the form will pass. In drafting and arranging the questions, note:

1 The design should be uncomplicated and functional — not forbidding to the completer — and convenient for retrieval purposes. Use lines, boxes, panels, and other devices for prominence, clarity and quick location of information.
2 Arrange the content in logical sequence, grouping related questions. Consider dividing the main sections of the form by unbroken horizontal lines right across the paper.
3 Choose simple, concise and unambiguous wording. Abbreviations are best avoided as they are liable to cause confusion.
4 Judiciously use the device of offering alternatives: invite the completer to delete, or to tick a box, as appropriate. This simplifies completion, ensures clear answers, is economical with space, and facilitates clerical operations.

```
I enclose cheque/postal order/cash* to
the value of £

* Delete as appropriate
```

```
Size          Colour
Small  [ ]    Red    [ ]
Medium [ ]    Blue   [ ]
Large  [ ]    Green  [ ]
PLEASE TICK BOX
```

5 Leave enough room for answers, but too much can give a false impression of the amount of information required. With items like qualifications, cater for an 'average' answer.
6 Any part of the form *not* intended for completion should be kept separate and marked, eg FOR OFFICE USE ONLY.
7 Give each form a short title and an identifying reference, with (or incorporating) the date of issue for forms which are periodically updated.

Typing forms

1 Centre the matter vertically and horizontally on the page. Where layout permits, keep a straight right-margin.
2 Lines are often made of lightly typed dots, or with the underscore. Unspaced hyphens give a less heavy appearance, but it is necessary, after the wording, to turn the paper on half a space before using the hyphen key.
3 At least one space should be left between typed wording and typed lines.
4 Line-spacing should be 1½ or double, for ease of reading.

However, questions and explanations of more than one line are usually typed in single spacing.

5   If the form contains columns and boxes it presents a neat appearance if you line up horizontal and vertical lines when possible. Similarly, items starting part-way across the form at different levels should be aligned vertically, if suitable, by means of the tabulator.

6   When typing a form designed by another person do not alter the design or wording without consulting the originator.

7   With complex forms intended for the camera or copier it may be faster to paste in certain parts.

Completing forms: general

1   Ensure that the inserted matter will run in line with the wording and lines on the form.

2   Set the margins to align with those on the form.

3   No word or part of a word should extend into the right margin.

4   No question should be left unanswered; this might suggest that it has been overlooked. Insert two or three spaced hyphens or type N/A (for 'not applicable') or None.

5   Make any deletions on the typewriter, using capital X for effective coverage.

Completing different types of forms

Lines for insertion of details   Leave at least one character space (consistently) between the wording and the typed insertion. Use the interliner or the variable line-spacer to ensure that no part of the words typed in (including descenders) touches the line or is more than ½ line-space above it. Where the form is typed, adjust your line-spacing to accord with it. If the form is printed, realignment will be necessary for each line.

With inserted information of more than one line (as with an address), the second and subsequent lines may go back to the left-hand margin (or start with an equal indent of two or three spaces from it); or they may be blocked under the first inserted line, as in the example below. Alternatively, all lines of all items may begin at the same point if there is room.

```
NAME (Mr/XXX/XXX/XXX*)  John Williamson ...............................................

ADDRESS  28 Darley Road ...........................................................

...............  SOUTHAMPTON  SO3 3GN ...............................................

TELEPHONE NO  0703 7486 ............  DATE OF BIRTH  12 Jan 1961 ................
```

Blank space for insertion of details   Leave at least one character space (consistently) between the wording and the typed insertion. A single-line insertion, or a first line, should line up with the wording, or be vertically centred to the print, or it may start on a new line. Insertions of more than one line should be blocked for neatness.

The open, undefined completion area can lead to straggling and untidy insertions. Locating and sorting information is a time-consuming task, so this method is often avoided.

```
SURNAME                    FIRST NAME

ADDRESS



TELEPHONE NUMBER           DATE OF BIRTH
```

Panel for insertion of details   A defined and limited area is provided for each item. In typed forms this method avoids the 'heavy' appearance of many lines for typing over.

Surname	Address
First name(s)	
Date of birth	Telephone number

Box for key entry   This method ensures that key information is given in a specified place for easy reference. Typed insertions should be approximately centred horizontally and vertically.

My upper price limit for a property is [ ]

Individual character boxes   Space is provided for each letter, character or digit. This device is often linked to computer use. Sometimes the top horizontal line is omitted.

My policy number is [ ][ ][ ][ ][ ][ ][ ][ ][ ][ ]

Columns for specified particulars   These may be ruled or unruled.

Quantity	Size	Colour

Forms of address: see Titles and forms of address pp181–7.
Fractions: see Technical typing pp 171–3.

Headings

Main headings of more than one line

Each part should be given suitable prominence.

Spaced capitals — one space between letters, three spaces between words.

Closed capitals — one or two spaces between words consistently within a single heading.

Initial capitals — one space between words. Except in a first word, the initial letter of minor words is usually in lower case.

Underscoring — can be applied to any of the above, and should extend the full length of the heading but not beyond it at either end. Initial and final punctuation (eg brackets) may be underscored or not — but be consistent. A heading in spaced capitals can be underscored half a line-space below.

> **Note**   A full stop is not used after a main heading unless the last word is abbreviated and full punctuation is being used.

> W O R L D   P O P U L A T I O N
>
> <u>A Study of Birth and Mortality Rates</u>
>
> by R C RODGERS

Headings to sections

Centred (to type)   Any of the styles above (except spaced capitals) can be used (consistently). Paragraphs underneath can be blocked or indented.

At margin   There are three kinds: paragraph, shoulder, and side (or marginal). Again, any of the styles above (excluding spaced capitals) can be used. Side headings stand out most, while shoulder headings are more prominent than paragraph ones.

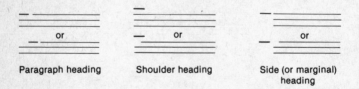

Paragraph heading   Shoulder heading   Side (or marginal) heading

Paragraph heading   The paragraph starts on the same line as the heading, and may be blocked or indented. The heading may or may not be followed by a full stop or colon (consistently). A uniform two or three character spaces should be left between the heading and the start of the text, unless the heading forms the first word(s) of the paragraph or is followed by a dash, when the usual single space is used.

Shoulder heading   This may be used over blocked or indented paragraphs. It is not followed by a full stop unless the last word is abbreviated and full punctuation is being used. A consistent one or two lines of space separates the heading from the text below it.

Side (or marginal) heading   This is typed in the space to the left of the paragraph, with each heading beginning (or exceptionally ending) at the same point. Paragraphs may be blocked or indented. Some drafters prefer a colon after side headings, regardless of the punctuation style being used.

At least two spaces should be left between the longest heading and the left edge of the paragraphs. Set the left margin for the paragraphs, and a tab stop for quickly finding the starting position of the headings. Where the heading runs to more than one line, the text starts level with the *first* line of the heading.

See also Oblique headings pp 124–6, and Vertical headings pp 190–3.

Highlighted matter

Price particulars, a quotation, a short tabulation and similar items can be made to stand out from the main text by the following methods. (At least one line of space is needed before and after highlighted matter.)

Indented paragraphs — by insetting the matter from both margins equally (ie by centring to the typing line).

Blocked or hanging paragraphs — by insetting at least five spaces on the left only *or* by insetting from both margins equally.

Varying the line-spacing — by using $1\frac{1}{2}$ or double-spacing for text in single-spacing; and single-spacing for text in $1\frac{1}{2}$, double or treble spacing.

House style

From the wide variety of styles available for most documents, organisations normally adopt their own 'house style', stipulating open or full punctuation, blocked or indented paragraphs, particular positions for date and reference(s), and so on.

A standard house style *a* denotes efficiency and order; *b* speeds up typing; *c* facilitates quick reference. A new typist will be given guidelines and typed models to work from (see an example of house style details in the memo on p 115.)

As part of a rationalised house style, many organisations use a standard printed heading for external documents such as letters, compliments slips and statements of account, often with a distinctive logo built into it (see the example on p 32).

Hyphen and dash

The same character is used for both. As a hyphen it is typed with no space before or after it; as a dash it has one space before and one after. A hyphen is *never* typed at the start of a line. A dash may be placed at the end of a line *or* at the start of a new line at the margin-position (with one space after it).

Useful tip: If you have difficulty in distinguishing between the hyphen and the dash, try substituting a comma: if it makes sense, a dash is required; if not, use a hyphen.

Use of hyphen

1 In line-end word division.
2 In many compound nouns, eg humming-bird, ice-floe. There are other compound nouns which have no hyphen, eg hothead, iceberg, yet others are correct with or without a hyphen, eg bookbinder, book-binder. (Where the hyphen is optional, follow copy and be consistent.)
3 Conventionally, to combine two words in adjectival (but not usually in adverbial) expressions.

```
The warmly-clad children went to school.
The children went to school warmly clad.
```

4 To distinguish between such pairs of words as: remark and re-mark (mark again); resort and re-sort (sort again).

```
Recover your composure and re-cover the chair.
```

5 After some prefixes, eg ex-boyfriend, pre-Christmas rush, post-natal examination, non-existent ghost.
6 Sometimes to break up an awkward sequence of vowels or consonants, eg good co-ordination, co-operative store, shell-less seafood.
7 After the first part of successive word combinations to avoid repetition.

```
Black- brown- and yellow-centred varieties are available.
```

8 Optionally, after a colon to introduce highlighted or inset matter that starts on the following line.

Use of dash

1 To mark a distinct break in a sentence.

```
There are other examples - see page 66.
```

2 To enclose a parenthesis, as an alternative to brackets or commas.

```
In winter - provided there is no snow - we take a daily five-mile walk.
In winter (provided there is no snow) we take a daily five-mile walk.
In winter, provided there is no snow, we take a daily five-mile walk.
```

3 To show hesitating speech.

```
Yes - er, I - will - if you - er - insist.
```

4 Sometimes, before the name of the author following a quotation or poem.
5 To replace an impolite word (two spaces before and after).

```
She's nothing but a  -  liar.
```

Use of hyphen or dash

Either can be used in expressions like the following, but the hyphen is quicker and neater.

```
68-72 High Street      pages 100-110      1979-1982
68 - 72 High Street    pages 100 - 110    1979 - 1982
```

Inferior and superior characters

(Also known as subscripts and superscripts.) These are numerals or letters which are placed below or above the normal typing line: use the half-spacer or the variable line-spacer. No space should be left before the inferior or superior numeral or letter. They are frequently used in chemical and mathematical formulae (see Technical typing pp 171–3).

Information: see Reference sources pp 151–5

Itineraries

These vary in style and in the amount of detail required, but they must always be clearly and systematically set out so that all the points may be taken in at a glance; a column arrangement is therefore recommended. If the itinerary is short it is best typed on A6 or A7 card for carrying in a wallet or handbag.

```
MR G BROWN'S VISIT TO AMSTERDAM   (11-12 November 19--)


11 November    1530 hrs   Depart HEAD OFFICE by car

(Tuesday)      1600       Check in at HEATHROW
                          BA desk - Flight BA 1820

               1650       Depart HEATHROW

               1740       Arrive Amsterdam (SCHIPHOL)
                          Met by Mr Van Kriek and driven to
                          RITZ HOTEL, Amstelveen Plaats

                          At Hotel Reception confirm cab
                          booking for Wednesday 1215 hrs

               1930       Dinner at RITZ HOTEL with Dutch
                          importers

                          Overnight at RITZ HOTEL

12 November    1000       Meetings at RITZ HOTEL with Dutch
                          agents
(Wednesday)
               1215       Cab from RITZ HOTEL

               1245       Luncheon at DEN HAAG RESTAURANT
                          with Amsterdam Chamber of Commerce

               afternoon  Meetings (to be arranged by you)

               1800       Car at RITZ HOTEL (Mr Van Kriek)

               1815       Check-in at SCHIPHOL
                          KLM desk - Flight KLM 1650

               1850       Depart SCHIPHOL

               1940       Arrive HEATHROW

Documents      New products specifications (VR-695, ER-274)
               Details of last 2 years' sales to Holland
               Luncheon and Dinner Guest Lists

Copy to Managing Director
```

Two-day itinerary

```
        Mr A Mann

        Lecture to the Lincoln Photographic Society

        Tuesday 10 September

        0930 hrs    Depart London (Kings Cross)
        1140 hrs    Arrive Lincoln (St Marks)
        1615 hrs    Depart Lincoln (St Marks)
        1830 hrs    Arrive London (Kings Cross)

        The Chairman of the Society (Mr B Brown) will
        meet you at Lincoln and drive you to the
        station after the lunch and lecture.
```

Short itinerary on card

Job advertisement

This will be based on the corresponding job description and job specification (for the example below see pp 75–6). When drafting a job advertisement:

- use note form and the minimum words needed to convey the essential points
- clearly state the basic requirements so that only qualified candidates apply
- encourage a response by making an attractive (but accurate) presentation, eg mention excellent prospects
- type the final copy as it should appear in print

```
ASSISTANT PRIVATE SECRETARY (male or female) in
Export Department of multi-national group of
companies.  Duties include telephone (home and
overseas), reception of visitors, liaison with
Government Departments, and assistance with typing
correspondence, copying documents, and filing.
Good general education, typewriting, shorthand
and/or audio-typewriting essential; secretarial
experience an advantage.  Although working under
general supervision, a person of initiative is
required, with pleasant disposition.  Prospects
excellent.  Salary: £6,000 - £9,000 depending on
qualifications and experience.  Applications by
letter to: Personnel Manager, Mentrose Products
(UK) Limited, 24-28 Hayes Road, London SW15 9PR.
```

Job applications

Sometimes there is a form for completion, but you may be asked to apply by letter with a curriculum vitae. The covering letter should:

- be carefully handwritten or typed
- use good, clear English
- refer to the source of the advertisement
- briefly state why the advertised post has more appeal for you than your present work

The following letter is based on the job advertisement on p 73 (See also Curriculum vitae pp 38–9.)

68 Poplar Drive
Westdale
Middx   TW8 3AG

24 March 1984

Personnel Manager
Mentrose Products (UK) Limited
24–28 Hayes Road
London   SW15 9PR

Dear Sir

    I wish to apply for the post of Assistant Private Secretary (Export Department) advertised in today's Morning Echo.

    In many ways I am very happy in my present job – which I have held since leaving Secretarial College – but there are no promotion prospects or opportunities for broadening my experience. I now wish to do something more challenging.

    I should welcome the greater contact with people which your post offers, and the prospect of making use of my ability in European languages.

    I enclose a brief curriculum vitae, which gives my educational and secretarial qualifications, an indication of my personal interests, and the names of two referees willing to vouch for me.

                    Yours faithfully

                  Mary Anderson

                  Mary Anderson (Miss)

Job description

Based on job *analysis*, the job description defines the main duties and responsibilities etc of a post, with its grade for salary purposes. Together with its corresponding job specification it helps recruiters to draw up an advertisement and select the best applicant: the successful candidate is given the job description as a definition of the post.

The job description is also useful to training departments for devising appropriate training. Jobs evolve with time and the introduction of new technology and work practices. A job description therefore needs to be reviewed periodically, and should include the originating reference with its date of issue. In a large organisation, a standard form would be prepared and used for a variety of job descriptions. Note the different category headings in the example below. (Compare this with the job specification, p 76.)

MENTROSE PRODUCTS (UK) LIMITED
Job description - secretarial

JOB TITLE:	SALARY GRADE:
Assistant private secretary	B or C
DEPARTMENT:	RESPONSIBLE TO:
Export	Export Director's private secretary

NATURE AND SCOPE OF DUTIES:

General assistance to the private secretary with the following:

1. Typing correspondence from manuscript or typescript draft/notes/audio/shorthand

2. Copying documents on copying machine or duplicator

3. Filing

Personal responsibilities:

1. Answering the telephone, and screening and connecting calls

2. Reception of visitors

3. Collation of information from, and correspondence with, Government Departments (Trade and Industry, Overseas Development, Export Credits Guarantee Department, etc)

HOURS OF WORK:	HOLIDAY ENTITLEMENT:
Normally 9.00 am to 1.00 pm 2.15 pm to 5.00 pm Monday to Friday (extra hours count for overtime payments)	15 working days

EFM/S/84

Job specification

Developed from its corresponding job description (p 75), the job specification defines the skills, qualities, qualifications, work experience, etc, needed to do a particular job well. Together with the job description, it helps recruiters to draw up an advertisement and select the best applicant. Like the job description, it needs to be reviewed periodically, and should include the originating reference with the date of issue. In a large organisation, a standard form would be used for various job specifications.

```
MENTROSE PRODUCTS (UK) LIMITED
Job Specification - secretarial
```

JOB TITLE:	SALARY GRADE:
Assistant private secretary	B or C (depending on age, qualifications and experience)

DEPARTMENT:	RESPONSIBLE TO:
Export	Export Director's private secretary

EXTENT OF JOB:

1. General assistance to the private secretary with correspondence, copying and filing

2. Personal responsibility for telephone and reception: also for collating information from and correspondence with Government Departments

PERSONAL QUALITIES AND APTITUDES REQUIRED:

1. Readiness to work under supervision

2. Good speech and manner with people

3. Willingness to work overtime when necessary

4. Discretion in dealing with confidential information

5. Interest in foreign countries and overseas trade, particularly with developing countries

MINIMUM EDUCATION, TRAINING AND EXPERIENCE:

1. Good general education, including GCE 'O' Level (or equivalent) in English

2. Intermediate Typewriting certificate

3.   "   Audio-typing   "

4.   "   Office Practice   "

5. Shorthand 80 wpm

6. One year's experience as a secretary

AGE: 18-25   SEX: Either

EFM/S/84

Justified right-margin

This gives an appearance similar to the usual appearance of print; and the basic method of achieving it is the same: varying the space between words. Without an electronic typewriter or a word processor (which can adjust the spacing automatically) it is very time consuming, and will only be worthwhile for special copy or as a display feature.

Method

First type a draft, keeping as close as possible to the length of line required. From this you can ascertain the number of spaces to absorb in each line.

1 Use the paper bail scale to define the typing line. Thus for a line length of 60 characters, set the left-margin at, say, 10 and the right at 70. At this point, hold a ball-point firmly at the printing point and turn the cylinder to draw a vertical ending-line for the type.
2 Take the type as close as possible to your drawn line but never cut through it or extend beyond it. It is difficult to absorb the extra spaces in any line falling very short, so use line-end word division to avoid this. The last line of a paragraph may, of course, be too short for extension to the right-margin.
3 For each line, count the spaces between the end of the type and your drawn line. Jot the figures in the margin.
4 Decide which are the best points at which to absorb spaces. An extra space will be less prominent after a punctuation mark, or between long words. Mark the chosen points on the draft. (If the typewriter has a half-space key you can distribute the spare spaces more evenly.)

When typing the final copy, insert the extra spaces at the points you have marked.

```
DRAFT

There/are several/reasons for the increase/in rates/this      4
year, and most of them are beyond/the control of your local   1
authorities./ The major/problem of inflation,/which faces     3
them as it does/you personally,/accounts for a significant    2
part of the rates bill. / Inflation for local/government is   2
mainly/due to labour costs,/which are agreed at a national    2
level.                                                        -
```

Leader dots

These lead the eye across the line from specified wording to
related figures or other tabulated matter, and their blocked effect
lends balance to a ragged column of words. Various methods
may be used:

- Continuous unspaced dots

       ....
      ....

- Regularly spaced single dots, eg one dot followed by four
  spaces

       .   .   .   .
       .   .   .   .

- Groups of two unspaced dots followed by three spaces

      ..   ..
      ..   ..

- Groups of three unspaced dots followed by two spaces

      ... ...
      ... ...

Points to follow:

1 At least one character space should be left before and after
  leader dots.
2 No line of type should project beyond the right-hand end of
  the leaders.

       _____   ....
       _____
       _____   .....
       _____   ...

3 Always end at the same point. Unspaced dots can line up
  exactly with the widest item in the column; groups of dots
  may have to extend slightly beyond the typing.

4 Grouped dots should be aligned under each other. Never start with part of a group: move the carriage to where the first complete group will begin. Except for continuous unspaced dots, errors in alignment may be avoided by starting at a point divisible by five on the scale (25 30 35 etc).

```
_____    ...   ...   ...
_____
_____      ...   ...
_____         ...   ...
```

5 After typescript extending to more than one line, use dots on the *last line only*. Matter can be blocked or typed in hanging style (consistently) irrespective of the layout style of the table.

```
_____
_____
_____  ........
_____    .....
_____      ........
_____
_____
_____    ........
```

Leaflets

A5 and A4 paper can be used unfolded, or variously folded into convenient sizes and shapes to suit the copy. Line-end word division is often necessary in the short lines of many leaflets. Sometimes continuous prose is well rendered with a justified right-margin. Ornamentation — tailpieces, borders, designs — may be effective. When typing on the folded leaflet, slip a sheet of strong paper between the pages to prevent pitting. All leaflets should be pleasing and eye-catching. Folded leaflets, which are in effect integrated groups of small displays, are a stringent test of display ability.

Four-page leaflets

1 A4 folded to give four A5 portrait pages
Front and back pages   The front page usually gives a prominent and well-spaced display of the title and main subject features of the leaflet. The back page can contain a variety of information, or be left blank. These two pages can thus be designed as quite separate entities and displays.
Two inside pages   The left and right sides should each form a well-displayed entity but, opening to view together, they should be as well balanced in layout and style as the content allows. Drafts of the inside pages should therefore be considered side by side.

Margins will depend on the nature and extent of the copy. Equal side margins are desirable at the left and right extremes. The inner margins (on either side of the fold) should be equal and, either singly or together, equal with the outer margin.

If two pages are similar in content and length, start both on the same level and use consistent line-spacing. If one side is longer, balance it with a tailpiece on the short page.

If the two pages are dissimilar in form and content, vary the line-spacing to equalise the length, or centre the shorter side on its page; these are good alternatives to using a common starting line and a tailpiece.

Marking pages   To avoid confusion when typing, lightly pencil F (for Front), B (for Back), IR (for Inside Right), and IL (for Inside Left) at the *tops* of the pages.

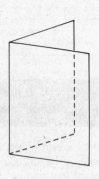

2   A4 folded to give four A5 landscape pages
This lift-up format is sometimes better suited to the shape and length of the copy than the A5 portrait format. Similar considerations as in **1** apply to the layout of the pages. Equal side margins are usually important in balancing the two inside pages.

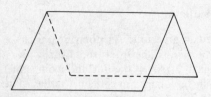

3   A5 folded to give four A6 pages
This provides a compact 4-page leaflet for short itineraries, travel information, etc. Again, the A6 pages can be used in portrait or landscape style.

Six-page leaflets

Take a sheet of A4, with the shorter side at the top. Fold it over twice from the bottom to form three equal sections.* Turn the longer side top to bottom in front of you (portrait) so that a single panel unfolds to your left. You now have a 6-page leaflet, with the front panel on top.

Mark each sheet at the top in pencil to ensure correct placement of the material. First mark the front panel F and the back panel B. Now open out the leaflet so that the front panel on your left is face down. From left to right number the three panels 1, 2, 3. Mark with 4 the reverse of panel 3. Page 3 thus folds back over page 2 and page 1 then folds over this.

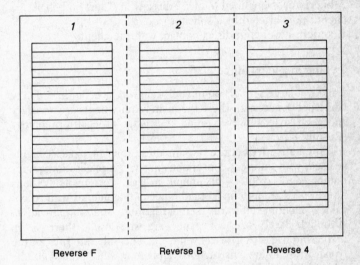

| 1 | 2 | 3 |

Reverse F   Reverse B   Reverse 4

Since each panel is long and narrow, the side margins can be narrow too, but preferably not less than three character spaces. If part of the copy requires more than a single panel, panels 1 and 2 or 2 and 3 can be typed across to read as one page.

---

*6 equal panels, each as follows:

99 mm X 210 mm (approx 4 in X 8¼ in)

Characters across panel
    Elite 46
    Pica 39

Lines down panel
      50 (Elite and Pica)

Legal typing

Legal work covers many areas including:

- Company and commercial law
- Conveyancing (transfer of property)
- Criminal law
- Family law (divorce, custody, probate, etc)
- Litigation (disputes and claims)

In the legal process:
A **barrister** is qualified to plead directly in Court on behalf of a client; he is briefed by a solicitor.
A **solicitor** works in direct contact with the client.

Typing in a legal office

Usually a large proportion of your time will be spent in ordinary correspondence, etc, where the main requirements are accuracy and good style; however, some knowledge of legal terminology is useful.

1 Specialised documents In these the language is highly stylised, with different conventions in style, capitalisation, punctuation, and layout — all unique to legal documents. Various house styles are used in a broad range of documents, with recent trends inclining towards standardisation and simplification. Although large sizes of paper are still used, there is an increasing use of A4 for convenience. The only safe rule for the typist is to follow instructions and copy with precision: the discretion available in other spheres is *not* permissible here. (A new typist will always have clear instructions and specimen guides.)

2 Standard wording Standard documents are available in printed form from law stationers, with blank spaces for the insertion of variables (see p 87). Word processors have revolutionised the production of documents with standard clauses.

3 Typing a legal draft Legal offices use drafts in the usual sense of a first rough copy for consideration and amendment within the office. Wide line-spacing and margins should be left for changes and insertions.

4 Travelling draft This is a draft sent to the other party's solicitors for their consideration; it, too, should have wide spacing and margins for amendment. One copy is retained and two are sent to the other solicitor. Of the latter, one passes to and fro between the solicitors with their respective amendments marked on it in identifiable ink (different colours — red, green, blue, brown, yellow — show the sequence of amendments). The copy retained by each solicitor is similarly amended until agreement has been reached. (Local solicitors may get together; then no travelling draft is required.) Where amendments are few, the engrossment (final copy) is typed from the amended draft; but if necessary a clean draft (fair copy) is prepared by the first solicitor for the other's agreement.

5 Typing an engrossment (final copy) This will usually be in double or $1\frac{1}{2}$ line-spacing. The left-margin should be $1\frac{1}{2}$ inches (for the stitching margin, see p 85); the right-margin should be $\frac{1}{2}$–1 inch. (If both sides of the paper are used, the margins will need to be reversed; see p 32.) However, many legal offices use specially-ruled paper, setting the confines for typing (see the specimens that follow pp 89–91).

No abbreviations must be used in the engrossment. Numbers, including dates, must be typed as words, with the exception of property numbers, postcodes, Acts of Parliament, and numbered paragraphs.

Punctuation marks are often omitted in case they confuse the sense, or lest the meaning be altered by the insertion of additional punctuation. Where lines end short of the right-margin, the space must be filled in by typed hyphens or a ruled line to prevent unauthorised additions. (This is not necessary at the draft stage.) The beginning of a new sentence is indicated by extra space in front of the first word, which begins with a capital letter or may be typed all in capitals.

Certain other words are also capitalised using closed or spaced capitals, and may be underlined for prominence. There are no hard and fast rules here; the use of capitals is largely dependent on house style.

Avoid line-end word division; indeed, many legal offices forbid it. No corrections are allowed (the typist must be exceptionally accurate). If the parties agree to alterations after the engrossment has been typed, the alterations must be initialled or signed by the parties concerned.

Legal vocabulary

This is important to the typist's role in legal typing. (See typed specimen documents pp 87–92.)

Abstract of title summarises the documents and facts constituting title (ownership) to real estate. It contains copies or abstracts of the documents in a specialised shortened form.

Affidavit is a written declaration given on oath before a Commissioner for Oaths, a duly authorised solicitor, or a notary public.

Agreement is a document signed by two or more persons agreeing to do what is specifically described and required.

Assent is concerned with the transfer of property into another's name, eg as the result of a legacy.

Assignment is the document of transfer of rights or property, eg of leasehold property.

Attestation is the act of witnessing a signature to a document. A witness may be required to attest to the authenticity of a signature (without regard to the contents of the document) by adding his or her signature, address, and occupation or description.

Brief is prepared by a solicitor for the use of counsel (a barrister) in Court; it contains full details of the client's case.

Conveyance is a document by which legal ownership of land or property is transferred from the vendor to the purchaser.

Deed is any document executed under seal (see below).

Defendant is the sued party in a legal case.

Document under hand is one signed by the interested parties but not bearing a seal, eg tenancy agreements for less than three years; wills.

Document under seal is a deed, signed by the parties concerned and bearing their seals. Sealing is done by placing one finger on the seal (see Locus sigilli below) and saying: 'I deliver this as my act and deed'. The deed is then signed, with the signature attested by a witness. Limited companies and corporations use a much larger seal, known as a common seal: signing and sealing in this case is performed by authorised members.

Execute a document means to sign and seal a deed or to sign a document under hand.

Lease is a contract in writing for a period of three years or more, under seal, whereby one person agrees to let land or premises to another for a specified period and a fixed rent. (The lessor grants the lease: the lessee is granted the lease.)

Locus sigilli is a Latin term meaning 'place of the seal'. When drawing up a document under seal, it is customary to type LS (in brackets or in a drawn circle) to the right of where the party(ies) will sign, and where the seal will appear.

Plaintiff is the party who commences litigation and sues another party (defendant).

Probate is the procedure by which a will is put into effect when a testator or testatrix dies; it is also called 'proving a will'. (See Will below.) The executors deliver to the Probate Registry the original will, together with an account of the estate; an oath that they will duly administer the estate; and the fee payable. The Probate Registry then issues a copy of the will, bound up with an order of court under its seal, stating that the will has been duly proved by the executors: this document is known as a probate.

Statement of claim is a formal document used in a legal action which sets out fully the facts on which the plaintiff supports his case.

Testimonium and attestation clause concludes most legal documents. It is concerned with signing and witnessing (see specimen documents pp 88–91).

Will sets out the wishes of a person concerning the distribution of his or her property and wealth after death. The person making the will is known as the testator (male) or testatrix (female). The executor (male) or executrix (female) is appointed by the testator/testatrix to carry out the terms of the will.

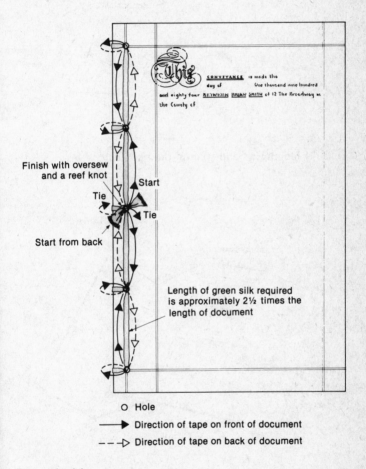

Finish with oversew and a reef knot

Start

Tie

Tie

Start from back

Length of green silk required is approximately 2½ times the length of document

O Hole

⟶ Direction of tape on front of document

- - -▷ Direction of tape on back of document

Sewing a legal document

Endorsement ('backsheet')

This gives the date, the names of the parties concerned, and a brief description of the document. The name and address of the solicitors are often typed at the foot.

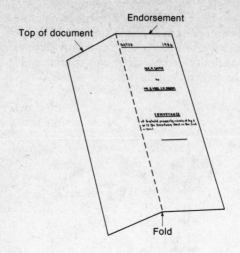

Fold A4 lengthways and type on the right-half.

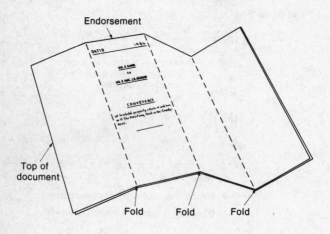

Fold the draft or brief paper into four crossways. With top of the document at the left, type on the second section from the left (make a pencil guidemark at the top).

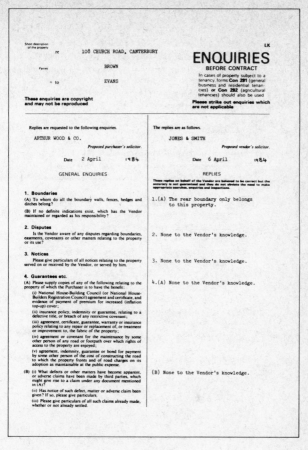

Short description
of the property

re   108 CHURCH ROAD, CANTERBURY

Parties   BROWN

" to   EVANS

LK

ENQUIRIES
BEFORE CONTRACT

In cases of property subject to a
tenancy, forms **Con 291** (general
business and residential tenancies) **or Con 292** (agricultural
tenancies) should also be used

**Please strike out enquiries which
are not applicable**

Replies are requested to the following enquiries.

ARTHUR WOOD & CO.

Proposed purchaser's solicitor.

Date   2 April   1984

GENERAL ENQUIRIES

The replies are as follows.

JONES & SMITH

Proposed vendor's solicitor.

Date   6 April   1984

REPLIES

These replies on behalf of the Vendor are believed to be correct but the
accuracy is not guaranteed and they do not obviate the need to make
appropriate searches, enquiries and inspections.

1. Boundaries

(A) To whom do all the boundary walls, fences, hedges and
ditches belong?

(B) If no definite indications exist, which has the Vendor
maintained or regarded as his responsibility?

1.(A) The rear boundary only belongs
      to this property.

2. Disputes

Is the Vendor aware of any disputes regarding boundaries,
easements, covenants or other matters relating to the property
or its use?

2. None to the Vendor's knowledge.

3. Notices

Please give particulars of all notices relating to the property
served on or received by the Vendor, or served by him.

3. None to the Vendor's knowledge.

4. Guarantees etc.

(A) Please supply copies of any of the following relating to the
property of which the Purchaser is to have the benefit:

    (i) National House-Building Council (or National House-
Builders Registration Council) agreement and certificate, and
evidence of payment of premium for increased (inflation
top-up) cover;

    (ii) insurance policy, indemnity or guarantee, relating to a
defective title, or breach of any restrictive covenant;

    (iii) agreement, certificate, guarantee, warranty or insurance
policy relating to any repair or replacement of, or treatment
or improvement to, the fabric of the property;

    (iv) agreement or covenant for the maintenance by some
other person of any road or footpath over which rights of
access to the property are enjoyed;

    (v) agreement, indemnity, guarantee or bond for payment
by some other person of the cost of constructing the road
to which the property fronts and of road charges on its
adoption as maintainable at the public expense.

4.(A) None to the Vendor's knowledge.

(B) (i) What defects or other matters have become apparent,
or adverse claims have been made by third parties, which
might give rise to a claim under any document mentioned
in (A)?

    (ii) Has notice of such defect, matter or adverse claim been
given? If so, please give particulars.

    (iii) Please give particulars of all such claims already made,
whether or not already settled.

(B) None to the Vendor's knowledge.

Page 1 of Enquiries before Contract (Ref LK)

<u>T H I S   C O N V E Y A N C E</u> is made the   day of

One thousand nine hundred and eighty four

<u>B E T W E E N</u> <u>JOHN SMITH</u> of 16 South Street in the City of Cardiff

Schoolteacher (hereinafter called "the Vendor") of the one part and

<u>WILLIAM STONE</u> of 10 The Strand Ramsgate in the County of Kent Builder

(hereinafter called "the Purchaser") of the other part

<u>W H E R E A S</u> :

(1) The Vendor is seised of the property hereinafter described for an

estate in fee simple in possession free from incumbrances

(2) The Vendor has agreed with the Purchaser for the sale to him of

the said property for a like estate at the price of Thirty thousand

pounds

<u>N O W   THIS   DEED   W I T N E S S E T H</u> as follows:-

1. <u>IN</u> pursuance of the said agreement and in consideration of the sum

of <u>THIRTY THOUSAND POUNDS</u> paid by the Purchaser to the Vendor (the

receipt whereof the Vendor hereby acknowledges) the Vendor as Beneficial

Owner hereby conveys unto the Purchaser <u>ALL THAT</u> piece or parcel of

land <u>TOGETHER</u> with the messuage or dwellinghouse erected thereon or on

part thereof situate at and known as Number 16 South Street in the City

of Cardiff <u>TO HOLD</u> the same unto the Purchaser in fee simple

2. <u>IT IS HEREBY CERTIFIED</u> that the transaction hereby effected does

not form part of a larger transaction or of a series of transactions in

respect of which the amount or value or the aggregate amount or value of

the consideration exceeds Thirty thousand pounds

<u>I N   W I T N E S S</u> whereof the parties hereto have hereunto set their

hands and seals the day and year first before written

<u>SIGNED SEALED AND DELIVERED</u> by)
the said <u>JOHN SMITH</u> in the   )
presence of:-   )

Draft Conveyance

This is the last Will of me

JACK SMITH of 10 The Causeway Newport in the County of

Gwent Schoolteacher ———

1. I HEREBY REVOKE all former Wills and testamentary

dispositions made by me ———

2. I GIVE DEVISE AND BEQUEATH all my estate both real and

personal of whatsoever nature and wheresoever situate to my

wife NORA ELIZABETH SMITH for her own use and benefit

absolutely and I APPOINT her to be the SOLE EXECUTRIX of

this my Will ———

3. I DESIRE that my body be cremated ———

I N   W I T N E S S whereof I have hereunto set my hand to

this my Will this   day of

One thousand nine hundred and seventy six ———

SIGNED by the said JACK SMITH as)
his last Will in the presence of)
us both being present at the   )
same time who at his request in)
his presence and in the presence)
of each other have hereunto   )
subscribed our names as   )
witnesses: —————)

Engrossment of Will

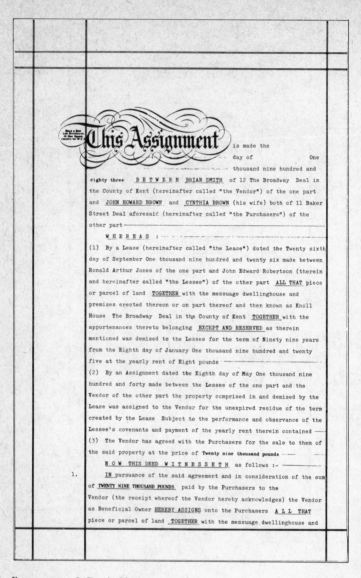

This Assignment is made the _____ day of _____ One thousand nine hundred and **eighty three** B E T W E E N BRIAN SMITH of 12 The Broadway Deal in the County of Kent (hereinafter called "the Vendor") of the one part and JOHN HOWARD BROWN and CYNTHIA BROWN (his wife) both of 11 Baker Street Deal aforesaid (hereinafter called "the Purchasers") of the other part ──────────────────────────────────────

W H E R E A S : ──────────────────

(1) By a Lease (hereinafter called "the Lease") dated the Twenty sixth day of September One thousand nine hundred and twenty six made between Ronald Arthur Jones of the one part and John Edward Robertson (therein and hereinafter called "the Lessee") of the other part ALL THAT piece or parcel of land TOGETHER with the messuage dwellinghouse and premises erected thereon or on part thereof and then known as Knoll House The Broadway Deal in the County of Kent TOGETHER with the appurtenances thereto belonging EXCEPT AND RESERVED as therein mentioned was demised to the Lessee for the term of Ninety nine years from the Eighth day of January One thousand nine hundred and twenty five at the yearly rent of Eight pounds ──────────────────

(2) By an Assignment dated the Eighth day of May One thousand nine hundred and forty made between the Lessee of the one part and the Vendor of the other part the property comprised in and demised by the Lease was assigned to the Vendor for the unexpired residue of the term created by the Lease Subject to the performance and observance of the Lessee's covenants and payment of the yearly rent therein contained ──────

(3) The Vendor has agreed with the Purchasers for the sale to them of the said property at the price of **Twenty nine thousand pounds** ──── ──

N O W T H I S D E E D W I T N E S S E T H as follows :- ──────────

1. IN pursuance of the said agreement and in consideration of the sum of **TWENTY NINE THOUSAND POUNDS** paid by the Purchasers to the Vendor (the receipt whereof the Vendor hereby acknowledges) the Vendor as Beneficial Owner HEREBY ASSIGNS unto the Purchasers A L L THAT piece or parcel of land TOGETHER with the messuage dwellinghouse and

Engrossment of a Deed of Assignment page 1

premises erected thereon or on part thereof situate at and now known
as 12 The Broadway Deal in the County of Kent T O HOLD the same unto
the Purchasers as joint tenants for the residue of the term of NINETY
NINE YEARS created by the Lease SUBJECT to the payment of the said
yearly rent of EIGHT POUNDS and to the performance and observance of
the Lessee's covenants in the Lease contained————————————————————

2.   IT IS HEREBY DECLARED as follows :————————————————

(a) The Purchasers shall hold the said property UPON TRUST to sell the
same or to postpone the sale thereof and shall hold the net proceeds of
sale and the net rents and profits until sale UPON TRUST for themselves
as joint tenants————————————————————————————————

(b) Until the expiration of Twenty one years from the death of the
survivor of the Purchasers the trustees for the time being of this
deed shall have full power to mortgage charge lease or otherwise
dispose of all or any part of the said property with all the powers
in that behalf of an absolute owner————————————————————

3.   IT IS HEREBY CERTIFIED that the transaction hereby effected does
not form part of a larger transaction or of a series of transactions in
respect of which the amount or value or the aggregate amount or value
of the consideration exceeds Thirty thousand pounds ——————————

    I N W I T N E S S whereof the parties hereto have hereunto
set their hands and seals the day and year first before written————————

SIGNED SEALED AND DELIVERED by)
the said BRIAN SMITH in the   )
presence of :————————   )

Engrossment of a Deed of Assignment page 2

IN THE HIGH COURT OF JUSTICE

QUEEN'S BENCH DIVISION

B E T W E E N :

ROBERT TAYLOR   Plaintiff

- and -

DAVID WILLIAM
JENKINS   Defendant

I ROBERT TAYLOR of 16 High Street Deal in the County
of Kent the above-named Plaintiff MAKE OATH AND SAY as
follows:-

1. By an Agreement dated the 17th day of August 1980 made
between me of the one part and the Defendant of the other part
I agreed to let and the Defendant agreed to take the premises
described as ALL THAT dwellinghouse and premises being
Number 26 Meadow View Road Deal in the County of Kent for the
term of One year commencing on the 1st day of September 1980
and thereafter on a quarterly tenancy at the yearly rent of
£2000 payable by equal quarterly payments on the 29th September
25th December 25th March and 24th June in every year

2. The said Agreement contains a provision for re-entry if
any part of the rent be unpaid when due

3. Four quarters' rent in respect of the said premises
amounting to £2000 were due to me on 25th March 1983 and have
not been paid and the said Agreement has become liable to
forfeiture

4. I am advised and verily believe that there is no defence
to this action

SWORN at   )
in the County of   )
this   day of   )
1983   )

Before me,

A Commissioner for Oaths

Affidavit

Letters

The good appearance of its letters is important to a firm's image. Special care is therefore expected when typing letters.

Use of standard letters and paragraphs

To save time and effort in letter writing, firms increasingly use standard letters and standard paragraphs (see pp 163–5) in routine correspondence. These are shown in an office correspondence handbook; with word processors they are typed out automatically as required, from the discs on which they are stored. However, there are still many one-off letters, which may be presented to the typist as manuscript/typescript draft, by audio, or by short-hand dictation.

Carbon copies

General At least one carbon copy must be made for the file, unless a copying machine is used. It may be preferable to type on both sides of flimsy paper, to achieve economy of paper and storage space. The flimsy must therefore be thick enough to show a legible transcript on both sides yet thin enough to take the required number of copies. Sometimes different coloured flimsy paper or carbon paper is used for different departments or individuals.

Distribution When copies of a letter are sent to persons other than the addressee, type: copies to; *or* distribution; *or* cc (copy circulated to) at the foot of the letter, followed by the recipients' names (usually in alphabetical order or in order of seniority). When the distribution should be known by all concerned, this appears on all copies, including the file copy. To ensure correct distribution, each person's copy is ticked beside his name, or the name is underlined.

Blind carbon copies It is sometimes inappropriate to show the distribution on the addressee's top copy. Then a 'blind' carbon copy distribution list is typed on the carbon copies only (pre-ceded by bcc), after the letter has been completed and the top copy removed. When the originator only should know the circulation, the bcc distribution is typed only on the file copy.

Preparing letters for signature

Ensure that the typescript is mailable. Then assemble all the papers (with the carbon(s) and enclosure(s) under the top copy, and the envelope flap folded over the uppermost part of the top copy) and secure them with a slip-on paper clip. It is wise *always* to keep together the letter and all the relating papers for enclosure. (Sometimes the typist may be asked to leave blanks for the salutation and complimentary close so that the originator may write them in (in personal terms) at the signature stage.)

Variety of layouts

House style preferences apply particularly to letters, and a wide variety of layouts is used. Fast, accurate typing requires automatised responses, which only come with the practice in similar style and layout which office work provides. It is necessary, however, to be familiar with the main distinguishing features of commonly used styles.

Even within a house style there are respects in which the typist should be flexible in his or her approach. For example, a few lines saved between the letter parts above the salutation, and/or in the signature block, could avoid an unduly short continuation sheet.

Between the two extremes of style — fully blocked (p 95) and fully displayed (p 99) — there are various intermediary styles. One example is shown on p 100; another, with the inside name and address at the foot of the letter, on p 101. (These four specimens use the same letter for ease in comparing styles.) See also the suggested layout for a personal letter under Job applications, p 74.

Circular letters

These have identical wording and are sent out in large numbers, often as an advertising mail-shot. A specific date is not usually given: 'date as postmark' or just the month and year are more common. Sometimes there is no inside name and address and the salutation may simply be 'Dear Sir or Madam'. However, circular letters are now usually produced on a word processor or memory electronic typewriter which, by merging the letter with a mailing list, produces 'personalised' letters, each one of top-copy quality. A circular letter is included under Cut-off slips on p 40.

Parts of a letter

In any layout style, certain parts are essential to every letter. Other parts will be added as appropriate (eg attention line, telephone extension number), and some parts are optional (eg designation of signatory). Most parts are illustrated in the fully blocked letter on p 95: this is followed by a description of the parts (including those not illustrated) in alphabetical order.
Attention line   It is sometimes requested that all correspondence be addressed to an organisation. The salutation is then Dear Sirs, but the writer may name a particular person to deal with the letter. This is shown on the envelope, and in the letter

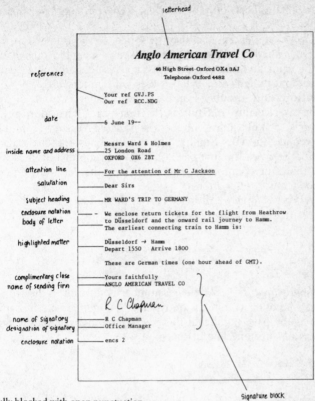

letterhead

references

Anglo American Travel Co

46 High Street·Oxford OX4 3AJ
Telephone: Oxford 4482

Your ref GVJ.PS
Our ref RCC.NDG

date

6 June 19--

inside name and address

Messrs Ward & Holmes
25 London Road
OXFORD OX6 2BT

attention line

For the attention of Mr G Jackson

salutation

Dear Sirs

subject heading

MR WARD'S TRIP TO GERMANY

enclosure notation
body of letter

We enclose return tickets for the flight from Heathrow
to Düsseldorf and the onward rail journey to Hamm.
The earliest connecting train to Hamm is:

highlighted matter

Düsseldorf → Hamm
Depart 1550   Arrive 1800

These are German times (one hour ahead of GMT).

complimentary close
name of sending firm

Yours faithfully
ANGLO AMERICAN TRAVEL CO

R C Chapman

name of signatory
designation of signatory

R C Chapman
Office Manager

enclosure notation

encs 2

Signature block

Fully blocked with open punctuation

by an Attention line. (An Attention line does *not* mean that the letter is personal [see Confidential line below]; it will be opened in the absence of the person named.)

It may be typed above the salutation at the left-margin or centred (whether paragraphs are blocked or indented); the typist may use closed capitals with or without underscore, *or* lower case with underscore. The wording varies: see examples in the letters above and on pp 99–101).

Body of letter   This should be divided into paragraphs and typed in single, 1½, or double spacing, with appropriate spacing between the paragraphs (see p 135).

Complimentary close   It should be separated from the body of the letter by at least one line of space. An initial capital is required for the first word only. For wording, see Salutation below.

Confidential (or Personal) line   The term Confidential (or Strictly Confidential) indicates confidential business for the eyes of the addressee (or other authorised person). The term Personal or Private indicates matter personal to the addressee and it should be opened only by him/her. The envelope is similarly marked.

The Confidential line may be typed at the left-margin or centred (whether paragraphs are blocked or indented), above the inside name and address; the typist may use closed capitals with or without underscore, *or* lower case with underscore.

Continuation sheets For these plain paper is used, of the same size, quality and tint as the first page. The addressee's name is spelt out fully as on the first page (eg Miss Ann Smith is *not* reduced to Miss Smith). The style and position of the date should be as on the first page. A consistent top margin must be left above the continuation sheet details, and at least one line of space (consistently) after it.

Fully blocked layout All lines start at the left-margin. A line of space between the parts is optional.

```
2
Messrs Ward & Holmes
6 June 19--
```

Fully displayed style The page number is centred to the typing line. The other two items are typed at the margins on the same line as the page number if there is room, otherwise on the line below or after one line of space.

```
Messrs Ward & Holmes          2          6 June 19--
```

Semi-blocked styles The addressee's name is placed at the left margin. The page number may be at the left margin or centred (a separating line of space is optional). The date will be placed as on the first page.

```
2
Messrs Ward & Holmes                      6 June 19--
```

Date The usual order is day, month, year (6 June 198–). The day and year are never spelt out in words. The month written in figures could cause confusion with the day — as the order of day and month varies from one country to another. The word 'Date' and the day of the week are not used. The month and year may be abbreviated (12 Jan 8–). The international system for all-numeric dates is as follows: 198–/1/12 (proceeding from the general to the particular). Dates occurring in the text of the letter must be typed in consistent form, though not necessarily according with the form at the head of the letter.

Designation This is typed on the line following the signatory's name. Closed capitals or initial capitals may be used, with or without underscore, but the name and the designation are seldom both typed in closed capitals, or both underscored.

Enclosure notation   The text of the letter usually mentions any enclosures, but a notation system provides a check to both sender and recipient that these have actually been sent. The word Enc(s), enc(s) or ENC(S) at the foot of the letter at the left-margin indicates that there are enclosures. The number of enclosures is best specified (eg Encs 3); also their nature (eg Enc leaflet).

Marginal marks may be made at points of reference in the letter, as an alternative or an addition to the enclosure notation. These may be in the form of one, two, or three unspaced dots, or a hyphen, or an oblique sign (there is a speed advantage in a lower case signal) in line with each mention in the text that something is being enclosed. Set a tab stop within the margin.

Highlighted matter   If more than one item is to be highlight-ed, there must be consistency of layout. (See also Highlighted matter p 69.)

Inside name and address   This ensures that each letter is inserted in the correct envelope and that the carbon copy is correctly filed. For speed, it is best typed as on the envelope (see p 52) but always with single spacing. Optionally, it may be placed at the *end* of the letter (see p 101); then if there is a continuation sheet, it may be at the foot of the first page *or* at the end of the letter. An enclosure notation at the foot of the letter may be typed above *or* below the name and address. Confidential and Attention lines must still appear at the top of the first page.

Letterhead   This will be printed in house style, often on expensive top-quality paper (with matching envelopes), signify-ing the importance attached to letters; avoid costly wastage from re-starts. It may include headed spaces for typing in refer-ence(s), date, and indicating enclosures.

Name of sending firm   This optional part may be house style; it may be typed in closed capitals, *or* with initial capitals and underscored. It should be typed on the line following either the complimentary close or the signatory's name/designation.

Name of signatory   This is typed under the space left for the signature. It is useful when the signature is unclear, and gives the precise name and initials for use in reply. Use closed capitals or initial capitals, with or without underscore (but the name and the designation are seldom both in closed capitals, or both under-scored).

Postscript   Sometimes this contains matter that the originator accidentally omitted, but it is also used to draw attention to a particular point. The signatory often initials it.

Reference(s)   This is used to trace and file correspondence. It often consists of the upper case initials of the originator, followed by the typist's initials (sometimes in lower case for differentiation). It may also indicate the department and/or the file number. Different parts of the reference are separated by a solidus or a full stop; there is no stop at the end. A letter sent in reply to one with a reference usually quotes this first. Where only the sender's reference is used, 'Our ref' is often omitted.

Salutation This is the opening greeting, with initial capitals. Commonly used forms are Dear Sir, Dear Madam, Dear Sirs (all formal, usually with Yours faithfully as the close); or Dear Mr Jones, Dear Mrs Smith, etc (informal, usually ending with Yours sincerely).

Signature block This consists of all the items from the complimentary close to the designation of the signatory. When the close starts just right of centre, the subsequent items are blocked to it, *or* each centred to it, *or* the signatory's name and designation are indented five spaces from the start of it.

Signing for intended signatory If authorised to despatch a letter in the absence of the originator, the typist signs in the signature space followed by pp (for 'on behalf of' or 'for'). If the secretary has been asked to write a letter on his or her own account, the secretary's signature appears above his or her own typed name and designation.

```
Yours faithfully
ANGLO AMERICAN TRAVEL CO

Norma Green

pp Mr R C Chapman
Office Manager
```

If the letter is already typed, 'pp' (or 'for') is written in after the signature or (more usually) in front of the originator's name.

```
Yours faithfully
ANGLO AMERICAN TRAVEL CO

Norma Green

Dictated by Mr R C Chapman, Office Manager, and signed
in his absence by his personal assistant
```

Alternative style

```
Yours faithfully
ANGLO AMERICAN TRAVEL CO

Norma Green

Personal assistant to Office Manager
```

Signature block when the typist has written the letter on his or her own account.

Subject heading This is typed in closed capitals with or without an underscore, *or* in initial capitals and underscored. When replying to a letter with a heading, repeat the heading. Headings provide a useful quick reference to the content.

Anglo American Travel Co

46 High Street · Oxford OX4 3AJ
Telephone: Oxford 4482

Your ref. GVJ/PS
Our ref. RCC/NDG   6th June, 19--.

Messrs. Ward & Holmes,
25 London Road,
OXFORD. OX6 2BT

               For the attention of Mr. G. Jackson

Dear Sirs,

                    Mr. Ward's trip to Germany

     We enclose return tickets for the flight from Heathrow to Düsseldorf and the onward rail journey to Hamm. The earliest connecting train to Hamm is:

               Düsseldorf → Hamm
               Depart 1550   Arrive 1800

     These are German times (one hour ahead of G.M.T.).

                         Yours faithfully,
                         ANGLO AMERICAN TRAVEL CO

                         R C Chapman

                         R. C. Chapman
                         Office Manager

Encs. 2

Fully displayed style with full punctuation

This style uses maximum centring and other features that make it the slowest style to type.

Note
- References at left-margin; date on same line as Our ref
- Attention line and subject heading centred and underscored
- Indented paragraphs

- Highlighted matter centred to typing line
- Complimentary close begins just right of centre; name of firm, signatory's name and designation centred to it, with the latter underscored
- *Full punctuation;* traditionalists who use displayed forms as house styles often prefer full punctuation with it, but display-ed styles can also be used with open punctuation

---

Anglo American Travel Co

46 High Street · Oxford OX4 3AJ
Telephone: Oxford 4482

Your ref GVJ.PS
Our ref RCC.ndg   6 June 19--

Messrs Ward & Holmes
25 London Road
OXFORD OX6 2BT

Attention: Mr G Jackson

Dear Sirs

                    MR WARD'S TRIP TO GERMANY

We enclose return tickets for the flight from
Heathrow to Düsseldorf and the onward rail journey
to Hamm. The earliest connecting train to Hamm is:

          Düsseldorf → Hamm
          Depart 1550   Arrive 1800

These are German times (one hour ahead of GMT).

                         Yours faithfully
                         ANGLO AMERICAN TRAVEL CO

                         R C Chapman

                         R C Chapman
                         Office Manager

encs 2 tickets

Semi-blocked with open punctuation

There are varying semi-blocked styles. The above is but one example.

Note
- Date on same line as Our ref, ending at right-margin. (Many who favour a blocked layout prefer this key item in this more prominent position)
- Attention line at left-margin, with initial capitals and underscored
- Subject heading in closed capitals, and centred to typing line for prominence
- Highlighted matter inset 5 spaces from left-margin for prominence
- Signature block starts just right of centre and is blocked

Anglo American Travel Co

46 High Street · Oxford OX4 3AJ
Telephone: Oxford 4482

Your ref GVJ.PS
Our ref RCC.NDG   6 June 19--

Attention of Mr G Jackson

Dear Sirs

MR WARD'S TRIP TO GERMANY

We enclose return tickets for the flight from Heathrow to Düsseldorf and the onward rail journey to Hamm. The earliest connecting train to Hamm is:

Düsseldorf → Hamm
Depart 1550   Arrive 1800

These are German times (one hour ahead of GMT).

Yours faithfully
Anglo American Travel Co

R C Chapman

R C Chapman
OFFICE MANAGER

Messrs Ward & Holmes
25 London Road
OXFORD OX6 2BT

Semi-blocked letter with inside name and address at foot

Letter writing

A well *written* letter is as important to a firm's image as a well *typed* letter, so give careful thought to composition.

- Assemble all points in logical order, and decide which need main treatment.
- The general tone of the letter must suit the situation and the firm's relationship with the addressee, but must *always* be courteous, however strongly worded or critical it is. Choose a suitable salutation and complimentary close.
- Avoid business jargon, eg *not* 'I am in receipt of your letter', but rather 'Thank you for your letter'. Use plain words and clear, uncomplicated sentences.
- Take care with punctuation, and remember that commas wrongly placed can be misleading.
- Use a subject-heading; this provides a useful quick reference to the content, both for the addressee and the file.
- In your introductory paragraph refer to the letter under reply (or to previous correspondence), or to a telephone call, etc, quoting the date. If there has been no previous contact on the matter, go straight into the subject of the letter.
- In the body of the letter, present all information and explanations point by point in compact paragraphs. (On moving to a new topic, start a new paragraph. This makes for ease and speed of understanding.)
- In your final paragraph, state the conclusion of your argument or suggest the next action to be taken.

Line graphs

Line graphs provide visual representation of a wide range of statistical data. They are frequently prepared for discussion at business meetings, often incorporated in typewritten reports. An expert typist is expected to cope with them.

There are two axes — a horizontal base line, joined at right angles by a left-hand vertical line (the x axis and y axis respectively). Scale points along the x axis (reading from left to right) indicate the independent variable, eg time period; those along the y axis (reading upwards) indicate the dependent or measured variable, eg the value or number of sales.

Single-line and multi-line graphs

Sometimes only one set of information is presented, by means of a single line. However, two or more sets of related data (for home/export sales, different departments, etc) can be shown on the same graph for instant comparison. The lines may be differentiated by colour, but this is effective only on a top copy. More often differently drawn lines (unbroken, broken, heavy, etc) are used, with a key.

Data presented by line graph can often be alternatively shown by bar chart, pie chart, or tabulation.

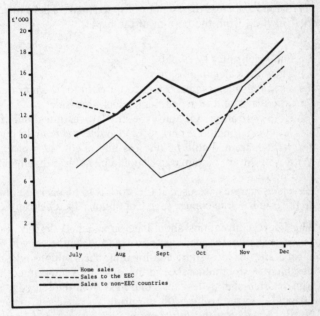

Multi-line graph

Line-spacing

Line space selector at 1	Line space selector at 2	Line space selector at 3

This is typed in single	In double spacing there	In treble spacing 2
line spacing. There is	*(space)*	*(space)*
no full line of space	is one full line of	*(space)*
between the lines of type.	*(space)*	lines of space are
But the lines are, of	space between the type.	*(space)*
course, clearly separated.		*(space)*
		left between the type.

2.5 cm (1 in) 6 lines

Some machines have intermediary line-space settings, eg
1½ (½ line of space between type)
2½ (1½ lines of space between type)

For line-spacing between different styles of paragraph see Paragraphs p 135

Margins

Top This should be not less than 1 inch (6 lines of space). On single page documents or where new sections or chapters begin on a new page, leave a little more than this (a 'dropped head').
Bottom Leave not less than 6 lines of space (make a light pencil mark 1 inch up from the bottom of the paper).

Side
- Left and right may be equal.
- Left may be wider than right.
- As a general rule, it is bad practice for right to be wider than left; the placement of typed matter looks lop-sided.
- With A4 portrait or A5 landscape, the left-margin should be not less than 1 inch (2.5 cm), ie 12 characters elite or 10 pica; the right-margin should be not less than 6 elite or 5 pica.
- With A5 portrait, both margins should be not less than 6 elite or 5 pica.
- Reversed margins are used if the work is to be backed either in the original or in copies. (See Continuous documents p 32.)

The above conventions should be approached flexibly. For instance, if slightly reduced margins would make the copy fit on one page and avoid a short continuation sheet, this would be preferable to a strict adherence to the 'rules'. Or if a printed A4 heading started slightly less than one inch from the left edge of the paper, align the typing with the print.

Note Always set the left-margin stop *where it will be most used*. For example, in hanging paragraphs this will be where the second and subsequent lines begin; use the margin release in conjunction with a tab stop for the first line of each paragraph.

Mathematical typing: see Technical typing pp 171–3
Measurements: see Metrication pp 118–20.

Measurements in continuous text

1 Measurements should not be divided at the end of a line.
2 Never use a full stop after a metric abbreviation.
3 Do not use s for plurals: 4 kg, 6 mm, 22 km.
4 One space should be left between the number and the unit of measurement.

5   A lower case x (with one space before and after) can be used
    instead of the words 'multiplied by'.

> ```
> The carpet measured 4 m x 3 m and was perfect.
> ```

Meetings

The purpose of most business meetings, large or small, is the
same: to reach decisions *by discussion*. Procedure varies only in
style and formality. The following vocabulary is essential to the
typist's role in meetings procedure.

Addressing the chair   All remarks must be addressed to the
Chairperson ('Mr Chairman' or 'Madam Chairman'), who
controls the meeting and the order of speaking.

Ad hoc   A Latin term meaning 'for this purpose'. Thus an ad
hoc committee is appointed for a particular task, as opposed to a
standing committee which is of a more permanent nature.

Agenda   This lists matters to be dealt with at a meeting. It may
be combined with the Notice of meeting, or sent separately.

Amendment   This is an alteration to the wording of a motion;
it must be proposed, seconded and put to the meeting in the
usual way.

Any other business (AOB)   This is usually included in the
Agenda, but only minor items should be raised without fore-
warning being given to members.

Attendance record   At large meetings, members sign an
attendance sheet or register. At small meetings, the secretary
might record the names of those present.

Casting vote   The Chairperson has a casting vote to decide an
issue when there is an equal number of votes for and against a
motion.

Chairperson's Agenda   This is a copy of the Agenda specially
prepared by the secretary for the Chairperson, with guidance
notes under items. The right side of the paper is left blank for
the Chairperson's additional notes.

Closure   To end a protracted discussion, any member may
move 'that the question be now put'. If the motion is carried, the
matter under discussion must be put to the vote forthwith.

Coopted member   This is a person appointed by a committee
to serve on it for a particular purpose.

Ex officio   A Latin term meaning 'by virtue of office'. Membership of a committee may be ex officio, ie automatic because of
a position already held.

Honorary officer or member   An honorary officer undertakes duties without payment, eg Hon Secretary, Hon Treasurer. Honorary membership of an organisation is granted as an honour, and no subscription is charged.

Lie on the table A motion that a matter should 'lie on the table' means that no action should be taken on it at the present time.

Memorandum and Articles of Association The Memorandum sets out the objects for which an organisation is formed. The Articles of Association are the regulations governing its business conduct and management.

Minutes See pp 111–12.

Motion This is a proposal put to a meeting. The mover (or proposer) speaks first and has the right of reply at the end of the discussion. He or she must have a supporter (seconder), who may speak only once. When put to the vote, a motion becomes the question and, if passed by the meeting, becomes a resolution for action.

Nem con An abbreviation of a Latin term meaning 'no-one dissenting'. A motion is passed nem con if no votes have been cast against it but some members have abstained (compare Unanimous below).

Notice of meeting This is sent by the secretary well in advance to everyone entitled to attend; it must state the day, time, and place (usually decided at the end of the previous meeting).

Out of order A member may be ruled out of order for a statement in breach of the governing rules. The statement must then be withdrawn.

Point of order Proceedings may be interrupted on a point of order regarding meeting procedure, standing orders or the Constitution. An immediate ruling by the Chairperson is required.

Proxy A person entitled to vote at a meeting may appoint another person to attend and vote on his behalf (by proxy), provided the regulations so allow.

Putting the question At the end of the discussion of a motion, the Chairperson 'puts the question' by announcing, 'The question before the meeting is . . .' Voting then takes place.

Quorum This means the minimum number of members (as laid down in the regulations) who must be present to make a meeting valid.

Resolution See Motion.

Rider This is an addition to a resolution; it differs from an amendment in that it adds to, rather than alters, the sense. A rider must be proposed, seconded, and put to the meeting in the usual way.

Standing orders These are the rules governing the conduct of proceedings in an organisation (also known as the Constitution).

Sub-committee   This is a group of persons appointed by a committee to undertake certain duties on its behalf.

Teller   A teller is a person appointed to count votes at a meeting.

Unanimous   A motion is carried unanimously if all members vote in favour of it (see also Nem con).

Meetings of a limited company

For legal and constitutional reasons, documentary procedure for the Annual General Meeting and other meetings of a public limited company is formal. The Notice of meeting and Agenda are expressed in stylised terms, eg 'Notice is hereby given . . .' They will be sent to shareholders with a form of proxy so that those who cannot attend may appoint another person to vote on their behalf. Formal Minutes record the precise wording of each resolution with the names of the proposer and seconder. All documents relating to this form of meeting must faithfully follow copy.

THE CENTRAL ENGINEERING COMPANY LIMITED

ANNUAL GENERAL MEETING

NOTICE IS HEREBY GIVEN that the Ninth Annual General Meeting of the Company will be held in the Rochester Hall, Hill Place, Coventry on Tuesday 24 May 19-- at 1100 hrs.

B U S I N E S S

1   To receive and consider the Directors' Report, Accounts and Balance Sheet for the year ended 31 March 19--.

2   To confirm the Preference Dividend paid in August 19-- and the Ordinary Interim Dividend paid in September 19--.

3   To declare an Ordinary Final Dividend.

4   To confirm the transfer of £250,000 to General Reserve.

5   To elect 2 Directors.

6   To transact any other business that may be brought before an Ordinary General Meeting.

BY ORDER OF THE BOARD

G Hammersmith
SECRETARY

21 March 19--

Notice and Agenda for Annual General Meeting of a limited company

Meetings of committees, boards, etc

In general, such meetings adopt a common procedure and documents follow a standard pattern, though the layout and language can vary with custom and preference in different organisations. There will be an advance Notice of the date, time, and place of the meeting; an Agenda (often combined with the Notice) including certain standard recurring items as well as items specific to the present meeting; and subsequently Minutes listing the topics discussed, with the decisions and main relevant arguments. The secretary might prepare a special Chairperson's Agenda. All these documents are typed from manuscript copy, shorthand notes or audio dictation. In the absence of guidelines, a blocked layout is recommended for speed.

CRAIGHALL RESIDENTS ASSOCIATION

A meeting of the Association will be held in the Valley Hotel, Craighall, on Tuesday 24 September 19-- at 7 30 pm. The Agenda will be circulated later.

Roger Steel
Hon Secretary

24 Greenhill Gardens
Craighall
(Tel 39765)

Notice of meeting

CRAIGHALL RESIDENTS ASSOCIATION

Meeting to be held in the Valley Hotel on Tuesday 24 September 19-- at 7 30 pm

A G E N D A

1 Apologies for absence.
2 Minutes of last meeting.
3 Matters arising from the Minutes.
4 Pedestrian crossing in Oak Road.
5 Conversion of the Crown Hotel.
6 Any other business.
7 Date of next meeting.

Roger Steel
Hon Secretary

Agenda of meeting

Sometimes the Notice of Meeting and the Agenda are combined:

Combined Notice of Meeting and Agenda

BIDMOUTH TENNIS CLUB

The Annual General Meeting of the Bidmouth Tennis Club will be held at the White Swan Inn, Bidmouth, on Tuesday 20 March 19-- at 1950 hrs.

A G E N D A

1 Apologies for absence.
2 Minutes of last meeting.
3 Matters arising therefrom.
4 Chairman's Annual Report.
5 Treasurer's Annual Report and Balance Sheet.
6 Consideration of plans for extending the Club's facilities.
7 Any other business.
8 Date of next meeting.

T Helpman
Hon Secretary

9 March 19--

Combined Notice and Agenda

```
CRAIGHALL RESIDENTS ASSOCIATION

Meeting to be held in the Valley Hotel on Tuesday 24 September 19--
at 7 30 pm

C H A I R M A N ' S   A G E N D A

1  Apologies for absence                        )
                                                )
   Vice-chairman still in hospital but          )
   doing well.                                  )
                                                )
2  Minutes of last meeting                      )
                                                )
   Secretary regrets omission of Mr Brown's     )
   name under those present.                     )
                                                )
3  Matters arising from the minutes             )
                                                )
   Any attempt to re-open the cycle path        )
   issue should be disallowed.                  )
                                                )
4  Pedestrian crossing in Oak Road              )
                                                )
   Council is resisting on grounds of           )
   proximity to Beech Road crossing.  See       )
   letter of 3 September.                        )
                                                )
5  Conversion of the Crown Hotel                )
                                                )
   Miss King's scheme for an old people's       )
   home seems impracticable - see Council's     )
   letter of 12 September.                       )
                                                )
6  Any other business                           )
                                                )
7  Date of next meeting                         )
                                                )
   Chairman and Secretary both away on the      )
   last Tuesday in October.  Suggest            )
   following Tuesday.                            )
```

Chairperson's Agenda: blocked style

```
THE 'PEGASUS' TRANSPORT & TRADING CO LTD              Form of Proxy
─────────────────────────────────────────────────────────────────

Before completing this form, please read the Notes on the reverse side.

I, the undersigned, being a Member of the above-named Company, hereby appoint
*the Chairman of the Meeting


as my Proxy to vote for me and on my behalf at the Annual General Meeting of
the Company to be held on Thursday 18 May 19--. ‡
This form of proxy is given in respect of      Ordinary Shares of 50p each.
The Proxy is to vote as instructed in respect of the resolutions specified
below:

                                                    For      Against
Resolution No 1 To adopt the Report of the Directors and
the Accounts and to declare a dividend               □         □

Resolution No 2 To re-elect as a Director

(a)  The Rt Hon Edward Armstrong PC                  □         □

(b)  Mr G S Blake                                    □         □

(c)  Sir James Browning KBE                          □         □

(d)  The Rt Hon Lord Livesy of Lamington PC GCB MVO  □         □

Resolution No 3 That the sum available for the remuneration
of the Directors be increased to £120,000 a year     □         □

Resolution No 4

(a)  To re-appoint Long & Masters as the Auditors of the
     Company                                         □         □

(b)  To authorise the Board to fix the remuneration of the
     Auditors for the coming year                    □         □

* Delete if it is desired to appoint any other person, and insert his or her
  name and address. A Proxy need not also be a Member of the Company.

‡ Insert the number of Ordinary Shares in respect of which the form of proxy
  is given. If the number is not inserted, the form of proxy will be taken
  to have been given in respect of all Ordinary Shares held.

Names of joint holders (if any) /IN BLOCK LETTERS/

1  ...........................

2  ...........................

3  ...........................

4  ...........................

Dated this      day of              19--

Signed .........................

Name and address /IN BLOCK LETTERS/
.................................................................
.................................................................
.................................................................
```

Form of proxy

Minutes

Methods of numbering   Some organisations number each minute
from 1 onwards for each meeting. Sometimes numbers run
consecutively through a series of meetings; eg minute 99.84 or
84.99 refers to the 99th minute of meetings held in 1984, or
minute 48.6 refers to the 6th minute of the 48th of all meetings
held.

110 Meetings

Action column   Sometimes the right-margin is headed Action, for insertion of the name or initials of the person who is to take follow-up action.

Indexing   Sometimes minutes are indexed for ease of reference. Index pages may be reserved at the front or back of the Minutes Book, or index cards used.

MINUTES OF MEETING

A meeting of the Entertainments Committee of the Shoreland Traders Association was held in the Committee Room of the Council Offices on Wednesday 12 January 19-- at 1800 hrs.

PRESENT

Mr John Lentern (Chairman)
Miss Angela West
Mr T Benham
Mr P Neames (Secretary)

1 APOLOGIES FOR ABSENCE

The Secretary reported that Mr Mountain was unable to attend as he was out of the country on business.

2 MINUTES OF LAST MEETING

The Minutes of the last meeting, held on 10 October 19-- were read, approved and signed by the Chairman.

3 MATTERS ARISING FROM THE MINUTES

The Secretary reported that the application for a bar licence at this year's Annual Dinner and Dance had been approved.

4 ARRANGEMENTS FOR THE ANNUAL DINNER AND DANCE

Miss West announced that she had made arrangements for the Paul Smithson Group to play at a fee of £200. She also stated that the printing of tickets was in progress.

After a lengthy discussion it was agreed to increase the price of a double ticket to £8.50.

5 ANY OTHER BUSINESS

There was no other business.

6 DATE OF NEXT MEETING

The date of the next meeting was fixed for 15 April 19--.

The Chairman declared the meeting closed at 1950 hrs.

(*Space for signature*)

J Brown
CHAIRMAN

(*Date of signing here*)

Minutes numbered from one onwards; shoulder headings

EXTRACT FROM MINUTES OF GENERAL PURPOSES COMMITTEE MEETING

(held on 2 May 19--)

OFFICE PREMISES	The Committee resumed their consideration of plans to improve the office premises. They examined 3 estimates from local firms for the partitioning of 2 large rooms and decoration of the entire ground floor. It was agreed to accept the lowest estimate and proceed at once with the work.
FIRM'S ANNUAL OUTING	The Secretary reported on the estimates of 3 firms in Seafield and 2 in Meadowland to cater for the firm's annual outing this year. The best offer at Seafield was £12 a head for 2 meals for a minimum number of 60. The meals would be served in a marquee on a suitable site. A limited bar service could be arranged. At Meadowland, a similar service could be had for £10 a head. The Committee nevertheless decided to use the Seafield firm.
DRAWING OFFICE REPRESEN- TATION	The Secretary reported on a request by the Drawing Office to be represented on the Committee by virtue of their increased numbers. This proposal was approved.

Minutes with side headings

MINUTES OF THE 23rd MEETING of the Board of Directors of Blackford Breweries Limited held on 7 December 19-- at the Registered Offices of the Company

Present

Mr L Blackshaw (Chairman and Managing Director)
Mrs D Clarke   )
Col J C Evans MC   ) Directors
Sir John Irvine KBE)
Mr P Ellis-Rees (Secretary)

23.1 APOLOGIES FOR ABSENCE   Action

   Apologies were received from Mr J Martin and Mr F Robertson.

23.2 MINUTES OF LAST MEETING

   The Minutes of the 22nd meeting held on 4 November 19-- were taken
   as read, approved, and signed by the Chairman - copies having
   been previously circulated to the Directorate.

23.3 REPORTS, ETC

   23.3.1 A summary of the Representatives' Reports was given by the
           Secretary. It was noted that in most parts of the country
           business was improving.

           The Secretary was asked to seek clarification of the con-
           flicting reports from the Western Region.   PE-R

   23.3.2 The trading figures for October were presented and dis-
           cussed. They were well down on last year's, but the
           forecast for the months ahead was better.

23.4 EXTENSION AND IMPROVEMENT OF THE BLACK BULL, OKELY

   23.4.1 The Secretary reported that work was proceeding on schedule
           and that the increased traffic through Okely now seemed
           more than likely to justify the cost of this venture.

Minutes (Note numbering method)

112 Meetings

Informal meetings

Especially within an organisation, many meetings are informal and not subject to full meetings procedure. A head of department might summon section heads to discuss certain matters. Notice and Agenda might then be done by memo. Still more informally, a manager might ask the secretary to arrange by telephone a meeting of selected staff. A secretary might attend informal meetings to take notes for the preparation of a record of conclusions. This would follow the order of the Agenda (if any) or simply record the main points made, and any decisions reached.

Where members of two firms reached agreement in discussion, one might record it by letter to the other, or each might record it separately on the file — as is done with decisions made by telephone.

```
MEMORANDUM

From  Dr J P Bradshaw                    Ref  JPB/as

To     Section Heads                     Date 18 January 19--

There will be a meeting in my office of all Section Heads on Friday
27 January 19-- at 1000 hrs.

A G E N D A

1  Budget for forthcoming financial year

2  (a)  Research programme for same period
   (b)  Proposed new laboratory and extension of existing ones

3  Staffing position

   (a)  Technical
   (b)  Clerical

4  Any other business


Circulation - Dr G Andrews
              Mr F Browning
              Dr P Smythe
              Miss S Williams
```

Notice and Agenda in memo

Memos

Being written communications within an organisation, recording facts, figures, requests, decisions, etc, these range from short simple notes to complex expositions of several pages.

Main features

- No salutation, complimentary close, or inside address is given; but the sender, receiver and date (and the reference when given) must be clearly shown.
- The sender authenticates the memo by signing or initialling it.
- Language can vary in formality according to the nature of the message and the relationship of sender to receiver.
- Enclosures (or attachments) are indicated as for letters; as are copies for distribution and blind copies.
- *Paper and style* Any of the standard paper sizes may be used (though usually A4 or A5 landscape), either with printed memo-heads or as plain paper. For speedy reference, filing, etc, a consistent house style is usually followed. This governs the layout, and the typing style of To, From, Ref and Date when plain paper is used.
- *Continuation sheets* Both sides of the paper are often used for the top copy of long memos (with reversed margins on the back). The printed memo-head is normally for the first sheet only, with plain continuation sheets. When printed memo-heads are used for continuation sheets, heading details must be inserted (consistently) on all pages.

  Plain paper continuation sheets are headed as for letters, with the sheet number, name of receiver, and date, all consistently positioned and styled. Note also:
  a paper of matching size and colour should be used
  b the continuation sheet should extend to at least a second line of text
  c the name of the receiver must be typed exactly as on the first sheet
  d the date should be consistent in style with the first sheet
  e at least one line of space should be left after the continuation sheet details

- *Carbon copies* At least one carbon copy must be made, for the file, unless a copying machine is to be used. It is preferable to type on both sides of flimsy paper for economy of paper and storage space; the flimsy must be thick enough to show legible typescript on both sides, yet thin enough to take the required number of copies.

- *Mailability or usability* As in-house documents, memos may have a lower standard of usability than letters, eg to save retyping a whole page, alterations in pen are usually acceptable.

- *Envelopes* Memos are usually delivered by hand, but they may be sent by inter-office van or by post to distant colleagues. Envelopes are typed only for memos to be sent by post. For inter-office circulation, memos may be placed in heavy-duty envelopes with a name grid, designed for frequent use.

```
                    M E M O R A N D U M

To:    Miss P Brown, General Office              12 May 19--

From:  Company Secretary                         TBS/aw/OT27


                 Telephone Extension Numbers

        I attach a list of additional extension numbers and names.
Kindly type a complete and up-to-date list of all our extensions,
in the alphabetical order of names.  Please send a copy to every-
one on the list.

                              HBSalt

                              T B Salt


Enc
```

Centred style plain paper memo

```
    M E M O

    Mrs F Matthews
    Head of Typing

    2 September 19--

    HOUSE-STYLE LAYOUT OF MEMOS

    For a number of reasons, we have decided to standardize the layout
    of our internal correspondence.  In particular, the tasks of reference
    and filing are made easier if key information can be quickly located
    because the position is standard.

    It is suggested that we adopt the following practices.

    1  The fully-blocked style, on plain paper.

    2  Open punctuation.

    3  Subject heading in closed capitals without underscoring.

    4  The words To and From omitted.  The name of the addressee will be
       typed at the top, and that of the sender at the foot of the memo.

    5  The reference will be the last item typed.

    This memo should be used as a guide.

    Since you have just joined the Company this would be a good time for
    the change.  It should make your work easier, and produce a higher
    output from our typists and secretaries.

    If you wish to discuss the matter, let me know.  Otherwise, please go
    ahead and put the scheme into practice.

    TST

    T S Thomas
    Company Secretary

    TST.bg
```

Fully blocked plain paper layout; recipient given at head, sender at foot

Menus

These may be centred or blocked, with or without an ornamental border. A5, A4, or any other suitable size may be used. Different courses should be clearly separated, as may alternative dishes within a course (using a half or full line of space). Vegetables are separated from the main dish(es) and are typed in single spacing.

Menu cards for special functions often give:
- name of the organisation and event
- name of the hotel or restaurant
- luncheon or dinner
- day and date
- price (if appropriate)

Some hotels and restaurants supply headed menu cards for typing or printing by the host organisation in their preferred style.

```
      THE COACH AND HORSES INN

      Lanchester


      Dinner Menu

      Tomato Soup
      Fresh Grapefruit
      Prawn Cocktail

      ****************

      Roast Beef and Yorkshire Pudding
      Roast Chicken with Bread Sauce
      Aylesbury Duckling with Orange Sauce

      ***********************************

      Roast and Boiled Potatoes
      Cauliflower
      Garden Peas
      Baby Carrots

      *************************

      Fresh Fruit Salad
      Cherry Tart
      Lemon Cheesecake
      Chocolate Gateau
      with Cream

      *****************

      Coffee or Tea
```

Simple menu in blocked style without border; rows of asterisks between courses extend to the width of the course above for balance

```
+:+:+:+:+:+:+:+:+:+:+:+:+:+:+:+:+:+:+:+:+:+:+:+:+:+:+:+:+:+:+:+:+:+:+:+:+:+:+:+
+                                                                           +
+                                                                           +
+                           THE CAVENDISH HOTEL                             +
+                                                                           +
+                               Dinner                                      +
+                                                                           +
+                        Chilled Fruit Juice                                +
+                           Prawn Cocktail                                  +
+                        Egg and Ham Vol-au-Vent                            +
+                           Hors d'Oeuvre                                   +
+                                                                           +
+                            * * * * *                                      +
+                                                                           +
+                      Cream of Watercress Soup                             +
+                          Consommé Olga                                    +
+                         Chilled Gazpacho                                  +
+                                                                           +
+                            * * * * *                                      +
+                                                                           +
+                      Fillet of Beef Grilled                               +
+                    with Tomato and Watercress                             +
+                                                                           +
+              Sauté of Chicken with Bacon and Mushrooms                    +
+                         and Madeira Sauce                                 +
+                                                                           +
+                   Escalope of Veal Cordon Bleu                            +
+                                                                           +
+                  Fried Salmon and Shrimp Pancakes                         +
+                         with Scampi Sauce                                 +
+                                                                           +
+                Runner Beans      Croquette Potatoes                       +
+              Spinach in Cream    Aubergines Sautées                       +
+                                                                           +
+                          Cold Buffet                                      +
+                                                                           +
+                            * * * * *                                      +
+                                                                           +
+                          Coupe Jacques                                    +
+                       Sweets from the Trolley                             +
+                        Various Ice Creams                                 +
+                                                                           +
+                            * * * * *                                      +
+                                                                           +
+                          Cheese Board                                     +
+                                                                           +
+                            * * * * *                                      +
+                                                                           +
+                             Coffee                                        +
+                                                                           +
+    ┌──────────────────────────┐  ┌──────────────────────────────────┐    +
+    │ DINNER CHARGE £9.50       │  │          SUPPLEMENTS             │    +
+    │ (including Service and VAT)│  │ Fresh Asparagus        £1.75     │    +
+    │                          │  │ Fresh Artichokes       £1.50     │    +
+    │ Wine by the glass 80p    │  │ Salmon Mayonnaise      £1.75     │    +
+    │ A la carte menu on request│  │ Strawberries and Cream £1.25     │    +
+    └──────────────────────────┘  └──────────────────────────────────┘    +
+                                                                           +
+:+:+:+:+:+:+:+:+:+:+:+:+:+:+:+:+:+:+:+:+:+:+:+:+:+:+:+:+:+:+:+:+:+:+:+:+:+:+:+
```

Menu in centred style with border

Message sheets

These systematise the handling of messages. Arrange the
skeleton so that inserted information can all begin at the same
point for ease in using the margin stop. The message is typed in
note form (see example on p 118).

```
MESSAGE

TO:    Mr T Andrews

ON:    10 December 1983

AT:    1130 hrs

IN YOUR ABSENCE

NAME:  Mr G King

OF:    British Plastics Ltd
       PORTSMOUTH

TEL:   0705 6906

       [ ]  called to see you
       [X]  telephoned
       [ ]  will phone again
       [X]  please phone him/her
       [ ]  urgent
       [X]  left the following message

       Most convenient date for your visit would
       be 5 Jan.  12 Jan if this not possible?


       Signed   Ellen Hill
```

Message sheet

Metrication

A new generation will know only the metric system; meantime, we have to convert. The more we *think* in metric terms, the easier this is. (See also Measurements in continuous text pp 104–5.)

Length

1 centimetre (cm) = 10 millimetres (mm) = 0.3937 in
1 metre (m)   = 100 centimetres (cm) = 1.0936 yd
1 kilometre (km) = 1000 metres (m)   = 0.6214 mile

1 inch = 2.54 cm   25 cm = 10 in (roughly)
1 foot = 0.3048 m   2 m   = $6\frac{1}{2}$ ft (roughly)
1 yard = 0.9144 m   100 m = 110 yd (roughly)
1 mile = 1.6093 km   8 km = 5 miles (roughly)

Area

1 sq cm (cm²) = 100 sq mm (mm²) = 0.1550 sq in
1 sq m (m²)   = 10 000 cm²   = 1.1960 sq yd
1 are (a)   = 100 m²   = 119.60 sq yd
1 hectare (ha) = 100 a   = 2.4711 acres
1 sq km (km²) = 100 ha   = 0.3861 sq miles

1 sq ft   = 0.0929 m² (for floor area, fabrics, etc)
1 sq yd   = 0.8361 m² (roughly 900 sq ft)
                      (100 sq yd) = 83 m²)

1 acre   = 0.4046 ha (for farmland, etc:
                      800 ha = 2000 acres)

1 sq mile = 2.59 km² (for any large area:
(640 acres)   area of Wales = 20 764 km²
                      (8017 sq miles)

Capacity

1 cubic metre (m³) = 1000 litres = 1.3080 cu yd
1 litre   = 1.7598 pints

1 pint   = 0.5683 litres
1 quart = 1.1365 litres
1 gallon = 4.5461 litres (6 gallons, eg of petrol
           = approx 27 litres)

Weight

1 gram(me) (g)   = 1000 milligram(me)s (mg) = 0.0353 oz
1 kilogram(me) (kg) = 1000 g   = 2.2046 lb
1 tonne (t)   = 1000 kg   = 0.9842 ton

1 oz   = 28.350 g   Watch grocery packages:
1 lb   = 0.4536 kg   500 g = 17.6 oz.
1 stone (14 lb) = 6.3503 kg   He weighs 76.20 kg
                                   (approx 12 stone).
1 cwt (112 lb) = 50.802 kg   A 50 kg sack of coal.
1 ton (20 cwt) = 1.0161 t   The metric tonne is slightly
                                   less than the imperial ton.

Thermometer scales (Fahrenheit and Celsius [centigrade])

Conversion can be effected by means of the following formulae:

$x\,°F = \frac{5}{9}(x - 32)\,°F$ $y\,°C = (\frac{9}{5}y + 32)\,°F$
Therefore   Therefore
$70\,°F = \frac{5}{9}(70 - 32)\,°C$ $20\,°C = (\frac{9}{5} \times 20) + 32\,°F$
$\quad\ = \frac{5}{9} \times 38\,°C$ $\quad\ = \frac{180}{5} + 32\,°F$
$\quad\ = \frac{190}{9}\,°C$ $\quad\ = 36 + 32\,°C$
$70\,°F = \underline{\underline{21.1\,°C}}$ $20\,°C = \underline{\underline{68\,°F}}$

On the Celsius scale, freezing point is 0 °C and boiling point is
100 °C; these are 32 ° and 212 ° respectively on the Fahrenheit
scale.

Equivalent sizes

1 *Shoes*

British	3½	4½	5	6	7	8	9	10
Continental	35½	36½	38	39½	40½	42	43	44

British	11	12	13
Continental	45½	47	48

2 *Women's clothing*

British	10	12	14	16	18	20	22	24
Bust (in)	32	34	36	38	40	42	44	46
Continental	38	40	42	44	46	48	50	52

3 *Menswear (suits, overcoats, sweaters)*

British	37–38	39–40	41–42	43–44
Continental	94–97	99–102	104–107	109–112

4 *Men's shirts*

British	14	14½	15	15½	16	16½
Continental	36	37	38	39–40	41	42

British	17	17½
Continental	43	44

Microwriter

Small in size, and weighing less than two pounds, the Microwriter can run for forty hours at a stretch off rechargeable batteries. By pressing five keys in different combinations, one for each finger, it is possible to input any character found on the traditional QWERTY keyboard. An extra thumb key gives word processor-style commands. A thin window panel displays a line of text as it is keyed-in, and it is possible to scroll in either direction to check for errors. The Microwriter's memory can store 1500 words of text, and format them in several ways. To produce hard copy of the text, the machine must be coupled to an electronic typewriter or computer printer.

The Microwriter is a useful machine for middle rank executives and self-employed professional people who do a great deal of 'think writing' (memoranda, notes of meetings, rough drafts of documents, etc) and want to bypass secretaries and typing pools more often. It is claimed that it takes an average user an hour to learn the alphabet and another fourteen hours to Microwrite as fast as handwriting: with further practice it is possible to key-in half as fast again as handwriting.

Money and numbers

Money and numbers in columns

Whole numbers only   These should line up from the right: units under units, tens under tens, etc; precision is important for reading and totalling. If any number in the column has *five or more digits*, a comma or space (consistently) is needed as a 'thousand marker', dividing digits into sets of three from the right. The marker must be maintained *throughout the column*, ie separating any number of four or more digits.

Numbers with decimal points   The decimal points must line up.

Pounds and pence   The decimal points marking off pounds from pence must be in vertical alignment. Two digits must always follow the decimal point to avoid confusion between amounts like 0.08 (8p) and 0.80 (80p).

£ (or other) currency symbol   At the head of the column the £ sign may be placed over any of the £ figures, or over the decimal point, or over the £ symbol before the total.

If the column is headed with a £ symbol, this is not repeated before each amount but may be given before the total. A £ sign can be typed close up before each item in *untotalled* columns.

Single spacing	1½ spacing	Double spacing
£ ←½	£	$
250.80	2,468,320 ←¼	6 432 186 ←ı
16.00	480,000	
203.08		24 624
.45 ←½	6,783	
———— ←½	1,024,086 ←¼	87
£470.33 ←¼	————— ←¼	
════	£3,979,189 ←¼	9 584 ←ı
		———— ←ı
		$6 466 481 ←ı

Dash, representing 'nil' or 'not applicable', may be blocked at the starting point of the column, centred, or typed under the units, irrespective of the layout style of the table. Use one, two, or three dashes or hyphens (consistently).

Line-spacing may depend on the space available. Where space is very limited, omit the space below the currency sign at the top of the column, and the space *above* the line over the total.

Totalling   Lines above and below the total may or may not (consistently) extend above and below the £ sign. Use the variable line-spacer or the interliner for double lines, *not* the half line-spacer which gives too wide a space.

Money in continuous text

General considerations are as follows:

1   No stop is used after the £ sign, nor after p for pence (except at the end of a sentence).
2   The decimal point (separating pounds from pence) is typed as a full stop in the normal position.
3   Always type two figures after the decimal point to avoid confusion in such sums as £12.05 (5p) and £12.50 (50p).
4   Use a comma *or* a space as a thousands marker:

> £33,250   £33 250
> £33,250,000   £33 250 000

5   The £ sign and p (for pence) are never both used in a single money expression: £22.80, 96p.
6   A money amount in figures is never divided at the end of a line.
7   Amounts in pounds only, and in pence only, may be rendered in words; but it is preferable to use words only for pound numbers up to one hundred, and for round hundreds, thousands, and millions thereafter.

There are a number of alternative methods:

Pounds only   £57 or   £57.00 or fifty-seven pounds
          £500 or   £500.00 or five hundred pounds
£5000 or £5,000 or £5,000.00 or five thousand pounds
Pence only   15p or 15 pence   or £0.15 or fifteen pence
          97p or 97 pence   or £0.97 or ninety-seven pence
Millions of pounds only These may be shown in various ways:

£3 million is a low figure.
£3m is a low figure.
£3M is a low figure.
Three million pounds is a low figure.
£3,000,000 is a low figure.
£3 000 000 is a low figure.

Sometimes figures *and* words are given, to ensure accuracy and to prevent alteration:

All for the sum of £5,000 (five thousand pounds).

Numbers within text (figures or words?)

1 **Cardinal numbers** (one, two, three, etc) It is difficult to lay down hard and fast rules. Except in money, dates, measurements, and such identification uses as page and house numbers — which always use figures — the RSA accepts cardinal numbers typed in any of the following ways:

- all in figures
- all in words
- one as a word; the remainder in figures
- one to nine in words; the remainder in figures
- a number at the start of a sentence as a word, or it may follow the scheme used for other numbers

Always use one system consistently within a piece of work.

Note
- In whole numbers of five or more digits expressing quantity, use a comma or space as thousand marker. (Remember the comma is used internationally to indicate a *decimal*.)

```
. . . a total of 3 207 107 men, women and children.
. . . a total of 3,207,107 men, women and children.
```

- In identification systems — STD telephone numbers, reference numbers, etc — follow the rules of the system for spaces, hyphens, full stops, etc.
- For numbers expressing a range, use hyphen or dash consistently (the former is faster and neater).

```
1880-1900      pages 24-29
1880 - 1900    pages 24 - 29
```

2 **Ordinal numbers** (first, second, third, etc) The numerical form (1st, 2nd, 3rd) is mainly used in such expressions as: 2nd class, 3rd edition, 5th amendment. The word form is preferred for such uses as: the first time we met, her second marriage, the third child in the family. Drafts will usually be written in the form to be copied, but look out for a numerical form used as a drafting abbreviation, but meant to be spelt out in the final copy.

  Note Numerical forms are *not* abbreviations; therefore they are never followed by a stop.

Oblique headings

These are used as an alternative to vertical headings; they are easier to read but more difficult to type, and the typist should be practised in vertical headings before attempting them.

All headings must slant to the right at the same angle, and must all begin at the same distance from the horizontal line below. Since the paper must be inserted diagonally, A4 can be used without folding only if the typewriter will take paper up to $14\frac{1}{2}$ in (37 cm) wide. (When the copy is intended for a camera or a copier, it may be faster to paste in oblique headings.)

According to whether the columns are of equal or unequal width, different methods will be used.

Typing method for columns of equal width

These headings take negligibly less space in depth than vertical ones, so the same method of calculation can be used (see p 191). Follow steps *a-e* only, of those suggested for vertical headings on p 191 (but when calculating the horizontal placement of the table, allow for a last heading overhang of one ruled column width). Then proceed as follows.

f Remove paper from the typewriter and rule the *body* of the table.

g Pencil rule the top horizontal line, extending it to the right of the last vertical line by one ruled column width.

h By placing a ruler along each vertical line in turn, in the body of the table, guidemark in pencil the points where each would meet the top horizontal line (shown on the example on p 125 by vertical broken lines).

i Rule the first oblique line to the guidemark where the *next* vertical line would meet the top horizontal line.

j Rule the other oblique lines in the same manner.

k Lightly rule a pencil guideline where the oblique headings will all begin (one line-space above the columns, as shown on the example by a broken horizontal line). On that line mark the positions where the first line of each oblique heading begins: each heading should begin at the same distance to the right of the oblique line as the first digit in the column below is to the right of the vertical line.

l Re-insert the paper diagonally into the typewriter, and adjust it so that the oblique lines line up with the paper-bail bar. Using your guidemarks, type the oblique headings as shown, all parallel to the oblique lines.

m When the ink ruling is complete, re-insert the paper the right way up, and type the heading (Town and District) at the left-margin position: centre it vertically in its space, *or* align it with the top *or* with the bottom of the oblique headings.

Hotel Rooms and Accommodation still available in July

Town and District	A Hotels	B Hotels	C Hotels	Houses	Bungalows	Flats	Chalets
Avignon	25	60	95	25	20	21	15
Nice	150	200	125	130	96	90	86
Toulouse	40	85	130	85	60	87	101
Marseilles	95	155	180	70	105	80	35
Nimes	80	120	90	65	55	45	36
Montpellier	35	80	95	62	45	65	29
Toulon	36	90	120	75	45	100	70

Oblique column headings (columns of equal width)

This method is suitable only if the columns are of equal width, since otherwise the oblique lines would run at different angles and the headings could not be slanted in parallel. It is, however, the *simplest method*. Therefore if the columns vary in width by only one or two characters, it is best to *make* them equal (ie calculate for and rule equal columns, geared to the widest one).

Centred style of layout
- The main heading and subsidiary heading are centred horizontally over the table
- The heading (Town and District) is centred over the column matter below; it is invariably centred vertically in its 'box'.
- Each oblique heading is centred to its column, eg a 1-line heading over a 3-digit-wide column is typed over the middle digit.

Typing method for columns of unequal width

Proceed as for columns of equal width above but for steps *h* to *j* substitute the following (before continuing with *k*).

h Ink rule the first oblique line at an angle of *roughly 70°* to the lower horizontal line. Too sharp an angle gives too wide an overhang; anything closer to the vertical scarcely justifies the use of oblique headings for easier reading. 'Get the feel' of the required angle.

i Place a ruler along the horizontal line at the *top of the body of the table*, and measure carefully the spaces between the vertical lines below. Work from left to right, starting with the first column after the descriptive column. Make a note of these measurements. Then move the ruler up to the top horizontal line (which you have already pencilled in) and mark along it the spaces between the vertical columns (as noted), starting at the top of the first oblique line (which is already ruled in).

j Rule the remaining oblique lines, in each case from the top of the vertical column to the corresponding mark on the top horizontal line. The oblique lines will then be parallel.

PARTICULARS OF SELECTED ELEMENTS

Element	Symbol	No of isotopes	Atomic weight	Atomic number	Specific gravity	Country of discovery	Date of discovery
Barium	Ba	10	137.36	56	3.5	England	1808
Chromium	Cr	5	52.01	24	7.1	France	1797
Magnesium	Mg	5	24.32	12	1.74	Scotland	1755
Nickel	Ni	7	58.69	28	8.90	Sweden	1754
Platinum	Pt	6	195.23	78	21.45	Italy	1557
Radium	Ra	4	226.05	88	5.0	France	1898
Uranium	U	4	238.07	92	18.7	Germany	1789

Oblique column headings (columns of unequal width)

Useful tip This needs just a steady hand and a good eye! After ruling the first oblique line as in *h*, slide the ruler down to the starting position of the next oblique line, and then of each further oblique line in turn, taking care to keep the lines parallel.

See also Vertical headings pp 190–3.

Open, full and optional punctuation

Open punctuation

Punctuation marks are omitted in or after:
- date
- reference
- name and address
- salutation
- dates, names and abbreviations in the text
- complimentary close
- name of the firm
- signatory's name and designation (but a comma or extra space will be required between separate items on the same line)
- enclosure notation

- times (but stops are included in 12-hour-clock times, eg 6.30 pm)
- letters and numbers in enumeration (but stops are included in the '1.2.1' method)

Full punctuation

Punctuation marks are included in and after:
- name and address
- salutation
- names and abbreviations in the text; but note the following:
  - a Names of firms, states, organisations, services, or individuals are acceptable with or without stops, eg ICI, USA, MCC, PAYE, MC (for Master of Ceremonies). Acronyms (abbreviations pronounced as a word not letter by letter) are always typed without full stops, eg UNESCO
  - b Metric items are always typed without stops, eg 10 mm, 24 cm, 3 kg, 15 kw
- between the surname and 'Esq' if used
- complimentary close
- abbreviations in the name of the firm
- enclosure notation
- times (but 24-hour-clock times are always typed without stops)
- letters and numbers in enumeration

Optional punctuation

You may choose whether or not to punctuate (consistently) in the following cases:
- dates
- after Ms
- after the name of the firm under the complimentary close (comma)
- after signatory's name when it stands alone (full stop)
- after signatory's name when it is followed by a designation (comma)
- after designation (full stop)
- after last word before the postcode (comma or full stop; but always use a full stop after an abbreviated county name).

Organisation charts

These are a valuable tool of management, showing the organisational structure, the chain of responsibility and the lines of communication. They are also useful to training departments in explaining these aspects to employees. Large organisations would have a main chart of the overall structure in broad outline, with sectional charts (for divisions or departments) showing functions and personnel in the detail required.

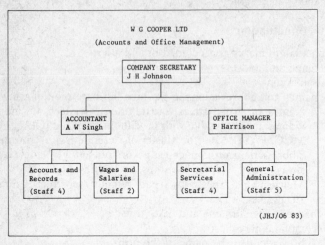

Vertically read chart: mixed centred and blocked style

Line of reading

Vertical Reflecting the hierarchical structure of most businesses, the organisation chart is often depicted as a 'pyramid', with the lines of command running down from the head of the organisation at the top. Space permitting, the different branches should be arranged so that posts of equal importance stand on the same horizontal level.

Horizontal Charts can also be presented so that the lines of command run from left to right. This style is easier to type and to rule because the matter appears in vertical columns; related groups can thus be clearly distinguished by line-spacing, without the use of boxes. Posts of equal importance will appear in the same vertical column. More material can be typed on the page with horizontally-read charts. (See example on p 130.)

Other features of organisation charts

- Items are linked by *unbroken* lines. Since the direction of reading is known, arrows are not necessary.
- *Broken* lines are used to show contacts outside the direct line of command, eg advisory or consultative services.
- The use of boxes is optional. All items, or selected items, may be enclosed, but some charts, especially horizontally-read ones, use no boxes.

- Periodic updating will be needed to reflect changes in the organisation's size and structure, or movement of staff. Therefore it is wise to include the date of issue with (or incorporated in) a reference.

Method

Analyse the draft to be sure that you understand the structure. Make preliminary calculations before starting to type.
Paper size will be governed by the shape and size of the chart, where a choice is allowed.
Line-spacing will depend on the number of items in the depth of the table, and sometimes on the shape and relationship of different branches. Where practicable, equal line-spacing between horizontal rows or vertical groups of items produces the most effective display. Once the line-spacing is decided, finalise your calculations for vertical centring of the chart on the paper.

Typing method

1 **Vertical charts** Work downwards when typing short simple charts. With a complex chart of four or more rows, you might find it easier (after inserting the headings) to *type the bottom row first* and work progressively upwards *level by level* (*not* line by line). This method could facilitate the suitable positioning of each item over its related items in the row below. Mark lightly in pencil, at the side of the paper, the point where the top line of each row will begin: do this as you return the carriage in working down the page to find the starting position of the bottom row of items. Make pencil marks to assist in centring single items over groups of items bracketed immediately under them.

2 **Horizontal charts** After the necessary calculations have been made and the headings inserted, type the extensive right-hand column first. Then type the other columns working to the left, with each item suitably positioned alongside its related items on the right; the overall shape will be that of a pyramid turned on its side.

3 **Pasting in** With complex charts intended for a camera or a copier, it may be faster to paste in certain parts.

4 **Ruling** This is best done last. Start by ruling the boxes, at an equal distance from the enclosed typescript on all four sides. Using a transparent ruler, pencil-rule first their top and bottom lines, extending them slightly beyond the points where they will meet the verticals: this makes neat corners. If two or more boxes are on the same level, draw their upper horizontal lines at the same ruling, and then their lower lines in the same way. Complete the ruling of the boxes in ink.

Mark with a pencil the centre-points of the box lines, where the connecting lines will meet them. Using these marks as a guide, pencil-rule horizontal connecting arms midway (or at any other suitable distance) between the levels of typescript. Complete the ruling in ink.

5 **Critical evaluation** of the completed chart is important, to confirm that it is clear and accurate.

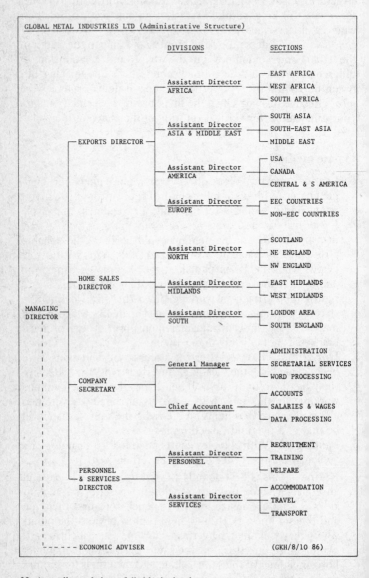

Horizontally read chart: fully blocked style

130 Organisation charts

Ornamentation

Tailpiece   This marks the end of a section or finished piece of work.

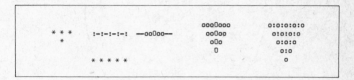

Tailpieces

Border   Notices, menus, programmes, etc, are sometimes 'framed' within a border. Sometimes just the four corners are ornamented: a simple method using asterisks is shown below. Equal space must be left between the border and the edge of the paper on all four sides.

When the pattern chosen is complex, care is needed on the corners. Suggested patterns follow, but there is wide scope for variation.

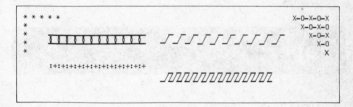

Borders

Designs and pictures   The typewriter may be used to produce many designs and pictures. For example, personal Christmas cards may be made using the typewriter and coloured with felt-tipped pens.

Pictorial outline   Sometimes wording is typed within an outline drawing, perhaps one traced from a book or magazine. If the work is intended for a camera or copier, it may be faster to paste in certain parts.

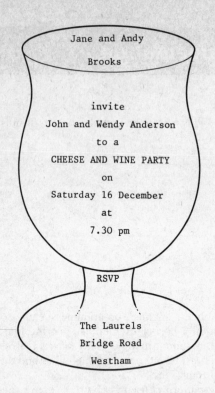

Inside the glass illustration:

Jane and Andy

Brooks

invite
John and Wendy Anderson
to a
CHEESE AND WINE PARTY
on
Saturday 16 December
at
7.30 pm

RSVP

The Laurels
Bridge Road
Westham

Pictorial outline

Paper

Quantities

Quire = 25 sheets (formerly 24)
Ream = 500 sheets (formerly 480)

Scales

To work out scales for *any* size of paper (and to spare your
memory) remember only this:

Elite pitch has 12 characters to the inch
Pica pitch has 10 characters to the inch
6 lines of type = one inch (elite *and* pica)

132 Paper

	Portrait					Landscape				
Spaces across paper	A4	⅔A4	A5	A6	A7	A4	⅔A4	A5	A6	A7
Elite	100	94	70	50	36	140	100	100	70	50
Pica	82	78	59	41	29	118	82	82	58	41
Lines down page	70	50	50	35	25	50	47	35	25	17

Sizes

The 'A' sizes of paper in general use (called IPS, for International-al Paper Sizes) are based on a rectangle that keeps the same proportions each time the size is halved. The original size is A0. A1 is half of A0; A2 half of A1, and so on. Thus the higher the figure, the smaller the paper; and the short side of any size equals the long side of the next size down. The diagram below makes this clear.

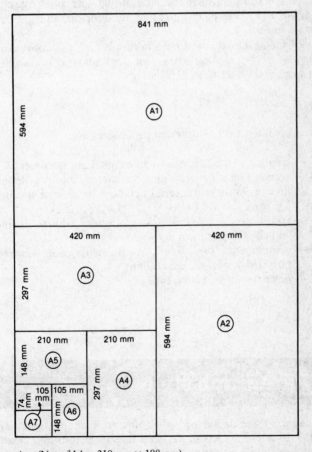

Paper sizes (Note: ⅔A4 = 210 mm × 198 mm)

Portrait means the shorter
side of the paper at the top

Portrait

Landscape means the longer
side at the top

Landscape

Types

A variety of types and tints is available. The most widely used
types are:

Airmail   Extra lightweight because of high airmail charges.
Bank (flimsy)   Low quality and thin; used for carbon copies and
sets of forms.
Bond   Good quality; used for letterheads and 'top-copy' work.
Duplicating   Semi-absorbent for ink duplicating; non-absorbent
for spirit and offset-litho duplicating.

Uses

Some common uses of different paper sizes are:

A3 — balance sheets, financial statements, legal documents
A4 — agenda, bills of quantities, estimates, invoices, letters,
memos, minutes, reports, quotations, specifications, literary work
A5 — credit notes, invoices (short), letters (short), memos
(short), statements of account
A6 — compliments slips, index cards, petty cash vouchers,
postcards, receipts, requisitions
A7 — business cards, labels, index cards

Paragraph styles

There are three paragraph styles: blocked, indented, and hanging. Use any one consistently in a document, but inset matter
may use a different style for differentiation.

Blocked

Indented (5 spaces or up to 1½")

Hanging (2 or 3 spaces)

Spacing between paragraphs With indented and hanging paragraphs the left-hand format shows the paragraph division. With blocked paragraphs, the sole indicator may be the space between the paragraphs. Hence the following conventions are used:

1 **Single spacing** One line of space between paragraphs in all three styles.
2 **1½, double, or treble spacing** With indented or hanging paragraphs, *no* additional space is needed between paragraphs. With blocked paragraphs, you may return the carriage twice between paragraphs; this is speedy but leaves an unnecessarily large gap. Alternatively, return the carriage once and use the half line-spacer to turn up an additional half or full line-space. Because of the space required to separate blocked paragraphs, many people avoid their use with 1½, double, or treble spacing.

Pie charts

These show at a glance the comparative size of the parts of any whole (slices of the pie). A wide range of statistical data can be presented in this way. Pie charts are frequently prepared for discussion at business meetings, often incorporated in typewritten reports. An expert typist is expected to cope with them.

Compasses are needed to draw the circle and a protractor to measure the angles. There are 360° round the centre point of a circle. Therefore a 25% ($\frac{1}{4}$) segment is formed by an angle of 90° ($\frac{1}{4}$ of 360), a 12½% ($\frac{1}{8}$) segment by 45°, and so on. It is simple to convert *any* percentage to the required angle, eg 5% requires an angle of 18°; found as follows:

$$\frac{5}{100} \times \frac{360}{1} = \frac{1800}{100} = 18\%$$

A description of the parts, perhaps stating percentages, can be shown within the segments (use pencil-guides to help position the typescript). To keep the pie chart itself simple and uncluttered, this may be amplified by a tabulation alongside (as in the example below).

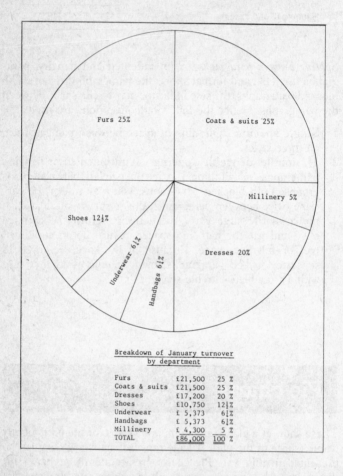

Breakdown of January turnover
by department

Furs	£21,500	25 %
Coats & suits	£21,500	25 %
Dresses	£17,200	20 %
Shoes	£10,750	12½%
Underwear	£ 5,373	6½%
Handbags	£ 5,373	6½%
Millinery	£ 4,300	5 %
TOTAL	£86,000	100 %

The different segments can be shown in different ways (accompanied by a key) with or without amplifying figures. Sometimes the segments are shaded with different colours — but this is effective only on a top copy. More often a combination of lines (horizontal, vertical and oblique), dots, white space, and shading is used.

Two or more pie charts (for home and export sales, different departments, different sales periods, etc) can be shown side by side for at-a-glance comparisons.

Data presented by pie charts can often be alternatively shown using bar charts, line graphs, or by tabulation alone.

Pitch

This term refers to the space occupied by each typewritten character. The two most common pitches are elite (12 point) and pica (10 point), shown below.

```
Elite type has 12 characters to the inch (2.5 cm).
Pica type has 10 characters to the inch (2.5 cm).
```

Typewriters used to be fitted with one *or* the other. Now, with electronic typewriters and word processors it is possible to change pitch at the touch of a key. For instance, on some machines the typist can rapidly alternate between 6, 10, 12 and 15 point. Daisy-wheel print elements, enclosed in cassettes, also enable the typeface style to be changed quickly.

With both elite and pica, 6 lines of type measure one inch. (See also Paper scales p 132.)

Plays

Plays for the stage

In general, the normal layout of printed plays is followed, with numbered Acts and Scenes, dialogue, and various directions. Publishers have different house styles for printing plays; in typing too there can be varied presentation. Unless instructed otherwise, the typist should conform to the style of the copy. The following are general guidelines only.

Paper and margins A4, typed on one side only. If pages are to be fastened at the side, leave a binding margin: the right-margin can be ½ inch.

Introductory pages Usually displaying the title, author's name, synopsis of Acts, and list of characters. There may also be a brief statement about the period, place and nature of the action. These pages are either numbered with small romans or not numbered at all.

Acts and Scenes When typing plays, there are two prime needs. First, to distinguish the dialogue of each character, which is done by typing the character's name in closed capitals in front of every speech, either as a side heading or as the start of a hanging paragraph. Second, to distinguish between spoken and unspoken matter (scene directions, stage directions, and speech directions), which is done by typing all unspoken matter with the red half of a bi-chrome ribbon (effective only on the top copy), or with underscore, or within brackets (or sometimes a combination).

- *Scene directions* appear at the start of the scene and run the full width of the dialogue line, using blocked or indented paragraphs.
- *Stage directions* between speeches can begin five spaces to the right of the start of the dialogue; or run the full width of the dialogue line. Blocked or indented paragraphs may be used. Stage directions sometimes occur at the beginning or in the middle of a speech, in which case they run on with the dialogue.
- *Speech directions* are often short (eg In quiet voice), and are typed in the dialogue, where they apply.

Pagination Pages are numbered at the top right. For ease of reference, Act and Scene number may be included, eg 1-2-10 for Act 1, Scene 2, page 10. Page numbering would then start afresh at 'one' in each Act.

Actor's part A theatrical company staging a printed play often supplies a copy to each speaking character for him to mark his own part and learn it in context. However, some producers prefer to use typed scripts (cost-effectively made on a word processor) so that their own interpretations and notes can be added, on interleaved blank sheets if necessary. In such cases the display and layout of the script may vary from producer to producer.

ACT TWO

(The room at the Tesmans', as in the First Act, except that the piano has been taken away and a graceful little writing-table with a book-case put in its place. A smaller table has been put by the sofa on the left; most of the bouquets are gone, but Mrs Elvsted's stands on the large table in the front of the stage. It is afternoon.

HEDDA, in an afternoon dress, is alone in the room. She is standing by the open glass door, loading a pistol. The fellow to it lies in an open pistol-case on the writing table.)

HEDDA   (looking down the garden and calling) How do you do again, Mr Brack?

BRACK   (is heard from below, at a little distance) And you, Mrs Tesman?

HEDDA   (lifting the pistol and aiming) I'm going to shoot you, sir!

BRACK   (calling from below) No, no, no! Don't stand there aiming straight at me.

HEDDA   That comes of using the back way in. (She shoots)

BRACK   (nearer) Are you quite crazy?

HEDDA   Dear me! I didn't hit you, did I?

BRACK   (still outside) Now stop this nonsense!

HEDDA   Well, come in then.

(BRACK, dressed as for an informal party, comes in by the glass door. He is carrying a light overcoat on his arm.)

Extract of a stage play: *Hedda Gabler* by Ibsen

A very short part might be typed as an *individual actor's part* (a cue script). This contains all the lines spoken by the actor concerned, with Act and Scene headings. The closing lines of the previous speaker are given as a cue (cues beginning at the middle of the page), typed or underlined in red to avoid confusion.

Plays for radio

Typed scripts are used by the speakers in radio plays, which may be specially written for the medium or adapted from a printed stage play. Since speech and sound effects alone must represent what might be visually conveyed on the stage, directions for voice inflection to convey mood, and the timing and quality of sound effects, become very important.

Radio plays are read in front of microphones — after exacting rehearsals. To avoid distraction during reading, there is no line-end division of words. The layout of radio plays can vary and, in the absence of specific instructions, the typist should follow copy. The points below provide a general guide only.

Paper and margins   A4, typed on one side only. Soft paper minimises rustling as the pages are turned over. The pages are often numbered in the centre both at the top and the bottom, but some producers prefer the numbers top right where they are more easily seen as the pages are turned over. The pages are attached at the top left corner with a pin binder (not a clip) or 'treasury tag'.

The left-margin is usually one inch, and the right-margin the same — to allow room for the studio manager's additions. Full pages of type reduce the turning over of pages, therefore single spacing is often used throughout, although double may be preferred for easier reading — particularly for long speeches. Likewise for ease of reading, pica pitch is preferred.

Page turnover is made at the end of a speech, sometimes resulting in a large bottom margin. Where a long speech must be divided, this is done at the end of a sentence and the remainder of the line filled in with spaced full stops. Below this, 'Continued' is typed at the bottom right-margin.

Dialogue and directions   The same two essentials as for stage plays apply: to distinguish the spoken lines of different characters, and to distinguish dialogue from directions.

- *Dialogue*   The character's name is typed in closed capitals in front of every speech, as a side heading. Speeches are numbered at the left-margin, in front of the character's name. Numbering often starts at 'one' on every page, but some producers prefer numbers to run consecutively throughout.
- *Sound effect directions* are typed in closed capitals within brackets. Between speeches, they can begin five spaces to the right of the start of the dialogue, or run the full width of the

dialogue line; blocked or hanging paragraphs may be used. Sound effects in mid-speech are typed within the speech.

- *Speech directions* are typed in underscored lower case, and enclosed within brackets. Place them within the speech.

1.

1. ANNOUNCER: In Paris - the Paris of 1884 - it has been a day of misty sunshine. The very pavements seem to give forth a pale and pearly radiance. The famous Parisian motor-horn has yet to sound its contemptuous farewell to the old era, its impudent welcome to the new. That day is coming very soon. The Paris of our story is removed merely by a decade and a half from the follies and conceits of the Second Empire. Leisure and grace still pervade the streets; and are to be observed in the elegant carriage of the lady in blue velvet, whose enormous hat hides her face, but cannot obscure completely the golden-red curls. One would say at once a lady of fashion - but that the blue of her dress is faded, and that the dress itself is in the mode of yesterday.

   (BRING UP STREET NOISES)

2. COCHER: Where to, Madame?

   (HORSE WHINNIES)

3. CORA: To the publishing house of Monsieur Levy.

4. COCHER: Surely. Gee-up there.

   (CLATTER OF HOOVES ON COBBLE STONES)

   (FADE THEN HOOVES UP AGAIN)

5. COCHER: Whoa! Whoa . . . there!

   (HOOVES STOP. IN THE BACKGROUND VOICES ARE RAISED IN STREET ARGUMENT)

6. COCHER: We have arrived, Madame. This is the house of Monsieur Levy, the publisher.

7. CORA: Thank you, driver. Please wait for me.

8. COCHER: Certainly, Madame.

   (THE VOICES STOP ABRUPTLY, THEIR OWNERS TOO INTERESTED IN WATCHING CORA ALIGHT)

9. MAN: Forgive me, Madame. You've dropped something - a piece of paper.

10. CORA: Thank you. (nervously) How careless of me.

    (DOOR SLAMS SMARTLY. THE BABBLE OF VOICES BREAKS OUT AGAIN)

11. WOMAN 1: Who was it, Pierre?

12. WOMAN 2: A hoity-toity piece, that's plain.

1.

Extract from a radio play script

Plays for TV

A full TV script is complex, with dialogue, verbal and general directions, sound effect directions, and camera directions. All must be clearly differentiated. TV scripts are therefore typed in two columns: a wide right column for dialogue, general directions, and sound effects; and a narrower column on the left for camera directions, suitably lined up.

140 Plays

Actors require only the material in the right column; but once all the camera decisions are made, the producer will want these inserted on his copy. The script is divided into 'frames', each numbered at the start of the right column. Then follow, on the same line, brief details that set the scene. The frame number and details are underscored the full width of the right column (or right across the page from margin to margin). Technical abbreviations are used, eg INT (interior), EXT (exterior), LS (long shot), BP (back projection), CU (close up), zo/zi (zoom out/ zoom in). As with stage and radio plays, the layout and style of TV scripts can vary. The typist should follow the style of the copy.

---

31. INT.   OLD PEOPLE'S CLUB   DAY

(THE SCENE IS A LARGE ROOM WITH SEVERAL TABLES
PILED HIGH WITH ARTICLES, CARDBOARD BOXES,
PAINTINGS, ETC. OLD AGE PENSIONERS ARE WORKING
AT THEM.

THE PRINCIPAL, MRS. WEATHERBY, A HANDSOME WOMAN
OF FORTY-FIVE, IS CONDUCTING THE NEWCOMERS
ROUND. SHE PUSHES MRS. HALLIDAY BESIDE A
SHARP-FEATURED SMALL WOMAN.)

MRS. WEATHERBY: This lady is making cardboard boxes.
Mrs. Williamson, show Mrs. Halliday how you do them.

MRS. HALLIDAY: We've met.

(PAN WITH MRS. WEATHERBY AS SHE GOES OVER TO
GRAN AND TAKES HER ARM, LOOKING FOR A SUITABLE
INTRODUCTION.

SHE REACHES A ROBUST LATE-SIXTIES HANDSOME MAN
NAMED MARSHALL, SMARTLY DRESSED, SMOKING A
CIGAR, ENGAGED IN A LOVE/HATE RELATIONSHIP WITH
A BASKET OF RAFIA WORK.)

GRAN: Please! Do carry on.   (POINTS TO BASKET)

MARSHALL: I was afraid you'd say that.

GRAN: Of course, if you have a car, and plenty of
spare time, you could be doing more important things.

MIX TELECINE

L.S. of an open old
Rolls speeding
through the country-
side, with four
people in it:
MARSHALL, GRAN,
MRS. HALLIDAY and
O'MALLEY.

END TELECINE

32. EXT.   DAY   B.P.

(MARSHALL IS ON HIS FAVOURITE THEME, BUT NO-ONE
IS LISTENING. THEY ARE ALL ENJOYING THE COUNTRY-
SIDE.)

MARSHALL: We're cluttering up the earth. Ought to
be done away with, everybody over sixty.

(Sound dubbed: car skidding)

(MARSHALL'S EYES NEARLY POP OUT OF HIS HEAD AS HE
SWERVES LEFT AND RIGHT.)

The idiot! He nearly killed me!

Extract from a TV play script

Poetry

There are no hard and fast rules for setting out poems. In the absence of instructions the typist should follow copy. The following points are intended as a general guide only.

Margins If a short poem is to occupy a page, it should be centred on it. Horizontal centring should be geared to the longest line. Any very long lines are 'hooked-in' for balance; ie some words (typed after a left-hand bracket) are carried to the following or preceding line, to line up on the right. Also for the sake of balance, very short lines can start further to the right or be centred to the width of the poem or the verse.

With a long poem, use a dropped head on the first page and leave at least six lines of space at the foot of all sheets.

Quotation When a poem or part of a poem is quoted, quotation marks are used only at the beginning and end. Quoted poetry is blocked at the left-margin, *or* indented, *or* centred to the typing line.

Line-spacing Use single spacing, with a consistent one or two lines between verses.

Punctuation Follow copy for commas, colons, full stops, etc. In most poetry every line begins with a capital letter, but this is not always so, particularly in modern poetry.

Chorus This sometimes begins or is blocked further to the right than the rest of the verse. It is often underscored in type (it would be italicised in print).

Indentation can be used to relate rhyming lines. Thus when alternate lines rhyme, the second, fourth, sixth lines, etc, may be indented a consistent two or three spaces from the point where the others begin. This is illustrated by the example below, which is the first verse of 'The Soldier' by Rupert Brooke. (With many poems, however, *all* lines start at the same point, regardless of rhyming.)

```
If I should die, think only this of me:
   That there's some corner of a foreign field
That is for ever England.  There shall be
   In that rich earth a richer dust concealed;
A dust whom England bore, shaped, made aware,
   Gave, once, her flowers to love, her ways to roam,
A body of England's, breathing English air,
   Washed by the rivers, blest by the suns of home.
```

Poem with indentation

Note the relationship between indentation and rhyming in the poem which follows.

```
                   THE OWL

     When cats run home and light is come,
       And dew is cold upon the ground,
     And the far-off stream is dumb,
       And the whirring sail goes round,
       And the whirring sail goes round;
         Alone and warming his five wits,
         The white owl in the belfry sits.
```

Poem with rhyming indentation

No indentation   Where there is no rhyming (as in blank verse) or where successive lines rhyme (as in the poem below) no indentation is used. Note that the poet's name lines up with the longest line.

```
                  SILVER

   Slowly, silently, now the moon
   Walks the night in her silver shoon;
   This way, and that, she peers, and sees
   Silver fruit upon silver trees;
   One by one the casements catch
   Her beams beneath the silvery thatch;
   Couched in his kennel, like a log,
   With paws of silver sleeps the dog;
   From their shadowy cote the white breasts peep
   Of doves in a silver-feathered sleep;
   A harvest mouse goes scampering by,
   With silver claws, and silver eye,
   And moveless fish in the water gleam,
   By silver reeds in a silver stream.

                            Walter de la Mare
```

Poem without indentation

Position at machine

A good sitting position is important for lengthy spells at the typewriter, to prevent aches and tiredness. Use a purpose-designed upholstered chair with a back support; adjust the seat height and your distance from the desk for relaxed comfort, neither stretching nor crouching. The feet should be flat on the floor for balance. Position the typewriter flush with the front edge of the desk. Place the copy so that it is sloping gently towards you, to avoid eye strain. When audio-typing, keep your eyes on the typescript, checking accuracy as you work.

Programmes

Programmes are used for many different purposes — concerts, conferences, lectures, exhibitions, induction courses, etc — in a variety of forms and styles. They may be typed on unfolded paper (as the examples that follow), or the paper may be variously folded to form four- or six-page leaflets (see Leaflets pp 79–81).

The display of a programme is particularly important because of the large circulation. Some are ornamented and/or given a typed border. Note the many display features illustrated in the following specimen programmes; Display (pp 42–6) elaborates on these.

```
BOLTON'S LTD SPORTS CLUB

Programme of Events for 19--


8 February . . . . . . . . Dinner and Dance

6 April  . . . . . . Annual General Meeting

2 June . . . . . . . . . Sports Day: Finals

3 September  . . . . . . . Barbecue Evening

9 December . . . Children's Christmas Party
```

Simple programme with right-margin aligned

NORTH SEA PETROLEUM COMPANY

Induction Course for Management Trainees
(18-22 June 19--)

Day	0930 - 1100	1130 - 1300	1430 - 1615
Mon	TOUR OF HEAD OFFICE DEPARTMENTS AS SHOWN		
	Personnel and Information	Exploration and Production	Finance and Administration
Tues	Talk and Discussion CAREERS IN OIL (Personnel Director)	Film and Talk DATA PROCESSING (Company Secretary)	Talk and Discussion COMPETITION (Marketing Director)
Wed	ALL-DAY VISIT TO RAVENSCROFT REFINERY		
Thurs	Talk and Discussion THE FUTURE OF ENERGY (Chief Scientist)	Film and Discussion NORTH SEA GAS PRODUCTION (Production Manager)	Talk and Discussion PLANNING AND BUDGETING (Finance Director)
Fri	Talk and Discussion OIL AND POLITICS (General Manager)	Talk and Discussion PERSONNEL MANAGEMENT (Personnel Manager)	Questions, Answers and Discussion PLENARY SESSION

Business programme: blocked style with no embellishment

```
THE   WESTERN   PLAYERS

present

A VARIETY CONCERT

including

The Gardener

(a comedy in 3 Acts)

by

Felicity Macdonald

PROGRAMME

Entrée ............................... The Company

The Strolling Minstrels ............. Janet Rolls
                                      Sylvia Waters
                                      Robin Whistler

The Gardener .................. Producer: Anne Day

Cast in order of appearance

Flora Forsythe    Rose Phillips
John Williams     Jack Barker
Bob Forsythe      Ralph Robinson
Daphne Brooke     Sylvia Waters
The Gardener      Robin Whistler

Act 1 - The Forsythes' Sitting-room

Act 2 - The Summer House

Act 3 - The Forsythes' Sitting-room

* * * * *

The Strolling Minstrels ................ As above

Finale ............................... The Company

A COLLECTION WILL BE TAKEN FOR

CANCER RELIEF
```

Concert programme with border (Note display features)

```
SPRING GALA CONCERT                              Saturday 16 April 19--


                    The Winter Gardens, Eastchurch

                    THE SOUTHBOURNE ORCHESTRA


                    ┌─────────────────────────────┐
                    │  Conductor Henry Woodford    │
                    └─────────────────────────────┘

                        P R O G R A M M E


Overture            THE MARRIAGE OF FIGARO                   Mozart

Selection               NUTCRACKER SUITE                 Tchaikovsky

Suite                        CARMEN                            Bizet

Selection       TALES FROM THE VIENNA WOODS                  Strauss

                    ─────────────────────────
                        I N T E R V A L
                    ─────────────────────────

Overture                    EGMONT                         Beethoven

Suite                      PEER GYNT                           Grieg

Prelude             AFTERNOON OF A FAUN                      Debussy

Minuet                     BERENICE                           Handel

Finale                   MARCHE SLAVE                    Tchaikovsky
```

Principal players include

Violins: Hans Richter (leader)   Flute: Brian Payne

         Dennis Atwal   Oboe: Gillian Wood
         Alan Brooks
         Stephen James   Clarinet: Wilfred Owens
         Mary Tanner
                                    Bassoon: Alastair Harrison
Viola: Robert Ackroyd
                                    Horn: Jean Rooker
Cello: James Hunter   Roger Skinner

Bass: Ronald Dicks   Percussion: Geoffrey Wright

                                    Harp: Miriam Martin

                        ┌──────────────┐
                        │   Tickets   │
                        ├──────────────┤
                        │   £6.50   │
                        │   £5.50   │
                        │   £4.50   │
                        └──────────────┘

Concert programme (Note display features)

Proof-reading

The onus is on the typist to ensure that any work is mailable or 'ready for use'. Check each completed page word for word against copy *before* removal from typewriter: corrections can be done faster and better at this stage. To proof-read for meaning, yet with any eye for the smallest details, requires great concentration. While checking, lightly pencil a mark in the margin against each error. Provided no major error necessitates re-typing, make the corrections. (Put a pencil X in the margin against any points needing the originator's attention, eg uncertain accents, mathematical symbols, etc.)

With important documents, make a double-reading check of the completed work, with a colleague reading the draft as you check the typescript. (For correcting errors after the work has been removed from the typewriter, see p 36.)

Errors to look out for

- Errors in spelling, punctuation and grammar
- Confusion of words: principal/principle, advice/advise, etc
- Common substitutions of letters and words (r for t, m for n; our for your, these for there; etc)
- Typographical errors of all kinds: some points easily missed are faulty spacing and transposed letters
- Incorrect and inconsistent use of capital letters
- Inconsistencies of all kinds
- Misinterpretation of drafting abbreviations (reading *for meaning* will show these up)
- Names, addresses and figures need special attention
- Words transposed or omitted, or complete lines or sentences omitted

See also Correcting errors pp 35–6 and Correction signs pp 37–8

Punctuation

The modern trend towards short, direct sentences simplifies punctuation. Those who do use complex sentence construction often dictate the main punctuation or make it clear in the manuscript, and there is room for much personal preference in the use of commas, semi-colons, colons, dashes, etc. Being part of command of language, punctuation is not susceptible to simple rules. The following suggestions are for guidance only.

1 **Full stop** (or its equivalent: a question mark or an exclamation mark) ends every sentence.
2 **Question mark** follows a direct (but not an indirect) question.

```
When is the account due?   (direct question)
He asked when the account was due.   (indirect question)
```

3 **Exclamation mark** is used after statements worthy of being exclaimed about. In business writing it is obviously restricted in use.

```
Do you really mean that?   You stagger me!
```

4 **Comma** has many uses
   • To separate items in a list (the final comma before 'and' is optional, so long as the sense permits)

```
Please bring paper, pen, ruler, and pencil.
```

   • Optionally used either side of, or after, such words as however, moreover, nevertheless
   • To enclose a parenthesis as an alternative to brackets or dashes (see p 71)
   • To mark a short pause, or a break in a sentence

```
He asked me to type the letter, and then keep it by me.
```

5 **Semi-colon** marks longer pause than the comma. Note that with two breaks in a sentence, the stronger punctuation marks the longer pause.

```
He asked me to type the letter, checking all the
figures with the file; and then keep it by me.
```

6   **Colon** marks a still longer pause.

```
He asked me to type the letter, checking all
the figures with the file; and then keep it
by me: I could lock it in his cabinet.
```

The foregoing sentences illustrate the build-up of ideas and punctuation. Possible alternatives in the last sentence might be a comma after file and a semi-colon after me; or a full stop and a new sentence after me.

The colon's other uses include the following.

- To introduce direct speech (as an alternative to the comma)

```
After swimming the Channel, Mary said: "This
is my happiest day".
```

- To introduce a list of items (as an alternative to the dash)

```
We stock the following colours: black, white, and tan.
We stock the following colours - black, white, and tan.
```

- To join two related or contrasting thoughts

```
It was a fine day: the best of the whole holiday.
Lessor grants lease: lessee is granted lease.
```

- To introduce (with or without a following hyphen) high-lighted or inset matter that starts on the following line

See also: Apostrophe p 15, Brackets pp18–19, Hyphen and dash pp 70–1, Quotation marks pp 150–1. Punctuation (spacing after): see p 159.

Quotation marks

1   Single *or* double (consistently in one document) are used at both ends of a quotation *or* of direct speech *or* of the title of a book, etc.
2   The alternative form is used for a quotation *within* a quotation or *within* direct speech.

3   Single *or* double quotes may be used to show that a word or phrase is being used in a special way.
4   *Placing of punctuation in relation to quotation marks*   If the punctuation mark belongs to the quotation or to direct speech (as at the end of the example below), it comes *before* the closing quotation mark(s); if it belongs to the sentence construction (as in the opening words of the example), it comes *after* the quotation mark(s).
5   When a quotation consists of more than one paragraph, quotation marks are placed at the beginning of *each* paragraph, but at the end only of the *last* paragraph.

The above points are illustrated in the example below.

```
"Our need", said the staff manager, "is for still greater
productivity.  I should like to quote the following points
from the Chairman's address to the staff last year:

    'Let us be punctual in arrival at work, and then
    lose no time in getting down to it.

    'Let us likewise down tools on time, but work
    right up to "knocking-off" time.

    'While we are at work, let us give our undivided
    attention to it.  When we leave work, we can then
    forget it, and enjoy our outside interests.'

"As your manager, what better advice can I offer than that?"
```

Note   Long quotations in either prose or verse *may* be inset without quotation marks.

Rearrangement of material

If radical changes are required to typescript, for example reversal of column headings and side items in a table, it is safer to redraft before typing.

See Alphabetical indexing pp 13–14 for a reliable method of rearranging a list in alphabetical order, price order, date order, etc.

Reference sources

Familiarise yourself with the scope and layout of your public library's Reference Section, to ensure that you can speedily locate any required information. Some important reference books are listed below, but there are many more.

Information	Source of reference
English language	
Definitions, spelling, pronunciation, abbreviations	Any good English dictionary
Abbreviations and initials	Everyman's Dictionary of Abbreviations
Synonyms and antonyms	Roget's Thesaurus of English Words and Phrases
Grammar, punctuation, and English style	Fowler's Modern English Usage
Finance, industry and trade	
Information on firms, their scope, structure, and personnel	Stock Exchange Official Year Book
Biographical details of directors of companies	Directory of Directors
Information on banks, insurance companies, building societies, etc	Bankers' Almanac and Year Book Insurance Blue Book and Guide Building Societies' Year Book, etc
Information on trades and professions	Trade and professional journals and directories published for each
List of manufacturers, merchants, and exporters	Kelly's Directory of Merchants, Manufacturers and Shippers (separate volumes for UK and other countries)
Trade lists for London postal area, and street directory	Kelly's London Directory
Products and their manufacturers	UK Kompass (vol 1, products and manufacturers: vol 2, information on firms listed)
Manufacturers, merchant shippers, business and professional firms (British and foreign)	Stubbs' Directory
Trade and professional associations, chambers of commerce, and trade unions	Directory of British Associations and Associations in Ireland
General	
Wide miscellany of information	Encyclopaedia Britannica Whitaker's Almanack
Periodicals and trade magazines	Ulrich's International Periodicals Directory
List of publications on trades, professions, etc	Willings Press Guide
List of newspapers and periodicals published in Great Britain (and some foreign publications); with advertising rates and circulation figures	Newspaper Press Directory

Information	Source of reference
Current affairs	The Annual Register (in 4 main sections — Great Britain, Commonwealth, Foreign, General (covering Art, Law, Finance and Trade)
Technical terms	Specialized dictionaries, eg Short Dictionary of Architecture, Authors' and Printers' Dictionary, Black's Medical Dictionary, Chambers' Technical Dictionary

Government

Verbatim record of parliamentary proceedings (Commons and Lords)	Hansard (issued daily) HMSO
Governments and international organisations	Statesman's Year Book
Members of Parliament	*The Times* Guide to the House of Commons
Local government, and population statistics	Municipal Year Book
Government statistics on health, population, production, trade, etc	Monthly Digest of Statistics (HMSO) Annual Abstract of Statistics (HMSO)
Government reports	Available from HMSO

Law

Barristers and judges	Bar List
Solicitors, courts, legal officers	Solicitors' Diary, Almanac and Legal Directory
Legal terms and definitions	Osborn's Concise Law Dictionary

People

Eminent people	Who's Who (specialist versions include art, literature, medicine, science, theatre and various foreign countries)
People of international eminence	International Who's Who
Peers and their families, and other eminent persons (biographical details)	Debrett's Peerage and Titles of Courtesy Kelly's Handbook to the Titled, Landed, and Official Classes
Forms of address, decorations, honours and qualifications	Black's Titles and Forms of Address
Church of England clergymen	Crockford's Clerical Directory The Church of England Year Book (similar publications for other denominations)

Information	Source of reference
Armed Services	Navy List
	Army List
	Air Force List
Registered medical practitioners	Medical Register
	Medical Directory (annual)
Nurses	Register of Nurses
Dentists	Dentists' Register

Post Office Services

Services provided by Post Office, eg savings, national Girobank, licences	Post Office Guide (published annually and kept up to date by supplements)
Addresses, telephone numbers of local tradesmen, manufacturers and services under alphabetical heading of trades and professions	Yellow Pages
London post offices with postal districts of roads	London Post Offices and Streets
Telex subscribers (with answer-back codes)	Telex Directory

Travel

Air services	ABC World Airways Guide
Air and rail services Europe	ABC Air/Rail Europe
Nationwide train timetables	British Rail Passenger Timetable
Rail services from London	ABC Rail Guide
Rail services of Europe, North Africa and the Near East	Cooks Continental Timetable
Coach travel	National Express Guide to Express Services
Shipping services and European car ferries	ABC Shipping Guide
	Lloyd's Shipping List and Shipping Gazette
Motoring information (maps, hotels, garages, distances)	AA Members Handbook
	RAC Guide and Handbook
	AA and RAC European guides
Hotels and restaurants	ABC Hotel Guide
	Hotels and Restaurants in Britain
	Good Food Guide
	Financial Times World Hotel Directory
London	London A–Z
Worldwide locations	Any good atlas
Information on countries and places	Any good gazetteer
Advice on foreign travel, entry, regulations, consular facilities, hotels and customs	Hints to Businessmen (series of booklets for different countries issued by Department of Trade)

154 Reference sources

Miscellaneous current information

Banking, foreign currency, rates of exchange	Any bank
Books, newspapers, magazines, etc	Reading and Reference sections of library
Court procedure and information	Local Justices' Clerk
Income tax	Local Inland Revenue office
Translations, interpreters	Local Chamber of Commerce
	Language department in local college
	Appropriate embassy or consulate
Local government information	Local Town Hall
Motor taxation, etc	Local Motor Taxation office

Roman numerals

- Seven symbols are used, divided into units and fives.

Units		*Fives*	
I	(1)	V	(5)
X	(10)	L	(50)
C	(100)	D	(500)
M	(1000)		

Note   Use a capital letter 'I' for the large roman 'one': for the arabic 'one' the top row figure must be used.
- Each unit symbol can be repeated once or twice, to indicate twice or three times its value.

I (1)	X (10)	C (100)	M (1000)
II (2)	XX (20)	CC (200)	MM (2000)
III (3)	XXX (30)	CCC (300)	MMM (3000)

- Units used after a symbol of higher value show addition.

VII (7)	LXX (70)	DCCC (800)
XII (12)	CIII (103)	MXXX (1030)

- Each unit symbol may be placed before its immediately following 'five' or 'ten' symbol to indicate subtraction.

IV (4)	XL (40)	CD (400)
IX (9)	XC (90)	CM (900)

- A horizontal stroke over a roman numeral multiplies it by 1000.

$$\overline{\text{VII}} = 7000 \qquad \overline{\text{IX}} = 9000 \qquad \overline{\text{M}} = 1\,000\,000$$

- In enumeration, roman numerals are lined up to the right *or* the left.

i	i		I	I
ii	ii		II	II
iii	or iii		III	or III
iv	iv		IV	IV
v	v		V	V

Changing arabic numbers to roman numerals

Take each digit in turn, as in the example below. In each case take the unit or five symbol immediately below, and add to it the remaining symbols. (The only six exceptions to this are given in the paragraph on p 155 on subtraction numbers.)

$$868 = 800 + 60 + 8$$

$$800 = 500 + 300 = \text{DCCC}$$
$$60 = 50 + 10 = \text{LX}$$
$$8 = 5 + 3 = \text{VIII}$$

Therefore 868 is represented as DCCCLXVIII.

Uses of roman numerals

Roman numerals are seldom used now except for some specific purposes.

1 To number sections, sub-sections, etc, in various documents (see also Enumeration pp 49–50).

> Counsel for the Defence quoted The Social Security Pensions Act 1975, Section III, Sub-section iv.

2 To designate monarchs.

> After the Union of the Crowns of England and Scotland in 1603, King James VI of Scotland became King James I of England.

3   To number school forms, examination stages, sports teams, etc.

> The Headmaster announced that German
> classes would be available to Forms V
> and VI, for examination at Stage I and
> Stage II.

4   To name a year (on monuments, etc, and at the end of TV programmes and films).

> MCMLXXXIV   (1984)

5   *Small romans* are often used to paginate prefaces and other preliminary pages of books, reports, etc.

Security classification of documents

In these times of rapid technological development, commercial and industrial espionage must be guarded against, and *all* sensitive material must be protected. The typist, who is in a position of trust, must understand the security procedure and her important role in it. Every organisation will have its own system. The following are some general points.

- Classified documents must clearly show their security category *on each page*, top and bottom. Use the red half of a bi-chrome ribbon or underline the classification with a red biro.
- Envelopes bear their security marking above the address. With top gradings, each envelope should be enclosed in an outer envelope *not* revealing the secret nature of the contents.
- When not in use, immediately lock away top security documents in a safe or in an approved secure container (desk drawers and office filing cabinets are *not* normally adequate).

- Drafts of classified documents (or audio tapes) must receive the same security treatment as typed documents.
- Protect vulnerable carbon paper and carbon typewriter ribbon from inquisitive eyes.
- When you are instructed to make copies of classified documents, always do this yourself.
- When you are asked to dispose of classified material, shred it or burn it yourself.
- If you are asked for classified information, politely refuse; at your discretion, report the incident to your superior.

Much may be learned from the following example of a firm's management instruction on security procedure.

HARRISON MANUFACTURING COMPANY LTD

Security Classification of Documents

1 The security classification of documents is a matter requiring intelligent application by all concerned in the initiation of paper containing either sensitive information concerning the Company's affairs, or information personal to an employee.

2 Revised gradings, approved for use throughout the Company, are as follows:-

2.1 STRICTLY PERSONAL — 'Company Secret' matters for the eyes of the addressee only, or matters of extreme sensitivity affecting personnel.

May NOT be opened by secretaries.

2.2 PERSONAL — Private matters addressed to an individual concerning his salary, terms of service and items of a like nature.

May NOT be opened by secretaries.

2.3 STRICTLY CONFIDENTIAL — Matters for which a high degree of confidentiality is required to protect the interests of the Company. The information is restricted to the addressees on the distribution list of the document and at their discretion to other employees strictly on a 'need to know' basis.

May, at the discretion of the addressee, be opened by secretaries.

2.4 CONFIDENTIAL — Staff and personal matters relating to terms of service, salary scales, etc, correspondence between offices on personnel and administrative matters, and similar documents requiring a degree of confidentiality, but where a higher classification is inappropriate.

May, at the discretion of the addressee, be opened by secretaries.

3 When correspondence bears no classification, discretion should still be exercised regarding disclosure of information outside the Company.

4 Documents classified STRICTLY PERSONAL may not be copied without the authority of the originator, and must be enclosed in good-quality envelopes. A further control can be provided by numbering each copy and requiring a receipt.

5 The responsibility for correct classification rests with the originator of the document. Over-classification can cause more problems than it avoids.

6 If further security is required for documents containing extremely sensitive material, they may be double-enveloped. Then only the name, designation and address of the recipient should appear on the outer envelope.

Page 1 of an office instruction on security classification

158 Security classification of documents

The inner envelope should bear the security classification, the name and designation of the addressee and, on the reverse, the letter reference and an indication of the office of origin. The top and bottom flaps of the inner envelope may be further secured with transparent adhesive tape. For transmission between two offices on the same site, the outer envelope may be an interdepartmental post cover.

7. In the case of STRICTLY PERSONAL and PERSONAL documents enclosed in a single cover, these should bear the security classification of the enclosure, the name, designation and address of the recipient, and on the reverse the letter reference and an indication of the office of origin.

8. STRICTLY PERSONAL and PERSONAL documents may NOT be opened by secretaries. If the addressee is away from the office for any reason, his secretary should contact the office of the originator of the correspondence and request instructions.

9. It follows from the foregoing that the normal top security grading for documents relating to Company matters is STRICTLY CONFIDENTIAL, and that the STRICTLY PERSONAL grading is for very limited use for highly sensitive documents.

10. Unless the originator and the recipient of a STRICTLY PERSONAL document deal with it themselves, a secretary will have to type the document, type a reply, and file the correspondence. It is at the discretion of the originator and addressee how each deals with this, bearing in mind the necessity for the complete confidentiality of a 'Company Secret' document.

11. In many cases, a STRICTLY PERSONAL or STRICTLY CONFIDENTIAL document need only bear a security classification up to a certain date. As the classification may only be downgraded with the authority of the originator, it is helpful if in such cases he includes this information on the document. This will keep to a minimum the prolonged safe custody of classified documents.

12. The following should be borne in mind:-

12.1 Arrangements for the filing and safe custody of STRICTLY PERSONAL and STRICTLY CONFIDENTIAL documents - originals, information copies, and file copies - must be made by originators and recipients.

12.2 STRICTLY PERSONAL documents are to be kept in a safe or an approved secure container. The normal pattern office filing cabinet and desk drawer are not 'secure containers'.

12.3 The files in which classified documents are placed must automatically be afforded the treatment required for the document with the highest classification enclosed in the file. This emphasises:

12.3.1 the need to avoid over-grading so that staff access to files is not unnecessarily restricted nor scarce secure container space wasted;

12.3.2 the need for originators and recipients of classified documents, in consultation, to derestrict security gradings as soon as they are no longer necessary.

JBD/SJ
April 19--

Page 2 of an office instruction on security classification

Spacing after punctuation marks

Six methods, distinguished as *a* to *f* below, are in current use. Whichever method is adopted, it should be used consistently.

Character spaces after:	a	b	c	d	e	f
Full stop, question/exclamation mark	1	2	2	2	3	3
Colon	1	1	2	2	2	2
Semi-colon	1	1	1	2	1	2
Comma	1	1	1	1	1	1

Specifications

A specification is a document in which building, engineering, electrical, and other contractors set out a detailed account of the work to be done and materials to be used on a project for which they tender. Alternatively, an architect may, on behalf of a client, submit a specification to the contractors for a price quotation.

The conventional form starts with a preamble stating the name and address of the work site, the nature of the job, and the date. Then follows a full description of the sequence of operations with materials to be used for each; these are often side headings within a wide left-margin. Some specifications have an endorsement (backsheet) like that used for legal documents (see pp 85–6). Contractors may also use standard specifications (see p 162) for recognised jobs which they will undertake on any site.

The typist should follow the layout, and copy accurately any unfamiliar technical language. Some examples with notes follow.

S P E C I F I C A T I O N of work to be carried out and materials to be used on offices at 128 Dalston Lane, London E8G 2NQ (in the provision of a second doorway to the front office) for and to the satisfaction of:

> R C Southgate FRIBA FRICS
> Architect & Surveyor
> 26 Essex Road
> London EC8 2AS

18 May 19--

NEW DOORWAY	Remove the cupboard and shelving at the end of the side passage (as shown on the attached drawing).
	Make door opening in the wall at the end of the passage to lead to the front office (as shown on the drawing) and provide and fix 7.5 cm x 7.5 cm deal rebated door frame extended to the full height. Provide and hang with 10 cm steel butts 2 deal doors to match existing doors. Put deal moulded architraves with plinth blocks to both sides and fix mortice lever lock with brass door furniture, all to match existing. Fill in space over the doors with 5 cm breeze rendered both sides in Portland Cement and sand and finished in Siraphite. Make good cornices, picture rails, and skirting as required.
CEILINGS, CORNICES AND FRIEZES	Cut out cracks and properly make good. Wash off and twice emulsion paint (Dulux).
WALLS	Cut out the defective plaster under windows and make good in Portland Cement and sand.
	Strip the dado to the passage and properly make good any defective plaster. Wash down, properly prepare, and twice paint walls.
WOODWORK	Wash down, properly prepare, and paint all wood and other work previously or usually painted, 2 coats Dulux. All new wood to be primed and painted an additional coat.

Specification with side headings and blocked paragraphs

S P E C I F I C A T I O N of work to be carried out and

materials to be used on offices at 128 Dalston Lane,

London E8G 2NQ (in the provision of a second doorway to

the front office) for and to the satisfaction of:

R C Southgate FRIBA FRICS
Architect & Surveyor
26 Essex Road
London EC8 2AS

18 May 19--

NEW DOORWAY

Remove the cupboard and shelving at the end of the side passage (as shown on the attached drawing).

Make door opening in the wall at end of the passage to lead to the front office (as shown on the drawing) and provide and fix 7.5 cm x 7.5 cm deal rebated door frame extended to the full height. Provide and hang with 10 cm steel butts 2 deal doors to match existing doors. Put deal moulded architraves with plinth blocks to both sides and fix mortice lever lock with brass door furniture, all to match existing. Fill in space over the doors with 5 cm breeze rendered both sides in Portland Cement and sand and finished in Siraphite. Make good cornices, picture rails, and skirting as required.

CEILINGS, CORNICES AND FRIEZES

Cut out cracks and properly make good. Wash off and twice emulsion paint (Dulux).

WALLS

Cut out the defective plaster under windows and make good in Portland Cement and sand.

Strip the dado to the passage and properly make good any defective plaster. Wash down, properly prepare, and twice paint walls.

WOODWORK

Wash down, properly prepare, and paint all wood and other work previously or usually painted, 2 coats Dulux. All new wood to be primed and painted an additional coat.

Semi-blocked specification with shoulder headings and blocked paragraphs: preamble and architect's name and address could also be at left-margin to make the style fully-blocked

```
                S P E C I F I C A T I O N

                for

                Replastering following damp proof course insertion


                The purpose of replastering following the insertion of a new damp
                proof course is to contain any hygroscopic salts introduced into the
                wall structure as a result of rising damp, and to prevent them
                migrating through to the surface of the new plaster.  An additional
                complication brought about by rising damp is that ground water
                invariably contains dissolved salts which will concentrate at the wall
                surfaces where evaporation takes place.

                The presence of these salts in the wall's surface means that even if
                the further rise of moisture is prevented there is still the strong
                possibility of decorations being spoiled.  This is because some of the
                salts present in concentrations on the wall's surface are hygroscopic,
                which means they have the ability to absorb moisture from the atmos-
                phere, so that the surface tends to become damp during wet weather or
                humid conditions.

                In this event it will become essential for certain replastering works
                to take place, which must be in strict accordance with the specifica-
                tion outlined below.

PREPARATION     Hack off all perished plaster up to an approximate height of 1.5 metres
                or cill height beneath windows.  Wire brush exposed brick surface and
                rake out the joints to remove all loose salt deposits.

RENDERING COAT  This coat should be composed of 3 parts sharp washed sand to 1 part
                Portland Cement.  A liquid salt retardant (eg Sika) additive should be
                incorporated with the mix in compliance with the manufacturer's
                instructions.

                Once this coat has been applied the surface should be keyed (scratched)
                and the following floating coat put on before the initial set begins.

FLOATING COAT   This coat should be composed of 3 parts sharp washed sand and 2 parts
                lime to 1 part Portland Cement, and should contain no additives.  It
                should be left 1.5 mm behind the level of the existing finished plaster.

SETTING COAT    This coat should be porous and must not be over-trowelled.  It can be
                composed of lime and Siraphite (1 to 1).

                                                            DPC DATA SHEET 4
                                                            May 19—
```

Standard specification: fully-blocked except for side headings and reference at foot

Speed and accuracy

Employers are concerned with *production speed*, but until the typist has practice on the production tasks and house style of a particular office, speed development on straightforward copy is a useful means of raising general speed. Fast keyboard dexterity frees the mind to concentrate on the problems of production tasks — and to deal with these more quickly too.

Some examining bodies offer an optional 'speed endorsement' to their typewriting certificates. For this the minimum standards are: intermediate 35 wpm over five minutes with not more than six errors; advanced 50 wpm over five minutes with not more than six errors (the speed in both cases is calculated on the amount typed up to the seventh error). Employers prefer typists to have a high speed qualification as evidence of training and ability.

Copy designed to improve your speed and accuracy should be 'standard' in difficulty so that your results on different passages can be meaningfully compared. Consistent syllabic intensity is one such measure; counting standard words (5 strokes) is another (see p 165).

Standard correspondence

Standard (or form) letters and cards with printed or duplicated *standard wording* are used to save repetitive typing. Blank spaces provide for the typed insertion of variable details. They will be reproduced and coded in the office correspondence handbook if their volume justifies this.

NATIONAL BUILDING SOCIETY

National House
85 Fleet Street
SOUTHAMPTON
SO3 4AK

Tel 0703 64281

```
Dear

ACCOUNT NUMBER

At the time of writing your          mortgage repayment
has not been received.  It is essential that payments
reach the Society by the due date.  If you have not al-
ready sent your monthly remittance of £          I must ask
you to do so at once.

Yours faithfully



A G Wilson
Finance Section
```

Standard letter with blanks left for date and inside name and address, completion of salutation, account number, month, remittance due

```
        EDGAR HARRIS Galleries, 28-34 South Street,
        SHEFFIELD  S6 2VF                    Telephone 0742 721346
        _____


        Our next Quarterly Sale by Auction will be held on

        It will start promptly at

        Viewing will take place over the two preceding days
        during the hours

        The usual range of high-quality articles will be offered
        for sale.  This Auction will specially feature


        Sale Catalogue  £          per copy (including postage)
```

Standard card with blanks left for date, time of viewing hours, sale feature and catalogue price

Standard paragraphs are used for routine letter compilation, and will also be shown in the office correspondence manual. They will be suitably categorised, eg Enquiries, Quotations, Quality/Account Queries, and coded. Within each category they will be arranged and numbered in the logical order of appearance in a letter, often with alternatives so that the most appropriate one may be chosen. A sequence of dots signal to the typist where variables will need to be inserted. By such means all necessary information can be clearly presented in the context and tone required.

Routine letter forms are used to systematise the use of standard paragraphs. Spaces will be left for the insertion of such details as:

- Number of carbon copies required
- Reference(s)
- Date
- Name and address of addressee
- Style of salutation
- Signature block details
- Code numbers of the standard paragraphs to be used, together with variable information for insertion

Advantages of standard correspondence

1 Managers are freed from routine correspondence, which can be handled by correspondence clerks.
2 Correspondence is speeded up, since both originators and typists work faster from a known correspondence manual than manuscript, audio, or shorthand input.
3 Correspondence is improved by expert drafting.

Word processors and standard correspondence

Matter is keyed-in, checked, coded, and stored on discs, and from these it is produced for high speed automatic print-out as required. The machine is programmed to stop where variables need to be keyed-in manually (or the variables can be 'merged'). There is no need to check the print-out except for the keyed-in variables.

Subscripts and superscripts: see pp 71 and 171–3.

Syllabic intensity (SI) and standard words

SI is the average number of syllables in the actual words in a passage. For instance, in the sentence 'When the sun shines, he likes to work in the open' there are 11 actual words and 12 syllables. Therefore the SI is 1.09 (12 ÷ 11).

As a general rule, the higher the SI the more 'difficult' the content of the passage (it is estimated that the average syllabic count is about 1.40). The following sentence has the very high SI of 3.00 (27 syllables; 9 actual words).

> Inexperienced candidates possessing minimum
> qualifications seldom secure good positions.

There has to be a recognised standard of difficulty to assess speed and accuracy in typewriting, so that results on different passages can be meaningfully compared. Syllabic intensity is one such measure. Counting 'standard' words (5 strokes) instead of actual words is another: each manipulative action counts as a stroke.

Tabulation

General layout

Full-page tables are centred horizontally and vertically on the paper. The space between columns must normally be equal, but it can be wider after a descriptive column. This column is often 'squared up' with leader dots; items of more than one line may be typed in blocked or hanging style, with leaders on the last line only (see p 79).

When typing unruled tables, or those with horizontal ruling only, leave at least two spaces between columns. In tables with vertical ruling, leave at least one space between columns, and more if there is room.

Blocked style   The main and sub-headings are blocked at the left-margin *or* are lined up with the vertical ruling. Column headings and their material begin at the margin and tab stops (figures must be aligned correctly).

Centred style   The main and sub-headings are centred over the table. Column headings are centred over their columns, and where the heading is the widest item in a column, the other material is centred under it. (See p 168.)

BRUNTSFIELD STORES, BIRMINGHAM

<u>Sales Analysis</u>
(January to December 19--)

Department	City Branch		Eastgate Branch	
	Cash	Credit	Cash	Credit
	£	£	£	£
Men's Wear	36,750	28,500	27,640	25,560
Ladies' Fashions	41,650	31,450	33,500	26,430
Furniture	40,140	65,400	35,610	55,380
Soft Furnishings	21,720	39,950	24,870	28,150
China and Glass	24,350	16,780	18,670	11,580
Kitchenware	18,670	7,460	14,580	6,230
Sports Equipment	12,190	3,650	8,390	2,170
TOTAL	£195,470	£193,190	£163,260	£155,500

Blocked tabulation: column headings with sub-divisions

Horizontal centring of table

1 *Backspacing method*   From the centre of the paper, backspace
 once for every two characters and spaces in the widest item in
 each column (including headings) and the blank space
 between columns. (If a character is left over, ignore it.) This
 will establish the left-margin position, where the first column
 begins.

  From there, tap the space bar for each character in the
 widest item of the first column, and for each space in the first
 inter-column gap. This will give the first tab setting, where
 the second column starts. The remaining columns are dealt
 with in the same way.

2 *Arithmetical method*   Count the total number of characters
 and spaces in the widest item in each column, then add on
 the total number of blank spaces between columns. Subtract
 this from the number of character spaces across the paper.
 Then divide the answer by two (to give equal margins) to
 arrive at the left-margin position.

  To that scale point, add the characters in the widest item
 of the first column, and the spaces in the first inter-column
 gap. This will give the first tab setting (where the second
 column begins). The remaining tab positions are found in
 the same way.

3 *Short-cut method*   For a draft, or if you are pressed for time,
 the trained eye need not 'count up' if the table consists of
 numerous figure columns after a descriptive one. The
 margins and the space between columns can be expertly
 'guessed' since the width of the descriptive column is
 flexible. Backspace from the estimated right-margin position,
 setting the tabs from right to left. If the resulting space for
 the descriptive column is too wide or too narrow, clear the
 tabs and adjust the margins and the space between columns
 before quickly resetting.

Vertical centring of table

- *Full-page table*   Add up the number of lines (of type and
 space) that the table will occupy; subtract the total from the
 number of lines down the page; and divide the answer by two
 (to give equal space above and below the table). Begin the
 table one space further down.
- *Table within copy* is centred by leaving an equal space of two or
 three lines above and below it. The table may end the page if
 there is room for a bottom margin, otherwise the whole table
 must be typed on the next page. The table is centred to the
 typing line, *or* blocked to the left-margin, *or* starts five spaces
 to the right of it.

Layout sketch   It is usually helpful to make a quick freehand sketch, setting out your calculations (using the backspacing method, noting the margin and tab settings). Check them with the number of characters across the paper, etc, before starting to type. Such a sketch is also useful for any restart.

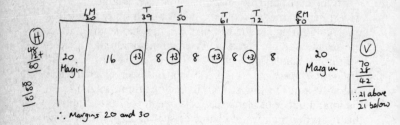

Layout sketch for table on p 166 (H = horizontal calculations: V = vertical calculations)

HOLIDAYS IN BRITAIN

See the Country By Coach

Some Selected Tours

Name of Tour	Days	Price	Hotels
		£	
Southern Country Houses	10	120	Hastings Southampton Exeter
The West Country	14	170	Bath Taunton Plymouth Truro
University Highlights	7	85	Oxford Cambridge
The Lake District	7	90	Keswick Kendal
Scottish Highlights	14	175	Oban Edinburgh Perth Inverness

Centred tabulation

168 Tabulation

Column headings of two or more lines

Use single spacing. In ruled tables headings are not under-scored. In unruled tables each line may be underscored, *or* last line only may be underscored either to its own length or to the maximum width of the heading.

Blocked style Each line begins at the start of its column. Differing numbers of lines may be vertically placed in a number of ways:

- All headings *finishing* on the same level.

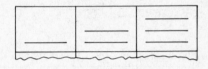

- All headings *starting* on the same level.

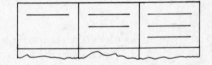

- All headings *centred vertically*, using the half line-spacer where necessary, eg in centring two lines to three.

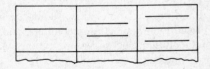

Centred style Each line is centred to its column. Differing numbers of lines may be vertically centred (see *Blocked style* above) *or* they may all finish on the same level.

Column headings with sub-divisions

(If a heading is wider than the combined columns below it, it should be divided at a suitable point.)

Blocked style   Each line of the heading starts at the tab position of the first sub-division (see p 166).

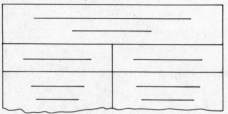

Centred style   The heading is centred over its sub-divisions.

Footnotes

Use footnote signs or figures or letters in the usual way. They are placed at the foot of the table, typed *below* the bottom line if the table is ruled. These may be blocked or centred with any layout style. They may be blocked with the start of the typescript *or* horizontal ruling (consistently).

Ruling

This assists a quick grasp of the material and the relationships within a table. Often horizontal ruling alone suffices.

On a well-typed table, full ruling is simple (some typists mark the positions of lines with light dots). The space between the typed material and the four outer lines should be equal. Inner verticals are placed mid-way between columns, and inner horizontals mid-way between blocks of typed matter. Major vertical divisions can be indicated by double lines or by heavy lines. Ruling may be done with the underscore key, a matching-colour pen, *or* with both.

- *Pen and transparent ruler*   Some typists prefer to pencil rule the four outer lines first to ensure that the lines are parallel to the typing, and to obtain neat corners. The inner lines are then ruled in ink; first those running the full width and length of the table, then any part-lines. Turn the table round to rule verticals, so that the ruling is always done from side to side: this gives better pen control.

- *Pen with paper in typewriter* Hold a ball-point pen firmly in a card-holder hole. Use the carriage release for horizontals, and turn the platen for verticals. This is the recommended method when carbon copies are taken.
- *Underscore* is used for horizontals as the work proceeds, and a pen used afterwards for the verticals. The verticals may also be made with the underscore by turning the paper round in the machine. The underscore method is recommended if horizontals only are required; they must extend equally at the left and right.

Redrafting

If radical changes are required to a complex table (reversing column headings and side items, etc) it is often safer to redraft before typing.

Note Data given in a tabulation can often be alternatively shown by bar chart, pie chart or line graph.

Technical typing (mathematical and scientific)

When copying mathematical, scientific or other technical matter which is not understood, type character by character to ensure accuracy, which is essential. The utmost care is needed when checking.

Offices engaged in specialised fields usually provide specialised typing elements for the typewriter. Occasionally mathematical and scientific matter has to be done on a standard keyboard, perhaps fitted with only a few needed symbols, the others being formed by combination characters (see p 29) or written in with matching-coloured pen. The many symbols that might have to be written in include:

> (is greater than)	∞ (infinity)
< (is less than)	π (pi)
∴ (therefore)	Σ (sigma — the sum of
∵ (because)	the terms indicated)
‖ (parallel)	△ (finite difference or
∩ (intersection)	increment)
⊥ (perpendicular)	∪ (union)

If the symbol, etc, is not clear in the copy, or you are uncertain about it, put a pencil x in the margin to remind the originator to deal with it.

Technical expressions and formulae

In all work which includes technical expressions and formulae, the typist must meticulously follow the copy in the ways listed below. Any of these may be of crucial significance to the intended meaning.

1 Distinguish accurately between lower and upper case characters. For example, carbon (C) and oxygen (O) may combine to form carbon monoxide (CO), but Co is the symbol for *cobalt* — a very different substance.
2 Ensure that subscripts and superscripts are clearly lowered below or raised above the line. A character typed on the line when it should be raised or lowered is a critical mistake.

$$HNaNH_4PO_4 = \text{hydrogen sodium ammonium orthophosphate}$$

$$Bi(HO)_3 + 3HNO_3 = Bi(NO_3)_3 + 3H_2O$$

3 When typing complex expressions and equations, maintain accurate alignment of the different levels. It is sometimes easier to type the different levels separately.

$$\frac{3a^4b^2c}{3a^2b} - \frac{9a^3bc^2}{3a^2b} - \frac{6a^2b^3}{3a^2b} = a^2bc - 3ac^2 - 2b^2$$

Note In the above example, minus and equals signs are centrally positioned, all on the same level.
4 Observe variations in spacing between characters (letters, figures, and symbols) both within and between groups.
5 Place brackets, and brackets within brackets, exactly as shown.

Typing fractions

Most keyboards are fitted with certain fractions; others can be made with the oblique stroke key (ie for sloping fractions). The mixing of keyboard and sloping fractions is unsatisfactory because of the disparity in size, therefore if several fractions are to be typed and the machine does not have keys for all of them, use the oblique stroke throughout. In offices where the work frequently includes a variety of fractions the appropriate specialised type element will be provided.

- *Fractions on the keyboard* No space is left between the whole number and its fraction, eg $10\frac{1}{2}$ and $8\frac{1}{4}$.
- *Sloping fractions* The numerator is separated from the denominator by a solidus (oblique stroke). One space is left between the whole number and the first figure of the fraction, as follows:

```
3 3/5      12 13/24
      or
3 ³/5      12 ¹³/24   (numerator raised)
```

Telex

Telex machines (teleprinters) use a QWERTY keyboard layout, therefore a conventional typewriting skill is easily applied to them.

Advantages of telex

- The speed of the telephone is combined with the authority of a printed record, both for the sender and the receiver.
- 24-hour-service: transmission may take place at any time of the day or night. In overseas communication, time differences are no problem: the machine may be left switched on (with an adequate paper-roll supply), and after the working day it takes incoming calls unattended.
- Clarity of the message: speech in a strange dialect or a foreign language is easily misunderstood, but telex provides a printed text for reference or translation.
- The automatic transmission facility enables the same text to be repeated to several destinations; technical and complex information can be checked beforehand.
- Up to six copies of each message can be obtained for office distribution.

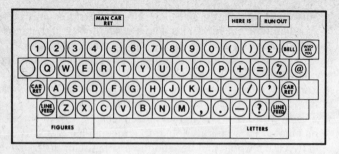

Telex keyboard

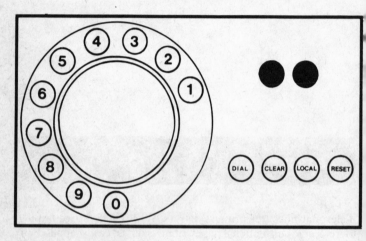

Traditional dialling unit

Operating procedure

1 Press the DIAL button: a green bulb lights to show that the machine is in use.
2 Dial the number required. (Businesses quote their telex number on their headed stationery, and subscribers are listed, with their 'answer-back' code, in the telex directory.)
3 On connection, press the WHO ARE YOU key. The distant teleprinter responds with its answer-back code for you to check that you have the right number. Then send your answer-back (using the HERE IS key) for them to identify you.
4 Type the message which will appear simultaneously (all in capitals) on the distant machine. The LETTERS key must be used before letters can be printed (this automatically locks

the figure and symbol keys to avoid mis-operation). The FIGURES key similarly enables only figures and symbols to be used.

5 At the end of the message, to confirm that the whole message has been received, send your answer-back code and obtain that of the distant machine (again using the HERE IS and WHO ARE YOU keys).

6 Finally, press the CLEAR button to switch off.

Incoming and outgoing messages are identified by the use of bi-chrome ribbon (black and red respectively).

Preparing telex messages   Use the telex message forms which are available from British Telecom. To asist the telex operator, write difficult words in capitals. Language should be condensed — but clear — to save transmission time. Call charges, like STD telephone rates, are based on time and distance.

Automatic transmission gives increased efficiency and cost-saving. Messages are sent by punched tape at a constant speed of about 120 wpm (against a good operator's 50 wpm). Tapes are made while the machine is 'off-line' (not transmitting); use the LOCAL button. Messages should be prepared and checked *before* starting to pay for line time; use the RESET button after LOCAL use.

Teleprinter development

As with other office machines, microprocessor technology is leading to rapid and fundamental changes in teleprinters. Electronic machine features include:

- Keyboard dialling so that no dialling unit is necessary.
- A memory which can be programmed with frequently-used telex numbers: in response to the code the required number is called automatically.
- 'Autocall' which enables messages to be transmitted from store automatically. In response to the Autocall button the machine tries to connect with the required number: if the number is engaged, it tries again at timed intervals until the number is connected and the message transmitted.
- A VDU (visual display unit) enables the operator to correct messages (and to add and delete text) as on a word processor (see pp 194–8). Word 'wraparound' automatically rearranges the amended text in lines of the correct length. VDUs have an adjustable tilting movement.
- Automatic printing of the date and time on all calls sent and received.
- Automatic line turn-up, allowing the operator to key continuously.
- Automatic justification of the right-margin.
- Operator prompting, to assist inexperienced staff.
- A central microprocessor which identifies machine faults.

Electronic teleprinter

Theses and treatises

The originator may ask for particular features which may be a
special requirement of his or her college. The following is a
general guide only to the typing of the final copy.
- The main text should be typed in $1\frac{1}{2}$ or double spacing.
- For the main text, indented paragraphs are often preferred to
  blocked ones, because the latter require extra space between
  paragraphs.
- The left-margin should be at least $1\frac{1}{2}$ inches (to form a
  binding margin). The right-margin should be $\frac{1}{2}$ to 1 inch.
- Use one side only of A4 bond paper.
- Pages should be numbered at the top centre.
- Use a consistent method of enumeration, according to the
  originator's preference.
- Use consistently open or full punctuation, as the originator
  wishes.
- Headings, sub-headings, and sub-division headings must be
  consistently typed in different styles.
- Use uniform dropped heads at the start of new sections.

- Quoted matter, etc, should be indented; it may be typed with single spacing for differentiation. Blocked or hanging paragraphs may also be used for differentiation.
- Footnote(s) should be typed at the foot of the same page as the reference (but long footnotes can extend to the following page). As footnotes are often numerous, it may be best to use numbers (1 2 3) for them. The following abbreviations are often used in footnotes referring to sources: *ib* or *ibid* (from the Latin *ibidem*, meaning 'in the same place'); *op cit* (from the Latin *opere citato*, meaning 'in the work quoted').

Preface This usually includes an attestation such as the following: This thesis is the result of my own work and includes nothing which is the outcome of work done in collaboration.

Bibliography This names the books and other sources used by the writer. Authors are listed alphabetically by surname, with the first name(s) or initial(s) following (see p 13); then come the title; and the place and date of publication. The length and complexity of the bibliography vary; it is sometimes divided into several sections.

Draft You may be asked to type first a draft from an amended manuscript or typescript, for further consideration by the author, before typing the final copy. In this case type the footnotes as suggested on p 59. (See the specimen page of a draft, and the corresponding final copy that follows pp 178 and 179.)

typewriter, the matter should be keyed-in with as even a right-hand margin as possible (using word division) to avoid excessive space between words.

(c) <u>For typing capital letters</u> the shift key can be used as on a typewriter. However, there may be in addition a 'capitals mode', which is particularly useful when capital letters and figures are mixed – since non-alphabet keys (including of course figures) <u>remain in lower case</u>.

(d) <u>Ending lines of type</u> Whereas the typist using a manual or electric typewriter must decide when to end each line of type and return the carriage, this operation is automatic on a word processor once margins have been set. She just types continuously, in the main ignoring line-end decisions. If the prescribed line would end in the middle of a word, the complete word is carried over to the next line.*

---

* If the operator sees on the screen that the line would end at an unsuitable point (as between two parts of a date) the machine can be instructed to treat the parts as a whole. Alternatively, the operator can choose to begin a new line whenever she pleases, by using the carriage-return key.

(e) <u>Underscoring</u> can be done as on a typewriter. Alternatively, the word processor can be <u>instructed in advance</u> to underscore – and will then do so automatically as each character is keyed-in, for as long as the instruction stands. The machine is also capable of automatically underscoring defined text <u>after</u> it has been completed.

(f) <u>Emboldening</u> (double typing) is not a very satisfactory operation on the typewriter and is therefore seldom used. With the word processor – which makes the second printing slightly to the side of the first – the effect is so distinctive as to make this device a genuine alternative to underscoring for emphasizing words or lines.

(g) <u>Making corrections and alterations</u> The typist using a word processor can throw away her eraser and correction liquid! Changes are made to the text electronically – <u>before</u> it is committed to paper. (If amendments <u>are</u> required later, the matter can be recalled on to the VDU from its storage disc, the necessary alterations made and the matter printed again.)

    (i) <u>Running corrections</u> – made as the operator keys-in the text – are carried out with ease. For large or small errors, the remedy is the same. The cursor* is moved back to the point of the error, the

---

* The cursor is a flashing signal which pin-points the working position on the screen. To facilitate speedy location, on some machines its horizontal position is also shown at the top of the screen.

---

    correction keyed-in, and the work continued from there. At the same time as the correction is inserted, the error is removed.

Specimen draft page of thesis (Note typing and asterisking of footnotes: final copy shown on p 179)

electronically – <u>before</u> it is committed to paper. (If amendments <u>are</u>
required later, the matter can be recalled on to the VDU from its storage
disc, the necessary alterations made and the matter printed again.)

    (i) <u>Running corrections</u> – made as the operator keys-in the text – are
        carried out with ease. For large or small errors, the remedy is
        the same. The cursor[1] is moved back to the point of the error, the
        correction keyed-in, and the work continued from there. At the same
        time as the correction is inserted, the error is removed.

    (ii) <u>Making corrections to finished text</u> is no more difficult. A <u>mis-</u>
        <u>keyed character</u> is corrected merely by moving the cursor to the
        point of the error, and keying-in the correct character.

        <u>Insertions</u> are simple – unlike on a typewriter where words or lines
        omitted entail retyping the whole page. The cursor is moved to the
        required position, and the appropriate function key depressed.
        Thereupon all the following text drops by one line to make room for
        the added matter – which is then keyed-in. If the insertion extends
        beyond the end of the line where it was started, the text drops down
        a further line – and so on until the insertion is completed. A key
        is then depressed to complete the operation and cause word wrap-
        around[2] to take place.

        <u>Deletions</u> are made character by character or by use of the 'delete'
        command sequence – after which the remaining text closes up (by word
        wrap-around) to avoid an unsightly gap.

        <u>Moving paragraphs</u> from one position in the text to another is
        possible with word processors. Where a paragraph move (or an
        insertion) would result in text spilling over from one page to
        another, many machines will automatically adjust for the new page
        endings and beginnings.

(c) <u>Ending lines of type</u> Whereas the typist using a manual or electric
typewriter must decide when to end each line of type and return the carriage,
this operation is automatic on a word processor once margins have been set.
She just types continuously, in the main ignoring line-end decisions. If
the prescribed line would end in the middle of a word, the complete word is

---

1 The cursor is a flashing signal which pin-points the working position on the
  screen. To facilitate speedy location, on some machines its horizontal
  position is also shown at the top of the screen.

2 Word wrap-around is the process by which the text automatically rearranges
  itself in lines of the correct length on the page after text-editing
  (correction) has taken place.

Specimen 'final copy' page of thesis (corresponding draft on p 178) (Note
numbering and placement of footnotes at foot of page of reference, ie draft and
final pages do not exactly correspond)

Time

Traditional 12-hour system

Figures The figures are always followed by am (midnight to midday) or pm (midday to midnight). A full stop always separates hours from minutes. With am (for ante meridiem — before noon) and pm (post meridiem — after noon) full stops are used in full punctuation, but not in open punctuation (see p 1).

```
We start work at 9.30 am.
The TV film ended at 10.30 pm.
```

Words This usage is mainly confined to continuous text. A figure with 'o'clock' is generally acceptable (eg 4 o'clock), but avoid bad mixes (half-past 9, etc).

```
Meet me at four o'clock this afternoon.
```

24-hour clock

This is increasingly used in business, and it is ideal for itineraries, programmes and other time schedules. There is less chance of ambiguity or error, and the system has been generally adopted in rail, sea and air time-tables.

Hours are numbered consecutively from midnight to midnight. Minutes follow hours without a separating full stop or space. There must always be four digits; two for the hours and two for the minutes, with noughts as required. The figures are followed by 'hours' or its abbreviation 'hrs'.

		spoken
Midnight	2400 hrs	twenty-four hundred hours
12.30 am	0030	oh oh thirty hours
1.00 am (or 1 am)	0100	oh one hundred hours
1.30 am	0130	oh one thirty hours
9.05 am (or 9.5 am)	0905	oh nine oh five hours
Noon	1200	twelve hundred hours
6.00 pm (or 6 pm)	1800	eighteen hundred hours
6.45 pm	1845	eighteen forty-five hours
11.25 pm	2325	twenty-three twenty-five hours
11.59 pm	2359	twenty-three fifty-nine hours

Titles and forms of address

Courtesy titles

Mr or Esq (Esquire)	use one *or* the other	Mr J C Smith J C Smith Esq
Senior and Junior (abbreviated)	to distinguish father and son; better used with Mr; precedes Esq	Mr J Ward Sen J Ward Jun Esq
Master	to address a boy (now seldom used); otherwise use no title	Master Charles Black Charles Black
Ms	if marital status not known or if she prefers	Miss L Barker Mrs B Adams Ms C Watson
The Misses	for unmarried sisters	The Misses A and J Lane
Messrs	when addressing a partnership (often omitted if there are three or more names). Comma shows 'Thomas' is a surname.	Messrs Willis & James Jones Lock & Brown Thomas, Lock & Brown
No courtesy title with	limited company public limited company impersonal name name incorporating a business	Modown Electrical Ltd Marks & Spencer plc Central Furnishings Helen Kay Fashions

Professional titles (replace courtesy titles)

Doctor	usually abbreviated	Dr J Little
Professor	sometimes abbreviated	Professor I D Ross Prof G Watkins
Navy, Army, and RAF ranks	often abbreviated	Lieut T Williams Maj S Gowers Sqn-Ldr P Harris
The Reverend or Reverend	usually abbreviated	The Rev Charles Gray Rev J Hislop

Note   Professional titles precede other titles:
Admiral The Right Hon Lord Strange
Professor Sir John Lang Bt

Addressing married couples

Mr and Mrs J C Smith (*not* Mr J C and Mrs E Smith)
Dr and Mrs J Little
Mr and Mrs J Young (even if Mrs Young is a Dr)
The Rev and Mrs C Gray
Sir John and Lady Sharp

Titles of Peers, Knights, etc

See selection on pp 186–7 (a full list is in Black's *Titles and Forms of Address*). The form of address given is customary, but simpler forms are accepted in informal correspondence (eg Dear Lady Sharp / Yours faithfully, instead of Madam / I am, Madam / Your obedient servant). The typist will be instructed.

Decorations, honours and qualifications

Use these in their correct order, as follows.

1	Decorations and honours (see pp 183–4)	VC (Victoria Cross) etc	Mr T Smithson VC
		CBE (Commander of British Empire) etc	Mrs E Toms CBE
2	Academic qualifications (see pp 184–5)	BA (Bachelor of Arts)	Mr B Maitland BA
		MA (Master of Arts)	Mrs S Andrews MA (unnecessary to add BA)
			Mrs Jane Banks MA BSc

Note A higher degree includes a lower one in the same faculty, but different faculties are shown (with the highest qualification first)

3	Professional qualifications (see pp 185–6)	FRCS (Fellow of Royal College of Surgeons) FRSA (Fellow of Royal Society of Arts)	Miss A Watson MD FRCS Mr A Ray MA FRSA
4	Other titles	MP (Member of Parliament)	Mrs A Swan OBE MP
		JP (Justice of the Peace)	Mr G Dunn MSc JP

Note Academic and professional qualifications are usually omitted except in formal correspondence, but decorations and honours should be used.

Order for decorations and honours

VC	Victoria Cross
GC	George Cross
KG	Knight of the Most Noble Order of the Garter
KT	Knight of the Most Ancient and Most Noble Order of the Thistle
KP	Knight of the Most Illustrious Order of St Patrick
PC	Privy Councillor
GCB	Knight Grand Cross of the Most Honourable Order of the Bath
OM	Order of Merit
GCSI	Knight Grand Commander of the Most Exalted Order of the Star of India
GCMG	Knight Grand Cross of the Most Distinguished Order of St Michael and St George
DCMG	Dame Grand Cross of the Most Distinguished Order of St Michael and St George
GCIE	Knight Grand Commander of the Most Eminent Order of the Indian Empire
VA	Royal Order of Victoria and Albert
CI	Imperial Order of the Crown of India
GCVO	Knight Grand Cross of the Royal Victorian Order
DCVO	Dame Grand Cross of the Royal Victorian Order
GBE	Knight Grand Cross of the Most Excellent Order of the British Empire
DBE	Dame Grand Cross of the Most Excellent Order of the British Empire
CH	Companion of Honour
KCB	Knight Commander of the Most Honourable Order of the Bath
KCSI	Knight Commander of the Most Exalted Order of the Star of India
KCMG	Knight Commander of the Most Distinguished Order of St Michael and St George
KCIE	Knight Commander of the Most Eminent Order of the Indian Empire
KCVO	Knight Commander of the Royal Victorian Order
KBE	Knight Commander of the Most Excellent Order of the British Empire
DBE	Dame Commander of the Most Excellent Order of the British Empire
CB	Companion of the Most Honourable Order of the Bath
CSI	Companion of the Most Exalted Order of the Star of India
CMG	Companion of the Most Distinguished Order of St Michael and St George
CIE	Companion of the Most Eminent Order of the Indian Empire

CVO	Commander of the Royal Victorian Order
CBE	Commander of the Most Excellent Order of the British Empire
DSO	Distinguished Service Order
MVO	Member of the Royal Victorian Order
OBE	Officer of the Most Excellent Order of the British Empire
ISO	Companion of the Imperial Service Order
MVO	Member of the Royal Victorian Order
MBE	Member of the Most Excellent Order of the British Empire
RRC	Member of the Royal Red Cross
DSC	Distinguished Service Cross
MC	Military Cross
DFC	Distinguished Flying Cross
AFC	Air Force Cross
ARRC	Associate of the Royal Red Cross
AM	Albert Medal
DCM	Distinguished Conduct Medal
CGM	Conspicuous Gallantry Medal
GM	George Medal
DSM	Distinguished Service Medal
MM	Military Medal
DFM	Distinguished Flying Medal
AFM	Air Force Medal
BEM	British Empire Medal
SGM	Sea Gallantry Medal
VD	Volunteer Officer's Decoration
TD	Territorial Decoration
ED	Efficiency Decoration

Thus Orders listed as follows:
  Garter
  Thistle
  St Patrick
  Bath
  Star of India
  St Michael and St George
  Indian Empire
  Victoria
  British Empire

Academic qualifications

(B = Bachelor: if Master or Doctor, substitute M or D for B)

BA	Bachelor of Arts
BAgric	Bachelor of Agriculture
BArch	Bachelor of Architecture
BCh	Bachelor of Surgery (Chirurgiae)

BCL	Bachelor of Civil Law
BCom	Bachelor of Commerce
BD	Bachelor of Divinity
BDS	Bachelor of Dental Surgery
BEd	Bachelor of Education
BEng	Bachelor of Engineering
BLitt	Bachelor of Letters, Literature
BM	(or MB) Bachelor of Medicine
BPhil	Bachelor of Philosophy
BSc	Bachelor of Science
BTh	Bachelor of Theology
BVM & S	Bachelor of Veterinary Medicine and Surgery
LAA	Licentiate of Central Association of Accountants
LLB	Bachelor of Laws
LRAM	Licentiate of Royal Academy of Music
LRCP	Licentiate of Royal College of Physicians
LRCS	Licentiate of Royal College of Surgeons
LSA	Licentiate of Society of Apothecaries
PhD	Doctor of Philosophy

Professional qualifications

(F = Fellow, M = Member, A or AM = Associate/Associate Member: placed before initials for institution or society)

BIM	British Institute of Management
CII	Chartered Insurance Institute
CIPFA	Chartered Institute of Public Finance Accountants
CIS	Chartered Institute of Secretaries and Administrators
FTCom	Faculty of Teachers in Commerce
GS	Geological Society
IA	Institute of Actuaries
IAE	Institution of Automobile Engineers
IB	Institute of Bankers
IC	Institute of Chemistry
ICE	Institution of Civil Engineers
IChemE	Institution of Chemical Engineers
ICWA	Institute of Cost and Works Accountants
IEE	Institution of Electrical Engineers
IL	Institute of Linguists
IMechE	Institution of Mechanical Engineers
IMunE	Institution of Municipal Engineers
InstAM	Institute of Administrative Management
InstM	Institute of Marketing
IOB	Institute of Builders
IPE	Institution of Production Engineers
IPM	Institute of Personnel Management
IPS	Incorporated Phonographic Society
IQPS	Institute of Qualified Private Secretaries

IQS	Institute of Quantity Surveyors
JI	Institute of Journalists
LA	Library Association
PS	Pharmaceutical Society
RAeS	Royal Aeronautical Society
RAS	Royal Astronomical Society
RCM	Royal College of Music
RCP	Royal College of Physicians
RCS	Royal College of Surgeons
RCVS	Royal College of Veterinary Surgeons
RGS	Royal Geographical Society

Title	Form of address
Baron	The Rt Hon Lord —
Baroness	The Rt Hon Lady —
Baronet	Sir Reginald Black Bt
Bishop (seat in Lords)	The Right Rev the Lord Bishop of —
Dame	Dame Mary Brownlow DBE (or other title)
Duke	His Grace the Duke of —
Duchess	Her Grace the Duchess of —
Earl	The Right Hon the Earl of —
Countess	The Right Hon the Countess of —
Judge (County Court)	His Honour Judge —
Judge (High Court)	The Honourable Mr Justice —
Knight	Sir John Sharp Kt (or other title)
Mayor	The Worshipful Mayor of —
Prime Minister	The Right Hon Margaret Thatcher PC MP
Her Majesty the Queen	Her Most Gracious Majesty, Queen Elizabeth II
Viscount	The Rt Hon the Viscount —
Viscountess	The Rt Hon the Viscountess —

RHS	Royal Horticultural Society	
RIBA	Royal Institute of British Architects	
RIC	Royal Institute of Chemistry	
RICS	Royal Institution of Chartered Surveyors	
RS	Royal Society	
RSA	Royal Society of Arts	
RSL	Royal Society of Literature	
SA	Society of Antiquaries	
SAA	Society of Incorporated Accountants and Auditors	
SCT	Society of Commercial Teachers	
ZS	Zoological Society	

Salutation	*Complimentary close*
My Lord	I have the honour to be, my Lord Your obedient servant
Madam	I have the honour to be, Madam Your Ladyship's obedient servant
Sir	I am, Sir Your obedient servant
My Lord Bishop	I have the honour to be, my Lord Bishop Your obedient servant
Dear Madam	Yours faithfully
My Lord Duke	I am, my Lord Duke Your Grace's most obedient servant
Madam	I am, Madam Your Grace's most obedient servant
My Lord	I have the honour to be, my Lord Your Lordship's obedient servant
Madam	I have the honour to be, Madam Your Ladyship's obedient servant
Sir	I am, Sir Your obedient servant
Sir	I am, Sir Your obedient servant
Sir	I am, Sir Your obedient servant
Sir	I am, Sir Your obedient servant
Madam	I have the honour to be, Madam Your obedient servant
Madam	I have the honour to be, Madam Your Majesty's faithful subject
My Lord	I am, My Lord Your obedient servant
Madam	I have the honour to be, Madam Your Ladyship's obedient servant

Titles and forms of address 187

Typewriter care

1 Never site a typewriter close to a hot radiator.
2 Keep the front of the machine flush with the edge of the desk so that it cannot be knocked by careless passers-by.
3 Before moving the machine, lock the carriage in the centre position (if there is no locking device, move the margin stops to the middle) to prevent it from sliding if tilted. Always lift the machine by the base from the back.
4 Use a backing sheet when typing on a single sheet of paper — this prevents pitting of the cylinder and improves the typescript.
5 When erasing, move the carriage to the extreme right or left (using the margin release key) to prevent particles from falling into the machine.
6 When using correction liquid, ensure that it is dry before typing the correction.
7 Dust the machine regularly with a soft cloth and a long-handled soft brush. Also, regularly dust the underneath parts by carefully raising the front base of the machine.
8 Each morning clean the typefaces with a hard brush dampened with a drop of methylated spirit.
9 Cover the machine overnight (and during other lengthy spells of non-use) to keep out dust — one of the typewriter's greatest enemies. Always lift off the cover carefully, making sure it is not caught up in the mechanism.
10 If the typewriter is not functioning properly and the fault is not obvious and easily rectified, call in an experienced mechanic; never tamper with it yourself.
11 Have the machine regularly serviced by experts.

Typing for print

Typists to authors and literary agencies type various forms of literary matter — stories, articles, novels, etc. The essential need is for consistency in layout and style throughout (see Continuous documents p 32). Several revised drafts may be needed before the final copy is typed for the printer.

Final copy

1 Publishers normally require two copies of the material (and the author will retain another copy).
2 Use A4 paper, typed on one side only.
3 Leave at least $1\frac{1}{2}$ inches for the left-margin.
4 Use $1\frac{1}{2}$ or double line-spacing for ease of reading and editing.
5 Number the pages (folios) consecutively.
6 Type the footnotes all together in a separate list: the typed pages will not correspond with the printed ones, so the publisher and printer will position the footnotes when the printed pages are made up.
7 Ensure that headings, sub-headings, and their sub-division headings are consistently typed in different styles, so that different 'weights' can be quickly interpreted by the editor for different styles of print.
8 Likewise, the enumeration system should be suitably graded and consistently applied (see Enumeration pp 49–50).

Invitations, leaflets, etc, for printing Clearly state your requirements: the quality, colour, and size of paper; the kind, size, and colour of print; the quantity required; etc.

Checking proofs

The printer supplies printed proofs for proof-reading. Sometimes these are *page proofs* which will accord with the printed pages. At other times *galley proofs* are supplied, from which the publisher will later paste-up the finished pages. The fewest possible alterations are sought at either stage as it is costly to make changes.

- Check the proofs very carefully, word for word, against copy. It may be helpful if a second person reads the copy aloud while you check the proof.
- Mark (in red ball-point for clarity) any corrections needed, using the list of correction signs on pp 37–8.
- Retain copy of the corrected proof for reference; carefully copy on to it all corrections made on the printer's copy.
- If the extent of the corrections is sufficient to require a second proof, mark it 'Further proof'. If the proof is satisfactory, mark it 'For press'.

Vertical headings

Vertical headings read sideways

Some tabulations have narrow columns (usually of figures) with much wider column headings. Here *vertical headings* enable more columns to be typed across the paper; and produce a more compact, balanced, and easily-read table, especially if it is ruled up. However, since vertical headings are more difficult to type and to read, they should be used only if the headings are considerably wider than their columns. (When the table is intended for a camera or copier it may be quicker to paste in vertical headings.)

Length of heading Very long vertical headings should be divided where possible. Signs (eg ampersand) and abbreviations may be used.

Mixed vertical and horizontal headings Often the first column is a descriptive one, much wider than the others. This heading is best typed horizontally; others may be typed horizontally too, but vertical and horizontal *should not be mixed indiscriminately*. Type a series of closely-related columns *all* with vertical headings even though one heading is short enough to type horizontally.

SOUTH OF FRANCE TOURIST ASSOCIATION

Hotel Rooms and Accommodation still available in July

Town and District	A Hotels	B Hotels	C Hotels	Houses	Bungalows	Flats	Chalets
Avignon	25	60	95	25	20	21	15
Nice	150	200	125	130	96	90	86
Toulouse	40	85	130	85	60	87	101
Marseilles	95	155	180	70	105	80	35
Nimes	80	120	90	65	55	45	36
Montpellier	35	80	95	62	45	65	29
Toulon	36	90	120	75	45	100	70

Measuring space for vertical headings The top headings and the body of the table must be typed before the paper is turned sideways for the insertion of the vertical headings. The correct amount of blank space must therefore be left *a* for vertical headings and *b* for the necessary line-spacing above and below them. Decide this depth as part of your calculations for the vertical placement of the table as a whole.

1 Blank space for headings themselves

- *Calculation method* First find the longest line in the headings (in the example, Bungalows with 9 characters). Convert this to vertical depth:

$$12 \text{ elite characters (10 pica)} = 1 \text{ inch horizontally}$$
$$= 6 \text{ lines of space vertically}$$

  Elite With a relationship of 12 to 6, the number of characters in the heading is halved to give the required number of vertical line-spaces. (Bungalows = 9 characters: half of 9 is $4\frac{1}{2}$.)

  Pica With a relationship of 10 to 6, take three-fifths of the number of characters, rounding up to the nearest half. (Bungalows = 9 characters: three-fifths of 9 is $5\frac{2}{5}$ ($\frac{3}{5} \times \frac{9}{1} = \frac{27}{5} = 5\frac{2}{5}$). Round up to $5\frac{1}{2}$.

- *Measuring with the line spacer* An alternative method is to type the longest vertical heading on a scrap of paper, then remove it and reinsert it sideways to measure the depth of the heading with the line-spacer. This method is useful when all the headings look similar in length, in which case *all* should be typed on the scrap of paper; otherwise just type the 'doubtful' ones. This is a reliable method of identifying the longest vertical line without the need for any counting.

2 Line-spacing above and below vertical headings This can vary in different tabulations. In the example given, three lines of space have been left (two between the top of the longest vertical heading and the main headings, and one between the bottom of the vertical headings and the first line of type in the body of the table).

Typing (blocked style)

a Complete, in the normal way, your calculations for the vertical placement of the table on the paper.

b Set the margin and tab stops for the body of the table.

c Type the main headings at the top of the table.

d Leave the correct number of lines of blank space for the column headings *and* for the spaces above and below them. (In the example: Elite $4\frac{1}{2} + 3 = 7\frac{1}{2}$; Pica $5\frac{1}{2} + 3 = 8\frac{1}{2}$.)

e Type the body of the table.

f Make a pencil guidemark where the first vertical heading will begin: one line-space above its column and over the first character in its column.

g Remove the paper from the typewriter and insert it sideways (feeding in first what *was* the left edge).

h Set the margin or the tab stop at your guidemark, where the first (and all other) vertical headings will begin. Start each one in line with the first character in its column.

i Remove the paper and rule up. (Horizontal lines can be made with the underscore as typing proceeds, if preferred.)

j Return the paper to the typewriter (right side up) and type the heading Town and District at the left margin position. This heading may *i* be centred vertically to the deepest column heading (as shown); *or ii* start level with the top of the vertical headings; *or iii* finish level with the bottom of the vertical headings.

When you are practised in the technique of vertical headings, you may prefer to type the horizontal headings before removing the paper from the typewriter at *g*.

Headings wider than their columns Sometimes one or more vertical headings will be 'wider' than the column(s) beneath. In these cases count the heading as the widest item in the column when calculating for the horizontal placement of the table. (Remember that lines in a vertical heading require more space than the same number of characters across a column below it, eg a 3-line vertical heading takes half an inch: as much as 6 elite characters *across* a column.)

Typing (centred style)

a The main heading and the subsidiary heading are centred horizontally over the table.

b The horizontal heading Town and District is *i* centred over the column matter below; and *ii* invariably centred vertically to the deepest column heading.

c Each vertical heading is centred to its column eg a one-line heading over a 3-digit-wide column would be typed over the middle digit.

Vertical headings read downwards

The upright letters are typed one below the other, normally all starting on the same upper horizontal level. The method is less satisfactory than vertical headings read sideways because *a* the headings are more difficult to read, since the eye is not accustomed to reading words downwards; and *b* the line-spacer must be used (at 1) after each letter, requiring far more vertical depth and giving a 'drawn out' appearance. Only 6 characters can be typed this way to each vertical inch, compared with 12 (elite) or 10 (pica) when the paper is turned sideways. The half-spacer cannot be used between letters because 'tall' letters (like l and h) and those with descenders (like g and y) would clash with the letters above and below them. This method is therefore best avoided on an ordinary desk typewriter unless it is specifically requested. A *word processor*, of course, can produce vertical headings *only* in a reading-downwards form.

Headings read downwards are more legible if they are all in capitals; and the solidity of capitals helps to counteract the drawn-out effect (see the last 4 headings in the example below).

OVERSEAS SALES IN JANUARY
(in £'000)

Category	Denmark	Eire	France	Germany	HOLLAND	ITALY	NORWAY	SPAIN
Foodstuffs	6	2	4	5	4	3	2	4
Clothing	8	3	4	6	7	4	3	4
Footwear	3	1	2	3	1	1	2	1
Furniture	10	12	9	11	7	6	5	8
Electrical	2	1	4	5	3	2	4	5

Weights and measurements: see pp 104 and 118–20.

Word division

Non-division of words For speed and simplicity, many typists do not use word division in normal work. By skilful reaction to the line-end bell they achieve a satisfactory right-hand margin.

Line-end bell Know the number of characters between the bell and where the carriage locks at the margin stop. This is the key to judging where to end each line, with or without word division. Since the number of characters varies on different machines, always check this on a strange one.

With margin stop set at the point of the desired margin, type right up to it and go a space or two beyond to complete a long word, rather than always stopping short, otherwise the right-margin will become wider than intended. Alternatively, set the margin stop two or three spaces further to the right.

Line-end division of words   There *are* times when all typists need to use line-end division. For example, with limited space and a narrow line length (as with folded leaflets) word division is often desirable. Another instance is when typing a draft for justifying the right-margin to the text.

Guidelines for word division

1   Pronunciation is the most important factor since words should be divided between syllables, eg win-dow, pic-ture. Many words can be divided in a number of ways, eg qual-ifying; quali-fying; qualify-ing. In such cases the determining factor will be the proximity to the margin position. Using syllables avoids misleading divisions like sip-hon and hyp-hen.

2   Divide between two similar consonants, eg neces-sary; excellent. However, if a root word ends in a double consonant, divide *after* the root word, eg miss-ing; tell-ing.

3   Divide between two different consonants if they are sounded separately, eg imper-fect; clandes-tine.

4   There is no sense in dividing a word to carry over only two letters, since the hyphen accounts for one letter. (Remember that the hyphen always appears at the *end* of a line; it is never carried over to the next line.)

5   Word division checks the flow of reading and understanding. Its *excessive* use is therefore undesirable even in the interests of a very even right margin.

6   Do not divide in the following cases:

- one syllable words (freight, brought)
- groups of numerals and associated units of measurements
- abbreviations (UNICEF)
- hyphenated words except at the permanent hyphen
- proper names
- specialist terms
- dates

Word processors

A word processor produces text that can be electronically edited, printed, stored, and retrieved. It can also transmit text over long distances to other compatible word processors and computer systems. Machines and software packages vary; the following is a general guide only.

Whether it is a 'stand-alone' (self-contained) system, or a shared-logic or mainframe system (with separate operating terminals linked to a common computer and printing unit) a word processor has four essential parts, as follows.

1 **Keyboard** This includes the QWERTY layout, together with groups of additional function keys which control such operations as: insert, delete, centre, justify, print, and so on. Keys that are frequently used in combination (such as the five cursor-control keys, which allow the 'typing-point' to be moved up, down, to the left, right, or back to the top) are grouped together.

2 **Video display unit (VDU)** This resembles a TV screen, and displays the text being keyed-in or edited. Some VDUs have an adjustable tilting movement. The characters on the screen may be illuminated green on a black background or black on white; and a brightness control adjusts for different lighting levels in the office. The 'format' line (usually at the top of the screen) reminds the operator of document name and page set-up — margin settings, tab stops, page length, etc.

'Scrolling' means running text over the screen, horizontally and vertically, so that the operator can see contiguous areas of pages containing more text than can be shown on the screen at one time.

3 **Central processing unit (CPU)** This is the computer that controls all the functions of the system.

4 **Printing unit** Roughly resembling a typewriter without a keyboard, this prints out the text on paper *after* it has been keyed-in, checked on the VDU, and after any necessary corrections and amendments have been made. Daisy-wheel print elements produce high-quality printing.

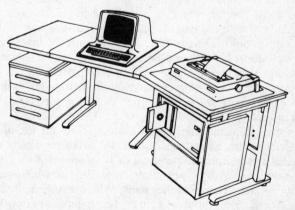

A stand-alone word processor showing keyboard, VDU, central processing unit and printing unit

Word processor keyboard

Speeding and simplifying the typist's work

Centring Without any counting or backspacing, the word processor operator merely keys-in the word, line, or block of text (in the line by line arrangement required) which is to be centred. The 'centre' command sequence is keyed, and the matter is centred automatically.

Corrections and alterations Changes are made to the text, electronically, *before* it is committed to paper. (For updating, the text is recalled from its storage disc on to the VDU, the necessary changes are made, and the matter is printed again.)

- *Running corrections* are made as the operator keys-in the text: the cursor is moved back to the point of error, the correction is keyed-in, and the work continues from there. At the same time as the correction is inserted, the error is removed.
- *Corrections to finished text,* such as a mis-keyed character, are corrected by moving the cursor to the point of error and keying-in the correct character.
- *Insertions* are made by moving the cursor to the required position and depressing the appropriate function key. Thereupon all the following text drops by one line to make room for the added matter, which is then keyed-in. If the insertion extends beyond the end of the line where it was started, the text drops down a further line, and so on until the insertion is completed. A key is then depressed to complete the operation and to cause 'word wraparound' to take place. (This is the process by which the text automatically rearranges itself in lines of the correct length after text-editing, ie correction, has taken place.)
- *Deletions* are made character by character *or* by the use of the 'delete' command sequence, after which the remaining text closes up (by word wraparound) to avoid an unsightly gap.
- *Moving text* Words, sentences, columns, or whole paragraphs can be moved as they stand. Where a paragraph move (or an insertion) would result in the text spilling over from one page to another, many machines will automatically adjust for the new page endings and beginnings.

196 Word processors

- *'Search and replace'* If an error has been repeated throughout a document (eg a name wrongly spelt, or a wrong price or date given), a global search and replace can be made: the machine will identify every instance of the wrong 'character string' and replace it with the correct one.

Ending lines of type is automatic on a word processor once the margins have been set. The operator keys-in continuously, and if any line would end in the middle of a word, the complete word is carried over to the next line. The operator must watch for any line that would end at an unsuitable point (eg between two parts of a date); the machine can then be instructed to treat the parts as a whole. Alternatively, the operator can choose to begin a new line whenever he or she pleases.

Underscoring can be done as on a typewriter. Alternatively, the word processor can be *instructed in advance* to underscore, and will then do so automatically as each character is keyed-in, for as long as the instruction stands. It is also possible to underscore defined text automatically *after* it has been completed.

Emboldening (double typing) is not very satisfactory on the typewriter and therefore is seldom used. With a word processor, which makes the second printing slightly to the side of the first, the effect is so distinctive as to make this a real alternative to underscoring for emphasising words or lines.

Typing capital letters The shift key can be used as on a typewriter, but there is also a capitals mode which is useful when capitals and figures are mixed, since the non-alphabet keys remain in lower case.

Justifying the right-hand margin can be carried out automatically at the print-out stage, but the matter should still be keyed-in with as even a right-margin as possible to avoid excessive space between words.

Arithmetic calculations In addition to automatic decimal alignment, some word processors have arithmetic facilities, which total columns of figures, carry out multiplication on a table of numbers, etc.

Spelling verification facility Some machines have built-in 'dictionaries' of 50 000 commonly used words. Up to 500 additional words can be entered by the user for the particular profession or industry. The machine 'checks' the operator's spelling of all the listed words. If a keyed-in word is not in the 'dictionary' or is spelt differently, it is highlighted; it can then be checked by the operator.

Some uses of a word processor

- Invaluable for the production of many copies of a document (circular letters, reports, advertising material, etc) since each is of 'top-copy' quality.

- Its versatility in correcting and amending text makes a word processor particularly useful for documents which may need to pass through several drafts — reports, articles, minutes of meetings, etc. The machine automatically reformats pages after text-editing.
- Price lists, mailing lists, telephone directories, etc, can be updated without the need to retype in full.
- Documents can be 'merged' from two separate files, eg a circular letter and a mailing list. The merge facility saves a great deal of time in preparing standard documents such as contracts and other legal documents.
- Invaluable for standard correspondence. Standard letters and paragraphs are keyed-in, checked, coded, and stored on disc for high-speed automatic print-out as required. The machine can be programmed to stop where variables need to be keyed-in manually — or the merge facility is used to include the given variables.
- High-quality display layouts are possible. Choices include different pitches and type-styles and reverse-tone effect (white print on a black background). Easy centring, justifying, and emboldening are useful in display work.
- A 'graphics mode' enables lines and boxes to be drawn. This feature greatly simplifies the drawing of flow charts, bar charts, and organisation charts: also the preparation of forms.
- Form-filling is made easy. Forms can be programmed with 'tab codes': as each item is filled in, the machine automatically tabs on to the position for starting the next one.
- Used in electronic mail systems for instantaneous transmission of documents to other compatible word processors and computer systems.

Index